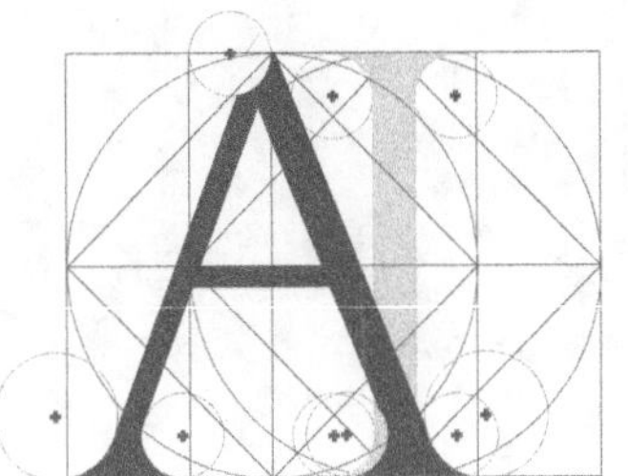

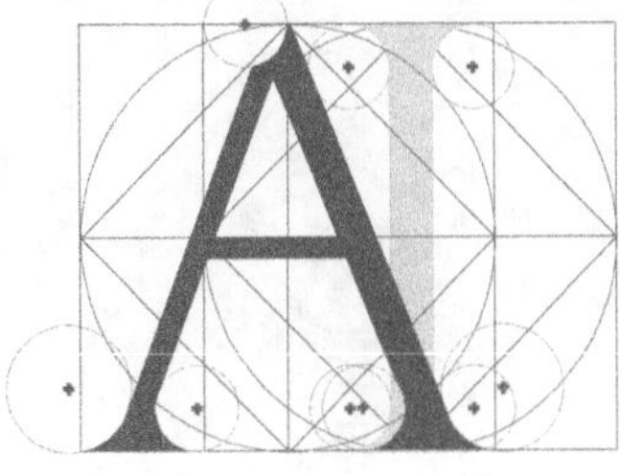

Assisting Intelligence

How to Build Authentic in the Age of AI

Mike P. O'Brien

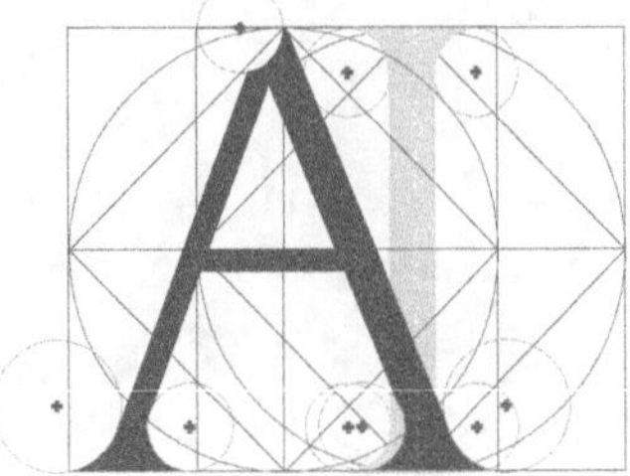

Welcome to
Assisting Intelligence
How to Build Authentic in the Age of AI

Assisting Intelligence is a practical guide for business professionals and educators, what you'll soon see as learners seeking to harness the power of AI for content creation and knowledge sharing. This book reframes AI as an assisting intelligence and explores innovative workflows for creating, crafting, preserving, and ultimately building authentic experiences that resonate with your ethos, perspective, and insight.

Assisting Intelligence examines the foundational principles for navigating the AI era and advancing learning and communication. It provides insights into how we can harness the power of AI to create a future where technology serves as a catalyst for building authentic learning and intelligence. By understanding and leveraging AI, we can unlock its potential to assist human development and progress.

Assisting Intelligence is available in hardcover, paperback, and digital formats.

For Elke and Sydney, who know all my stories and listen anyway, and whom I learn from every day.

Ancora Imparo.

Copyright

Copyright © 2024 By SmarterMedium, LLC

Limit of Liability / Disclaimer of Warranty:

Citations and Copyright:

Library Of Congress Classification

Library of Congress Control Number: 2024924093

Publisher

Published by SmarterMedium, LLC

Hull, MA USA

www.smartermedium.com

Versions of this Book

Embrace the future, informed by the past, to build authentic. A book for every bookshelf, digital or tangible. Assisting Intelligence is available in a variety of formats in print and accessible digitally in your preferred reading app. Below are the common formats and places to purchase or download.

Hardcover ISBN 979-8-9919867-0-0

Paperback ISBN 979-8-9919867-1-7

eBook ISBN 979-8-9919867-2-4

Full Color Incunabula Version ISBN 979-8-9919867-3-1

Digital Formats

This book is available digitally on many platforms, including Apple Books, Google Play, Amazon Kindle, B&N Nook, and other ebook platforms.

Custom Versions

Playbook, Presentation, and Personalized Formats are available on AssistingIntelligence.com. Discover how to build authentic knowledge by harnessing Assisting Intelligence in your corporate training or education program.

Ordering Information

Special discounts, enterprise licensing, and custom programs are available on quantity purchases by corporations, associations, and others. For details or questions, contact us or visit the custom solutions section of this playbook for ideas on how these works can be branded and customized for learning development.

info@assistingintelligence.com

Visit https://www.assistingintelligence.com for more information.

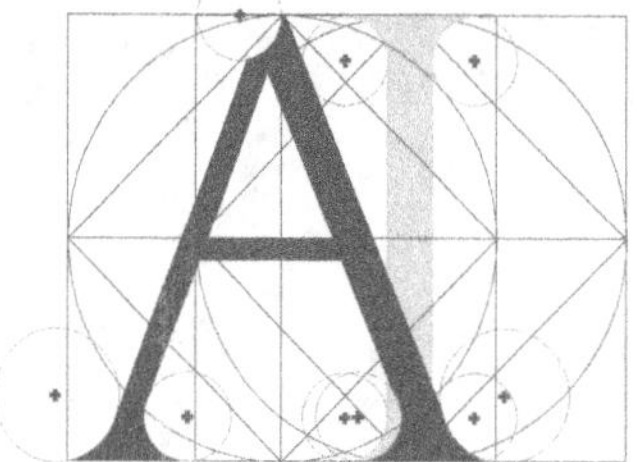

Table of Contents

A Golden Retriever, a 15th-Century Printer, and a Generative AI Model walk into a bar … No, this isn't the setup of a joke or an AI hallucination. It's the beginning of an extraordinary journey through time and technology, exploring how to build authentic knowledge and harness AI's power to assist us.

Five centuries ago, four books helped ignite the Renaissance. Today, they offer a roadmap for the future of AI.

Authentic Approach to the AI Age

As AI reshapes the world, we must choose our path. Will we delegate, experiment, or innovate? Part 1 offers an approach and understanding of AI's power for authentic learning and knowledge creation.

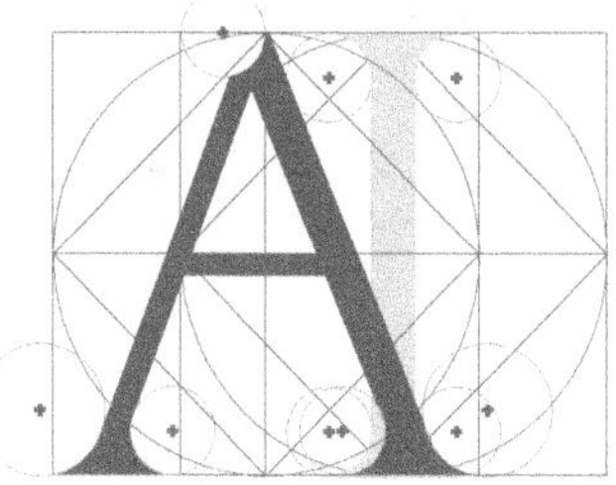

Assisting Intelligence

How to Build Authentic in the Age of AI

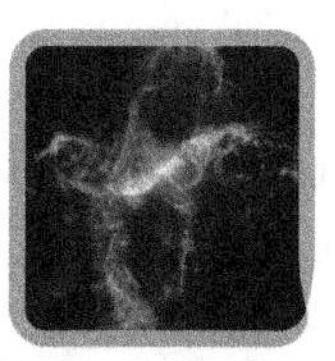

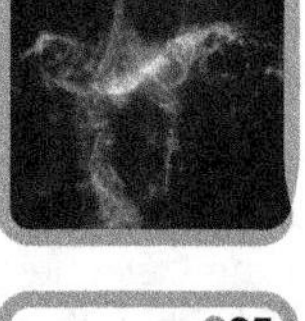

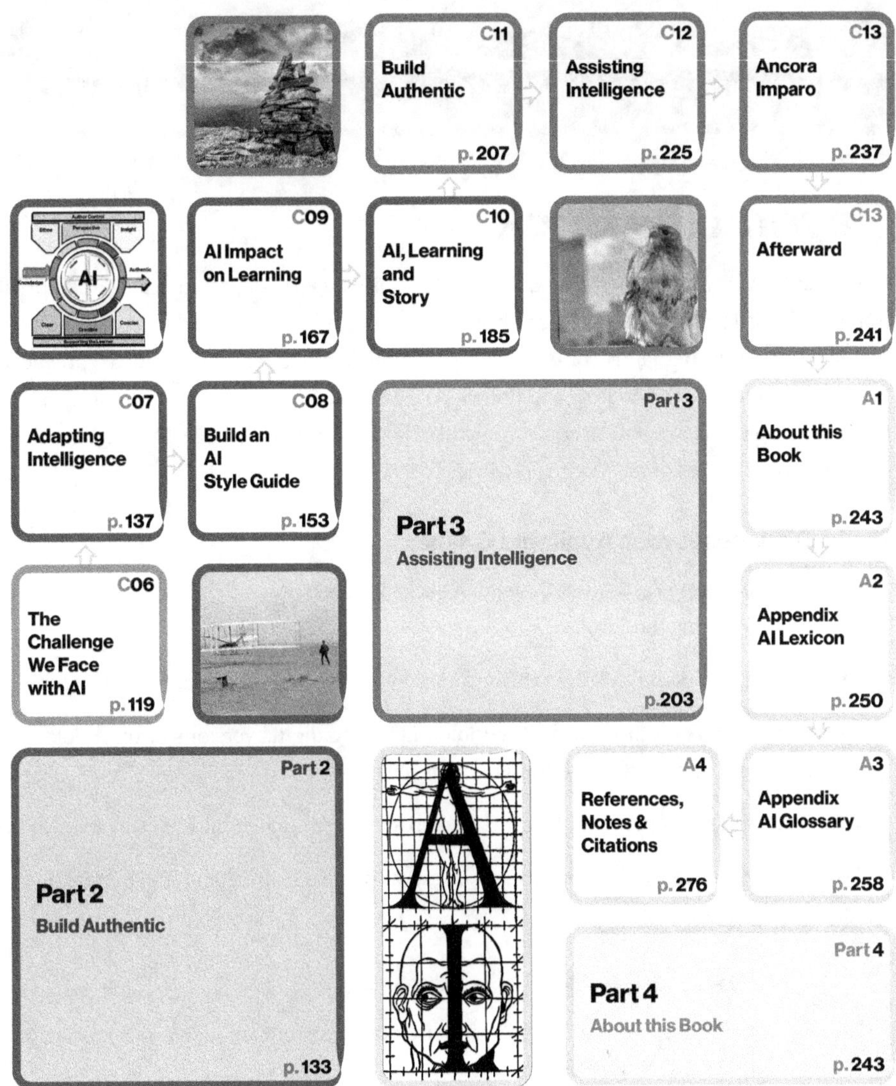

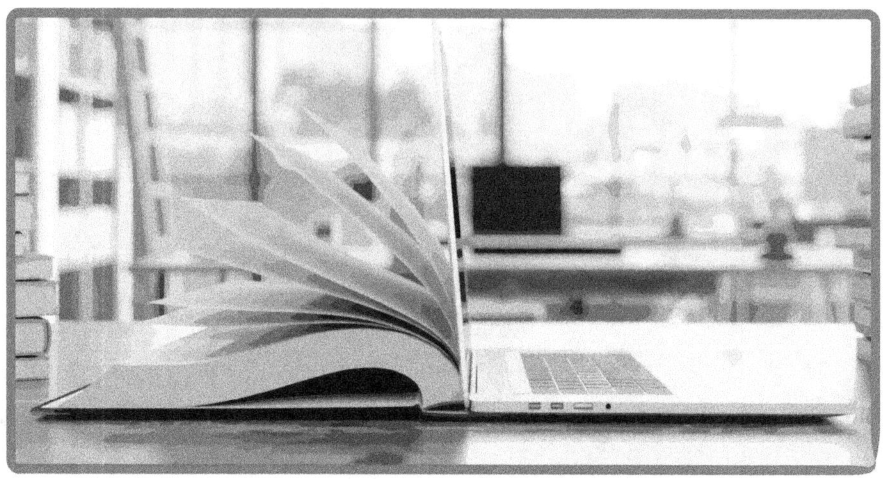

Beyond the Book

Assisting Intelligence: How to Build Authentic in the Age of AI provides a foundational framework for leveraging AI as a catalyst for growth and connection. However, the dynamic nature of AI demands continuous exploration. We're offering fresh ideas, practical tips, and inspiring stories to help you unlock AI's full potential. By staying current with the latest developments, we aim to equip you with the tools and knowledge necessary to navigate the complexities of an AI-driven world.

Up-to-Date Resources Available Online:

- **WRLD Resources**: Watch, Read, Listen, Discuss. Access a wealth of information on AI, learning, storytelling, and more.

- **Newsletters and Social Media**: Stay informed with the latest news, tips, and trends.

- **Downloadable Templates and Playbooks**: Leverage digital versions of playbook and practical tools to create effective training materials.

- **Online Courses**: Deepen your knowledge and skills with our comprehensive courses.

By visiting our website, you'll gain access to these valuable resources and much more. Let's continue the journey together.

Visit AssistingIntelligence.com

For more information or to inquire about custom solutions, please contact: info@assistingintelligence.com.

AI Usage and This Book

This book is about being authentic with the assistance of an AI. This book started as an experiment to learn more about generative AI while researching a book on an entirely different topic. For Assisting Intelligence, I tried to incorporate the use of AIs into each stage of the writing process. I found that it could accelerate brainstorming; however, the real research, writing, perspective, and most of the content had to be created outside of an AI, made with authentic sources, and curated independently. For any improvement an AI offered, it detracted from what was authentic and real about my content—my ethos, perspective, and insight.

Generative AI proved quite capable of copyediting, but I did not allow it to make substantive changes that altered the intent, meaning, or direction of the content. In every instance where I could, I tried to verify any conjecture made by AIs with authentic sources and curated content to further research outside of the AI.

It's important to note that this book does not feature AI-generated artwork. All images and illustrations were created by SmarterMedium using 'traditional' digital tools or were properly licensed from their copyright owners. Generative AI is still not ready for professional use and raises ethical concerns regarding copyright and authenticity.

The hallucinations and shenanigans in this book are entirely my own. One of the challenges and joys of writing in the AI era is finding ways to create content that AI simply cannot replicate. This is what makes this book unique and the perspective my own. I tested ideas, sought alternative arguments from AI, improved grammar and editing, and had fun crafting prompts that challenged the deep-learning neural network to think more like I do.

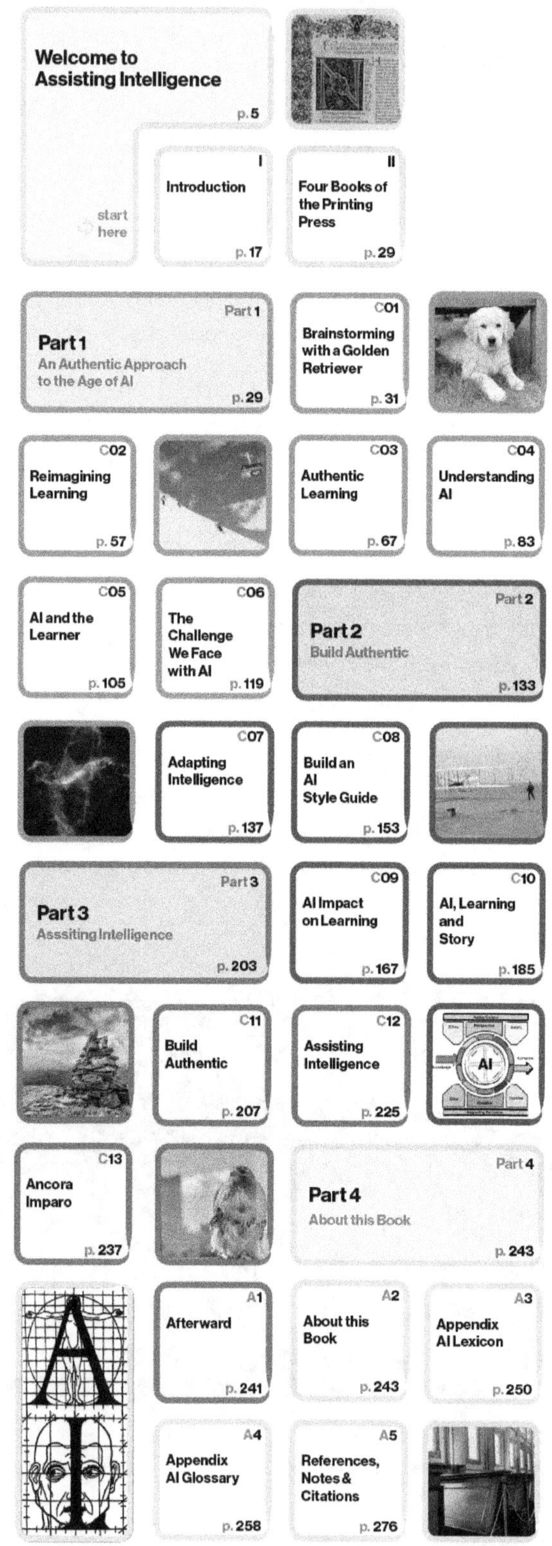

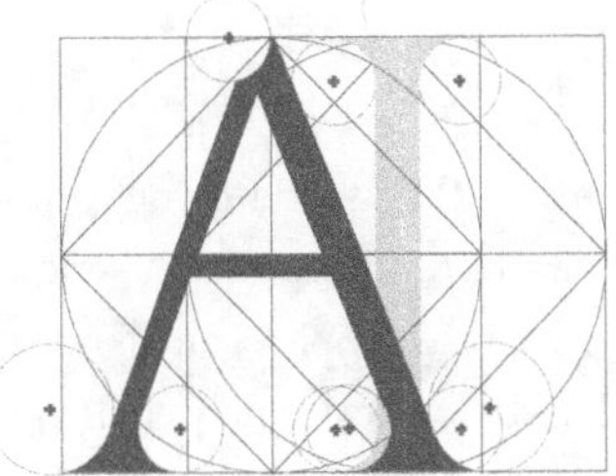

Introduction

What Can Four Books from a Pre-Renaissance World Teach Us About Our AI Age?

Five hundred years separate four books from the age of AI. Four books that transformed knowledge sharing after the printing press. Four books that ignited the Renaissance. Four books that offer a roadmap for our AI future.

Before printing was discovered, a century was equal to a thousand years.
— Henry David Thoreau

AI's Go Spark

In March 2016, Google's computer program AlphaGo captivated the world by defeating South Korean Go champion Lee Sedol in the first game of a historic five-match series.[1] This victory marked a breakthrough for Artificial Intelligence. Go, a complex game known for its reliance on intuition and creativity, was previously considered "extremely challenging" for AI. Unlike past AI victories like Deep Blue in chess, AlphaGo wasn't just replicating human play.[2]

In the second game, a move by AlphaGo, deemed a 'mistake' by analysts, was later hailed as a 'beautiful' breakthrough. This unexpected move, calculated as highly unlikely by human standards, showcased AI's ability to learn and innovate. AlphaGo wasn't just replicating patterns; it was developing new strategies.

In the fourth game, Lee Sedol elevated his play, executing a surprising strategy that defied AlphaGo's probability calculations. This move, later hailed as "God's Touch," secured a victory for Sedol. Lee Sedol's ability to rise to the occasion and adapt to the new paradigm presented by AI demonstrated the potential for humans and machines to learn from each other.

AlphaGo's overall win underscores a collaborative future. AI isn't a replacement for human ingenuity; it can be a spark. Humans and AI can work in tandem to unlock new levels of creativity and problem-solving, reshaping our world.

Centuries before AlphaGo, another innovation revolutionized knowledge: the printing press.

Book 1. The Bible

Johannes Gutenberg, 1455

Just as AlphaGo's victory marked a leap for AI, the publication of the Gutenberg Bible in 1455 sparked a pivotal moment in human history. Gutenberg and his Bible were more than a new printing method; they were a fountainhead for knowledge democratization, powering the Renaissance, Reformation, and Enlightenment. The Bible was the debut project of this transformative technology to the Western world.

Like AlphaGo, Gutenberg aimed to showcase his invention through a challenging project. Gutenberg was refining the printing process with his press, which was invented some 15 years before the Bible's publication. And his Bible was an ambitious undertaking, aiming to show that the new technology could create and compete with the hand-scribed masterworks of the day. Printed solely in black text, ornamentation, and flourishes were manually added by artisans and scribes. Pages from the new press were displayed, and a Cardinal in correspondence with the future Pope Pius II viewed some in Frankfurt. He wrote, "The script is extremely neat and legible, not at all difficult to follow. Your grace would be able to read it without effort, and indeed without glasses."[3] The Bible was a testament to the press's capabilities. It showcased a new standard of typography and layout— a fusion of technology and human artistry. The Bible was a masterpiece.

Much like the match with AlphaGo, it marked one of the first public demonstrations of content created by mechanical means that previously could only be done by hand.

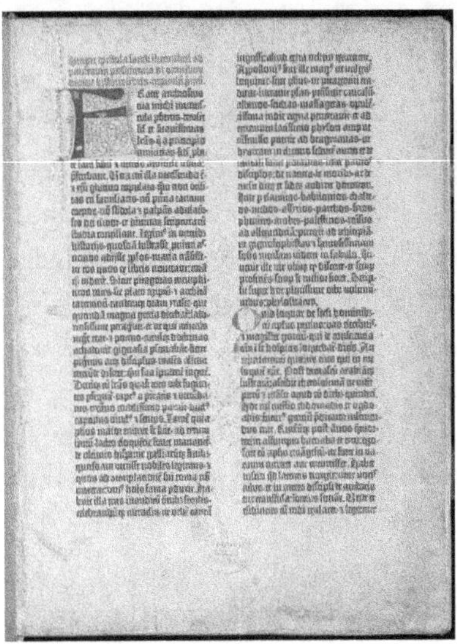

A page from the Gutenberg Bible featured hand-drawn flourishes added to the production.

Printed Incunabula

The Gutenberg Bible, weighing 60 pounds and spanning 1300 pages, was meant to be read aloud from the pulpit. What was to come in terms of the knowledge revolution was not yet on display or foretold.[4] In the beginning, printers aimed to make "incunabula" printed books to look like handwritten manuscripts, prioritizing aesthetics over the potential of the new technology.[5] Similarly, AI is often used to imitate human capabilities. While this approach is useful for specific tasks and can boost productivity, it might hinder us from fully exploring AI's potential for innovation.

Graphic artists refine AI-generated drafts much like the scribes of the Gutenberg era. While this approach assists with tasks traditionally done by hand, it may not fully utilize the technology. The emphasis on imitation rather than innovation could limit our ability to leverage AI's true power to transform our world. As we stand at the crossroads of this next technological revolution, the challenge lies in moving beyond mere replication to truly harness the innovative power of AI.

Book 2. La Commedia

Cristoforo Landino, 1481

In February 2023, Google unveiled Bard, an AI platform capable of explaining the James Webb Space Telescope discoveries to a child, aiming to compete with the media attention surrounding OpenAI's ChatGPT release months earlier. However, The New Scientist pointed out that Bard's demonstration contained inaccuracies quickly revealed by a simple Google search. This episode underscores the risks of pushing immature technology before it's fully developed.[6]

Bard's launch mirrored the aspirations of Cristoforo Landino, a scholar under Lorenzo de Medici's patronage in Florence. In 1481, Landino sought to enhance the city's literary prestige by publishing a groundbreaking edition of the Dante's Divine Comedy. Landino's ambitious La Commedia project required cutting-edge innovations: renowned artist Sandro Botticelli designed illustrations etched onto copper plates by Baccio Baldini – one for each canto. Plans called for printing 1,125 copies of the Divine Comedy, a monumental task given the extensive commentary and over 100 copper engravings.[7] Landino's initial contract, detailing the production process and daily proofing, seemed achievable. Despite advancements in printing and the ingenuity of those involved, challenges arose. The press's core strength in replicating text worked well, but the scale of Landino's commentary and one hundred engravings proved overwhelming. Copper engravings offered unprecedented detail, but including all hundred proved impractical. Today, only a fraction of the surviving copies contain engravings, often misplaced – one even upside down.[8]

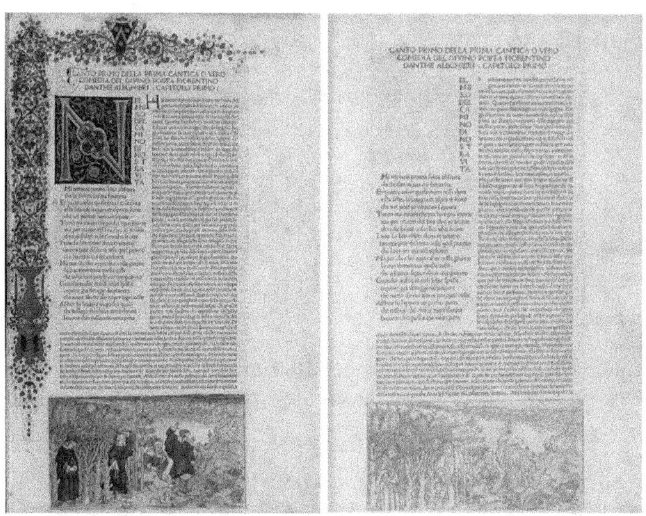

The ambition and reality of the printing of La Commedia were different.
Many of the books were missing engravings or contained mistakes.

The launch of Google's Bard AI and the ambitious 1481 printing of La Commedia in Florence serve as potent reminders of the perils of overextending nascent technology. In both cases, the desire for advancement clashed with technological limitations. Pursuing innovation is crucial, but so is acknowledging the limitations and potential errors in untested technologies. The path forward for AI development may lie in a balanced approach. The lesson from La Commedia is clear: ambitious goals must be balanced with a realistic understanding of what's achievable. Progress is often found not in audacious overreach but in the steady march of incremental improvements.

Book 3. The Aldine Virgil

Aldus Manutius, 1501

Following the publication of the Gutenberg Bible, Europe experienced a boom in printing houses and publishing centers. These hubs were strategically located around ports and trade routes, enabling the spread of knowledge. Venice, a thriving Mediterranean commerce hub, swiftly emerged as a publishing leader, its success fueled by its wealth, established trade routes, and skilled workforce.

This historical trend mirrors the rise of AI within today's digital commerce hubs. Leading AI technologies, such as Microsoft Copilot, Google Bard/Gemini, and Adobe Firefly, are closely tied to these hubs. These tools transcend automation, helping users find and organize information and leveraging established networks to accelerate adoption and enhance human capabilities.

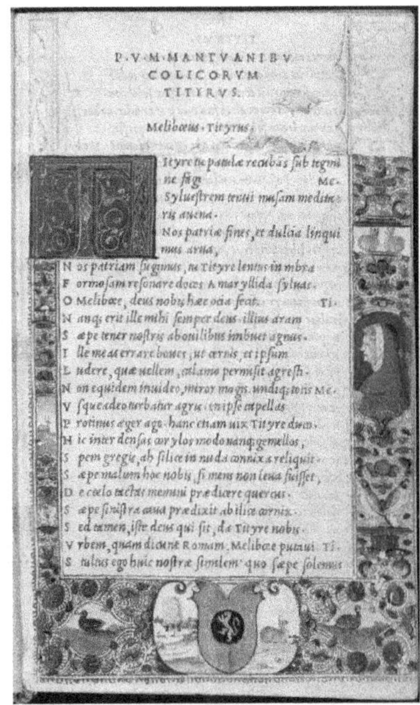

A page from the Aldine Virgil that included all the artistry of an incunabula but and a significantly smaller size.

In 1494, Aldus Manutius founded the Aldine Press in Venice, initiating a shift from mere replication to innovation. He introduced a new book design tailored for wider distribution and optimized for the printing press.[9] His publication of the "Virgil, Eclogues"—The Aldine Virgil—in 1501 was groundbreaking. It introduced the "octavo" format, a book one-eighth the size of a standard printed page, and boasted an unprecedented print run of 4,000 copies. This innovation echoes the transformative potential of AI today.[10]

Gutenberg Bible

La Commedia

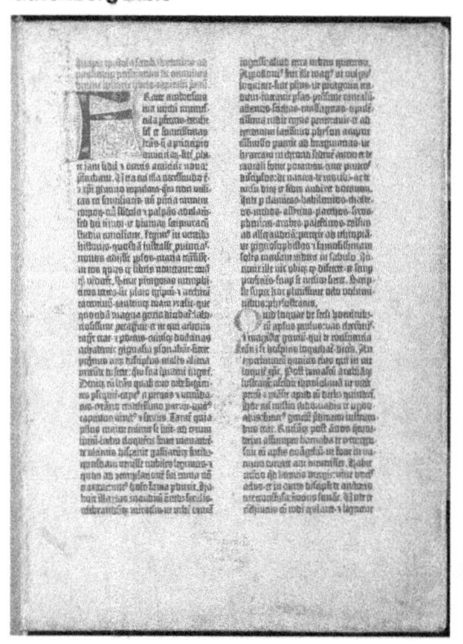

Aldine Virgil

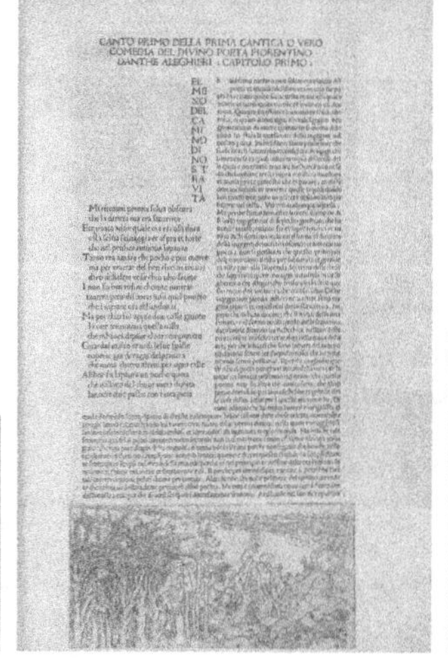

Aldine Divina Commedia

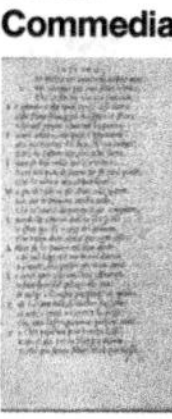

Comparing the sizes of the Gutenberg Bible, the octavo format Aldine Virgil, to the La Commedia, and the Aldine Divina Commedia. Note that the Aldine version of the Commedia displays the same Canto. Aldine is able to save space by eliminating all the commentary.

Book	Size (cm)	Pages
Gutenberg Bible (1455)	43.2 x 30.5 cm	1288
The Aldine Virgil (1501)	15.4 x 9.4 cm	228
La Commedia (1481)	43 x 31 cm	744
The Aldine Divina Commedia (1503)	15.7 x 9.4 cm	486

Aldine Virgil contrasted sharply with the massive Incunabula, like the Gutenberg Bible. Before Manutius, small books, known as "devotions," were primarily religious. The Aldine Virgil, however, was one of the first secular books printed for personal knowledge dissemination. Manutius innovated with the italic font to reduce size while maintaining readability. He also removed excessive commentary from the text, a technique exemplified by the Aldine version of La Commedia. This compact, portable format revolutionized personal reading and paved the way for the printing of numerous classical Greek and Roman works.

These books graced the personal libraries of luminaries like Leonardo da Vinci and Galileo Galilei.

Just as the Aldine Press democratized access to knowledge, AI tools enable us to search through vast amounts of information more quickly and efficiently. They empower us by aiding in the interpretation, discovery, and creation of new knowledge. AI also enables the creation of vast amounts of content. Aldus Manutius' focus on creating high-quality content leveraged the potential of the printing press, opening new markets and opportunities. Similarly, to achieve success with AI's generative power, we must prioritize focus, authenticity, and quality.

Sidenote: The "Aldus" name found new life in the digital age as Aldus PageMaker, a groundbreaking desktop publishing tool that transformed book publishing and laid the foundation for Adobe's success. This brief historical echo underscores the enduring impact of innovation. [11]

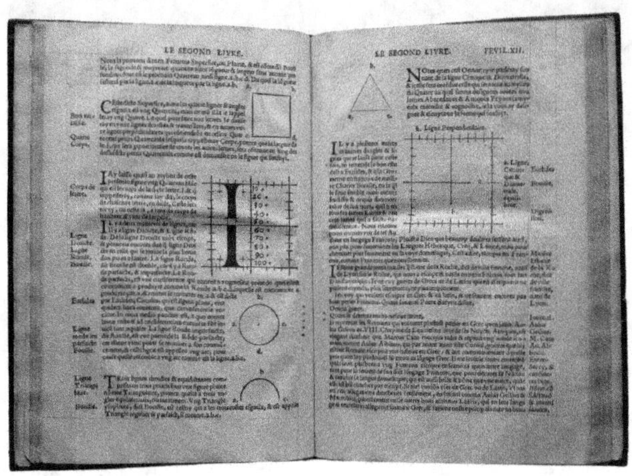

Book 4. Champ Fleury

Geoffroy Tory, 1529

To fully realize the latent transformative power of the printing press, further innovations were necessary. Nicholas Jenson, a pioneering printer, made a significant contribution by replacing the ornate blackletter script with the more legible Roman typeface.[12] This pivotal shift showcased the printing press's ability to produce sharper, more consistent letterforms, boosting legibility and visual harmony, laying the groundwork for future developments.

The 16th century witnessed an explosion of printing presses, yet consistency in language, texts, and fonts remained elusive. Geoffroy Tory emerged as a pioneering figure, championing standardization. His seminal work, "Champ Fleury," marked a pivotal shift from the chaotic Incunabula era to a more systematic approach. Tory introduced rules for

French spelling and grammar and innovated typeface design grounded in geometric principles. This approach aimed to standardize print and fonts, imbuing Roman type with a repeatable sense of natural beauty and harmony, all for the reader's benefit.[13]

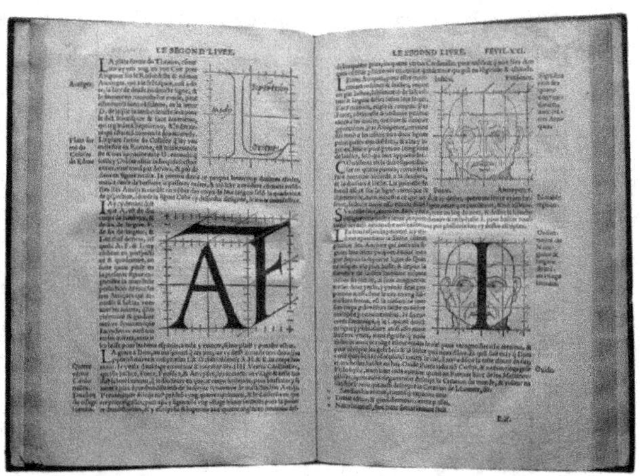

Pages from the Champ Fleury depicting Tory connecting typography to both nature and geometry.

Tory's emphasis on geometrically driven consistency aligns with the growing need to establish AI style, design, and usage standards today. AI excels at applying mathematical precision to content and design, enabling unparalleled consistency. Just as Tory harnessed the printing press's unique capabilities, we must recognize AI's distinct strengths. The goal is not to replace human creativity but to leverage AI as a powerful tool to enhance our abilities, ultimately benefiting the learner.

The printing press's impact unfolded through continuous innovation. Comparing Tory's work to AI reveals a shift from manual craftsmanship to digital automation, yet not a competitive one. We must set standards to elevate AI beyond mere human mimicry, similar to how Tory moved printing beyond the Incunabula era. By understanding AI's strengths, we can forge a collaborative future, building upon human creativity with AI's analytical power to achieve greater heights.

The Printing Press and the Trajectory of AI:

The claim that Artificial Intelligence will mirror the impact of the printing press may be overstated. Examining the historical development of print offers valuable insights into AI's trajectory. The printing press wasn't a singular invention; it was an enabling technology that unleashed a cascade of advancements in knowledge creation and dissemination.

What we can learn from each of the four books:

- **Gutenberg's Bible**: Just as Gutenberg's invention ignited a chain reaction of innovations studying its impact can provide a roadmap for navigating the coming wave of AI-driven advancements.

- **La Commedia**: Not all early endeavors will be groundbreaking. However, continued research and development have led to significant improvements.

- **Aldine Virgil**: Recognizing the true capabilities of AI, like the printing press, has the potential to democratize access to information. Aldus Manutius' Aldine Press transformed books into more personal knowledge devices, leveraging the technology to maximize reach and impact.

- **Champ Fleury**: Building upon existing strengths, figures like Geoffroy Tory used the printing press to establish standards and best practices, such as typeface design and page layout. Similarly, we can expect AI to lead to the development of new conventions for its control and integration.

AI has the potential to accelerate knowledge creation, technological advancements, and innovation, mirroring how these books shaped the printing press era. While AI's transformation will be long-lasting, significant changes may occur swiftly.

Da Vinci, a Gen-PrintPress Native

In 2019, a digital exhibition by the Museo Galileo in Florence sought to recreate the library of the universal genius. The exhibition offered a glimpse into Leonardo da Vinci's personal library at various times. Da Vinci, a towering figure of the Renaissance, emerged into a generation transformed by a revolutionary invention: the printing press.[14]

Da Vinci was born on April 15th, 1452, when Gutenberg was already at work creating his Bible using the printing press technology that would open knowledge to Da Vinci and the world. Unlike previous generations reliant on rare, hand-copied manuscripts, Da Vinci entered a world where books were becoming increasingly accessible. The printing press arrived in Florence in 1471, and by the time La Commedia was published, Da Vinci owned several books and even designed improvements for the press itself.

By 1501, his library had expanded to 140 titles, encompassing a diverse range of subjects. Works from the prestigious Aldine Press provided access to cutting-edge scientific texts, classical literature, and contemporary scholarship. At his death in 1519, his collection likely numbered around 200 volumes, a testament to his insatiable curiosity. The staggering growth of book publishing during Da Vinci's lifetime—from 5 million to 80 million titles by 1550—underscores the printing press's transformative power. This unprecedented access to knowledge undoubtedly fueled Da Vinci's polymathic genius, making him a quintessential product of his era. [15]

Age of Artificial

Learning from the Dawn of Printing

The internet and advancements in data processing have democratized information access, mirroring the transformative impact of the printing press. However, the true power of the press wasn't just the technology itself, but the explosion of learning and knowledge it enabled. Similarly, AI's potential lies in its ability to unlock significant changes across numerous fields.

We are currently in a transitional phase for AI, akin to the period following Gutenberg's invention. Just as the early printing press revolutionized knowledge sharing, AI is now moving beyond initial imitations to establish the necessary frameworks for its control and integration into society, markets, and daily lives. This period of uncertainty reflects the nascent stage of AI development, offering the potential to discover applications beyond mere automation or mimicking existing tasks.

By embracing AI as an "assistive intelligence" tool, we can usher in a new era of creativity, productivity, and innovation. Similar to how Da Vinci leveraged books off the printing press to fuel his endeavors, we can consider these guiding principles:

Guiding Principles for AI Use

Principle	Description
Focus on AI's Early Strengths	Leverage AI for tasks and questions that benefit from its analytical capabilities.
Balancing Innovation with Pragmatism	While pushing boundaries is crucial, understanding current capabilities is equally important. Setting realistic expectations allows us to manage initial limitations.
Discipline and Purpose	Maintain authenticity in endeavors that seek to utilize AI effectively.
Assisting Intelligence	Don't view AI as a replacement, but rather a collaborative tool. Building standards and guidelines for its practical use and collaboration is vital.

The Gutenberg Bible showcased the potential of the printing press. Publishers who followed him recognized the need to create something new, not simply replicate existing methods. While some early printed materials faded into obscurity, others, like Aldine Virgil, sparked a revolution in learning and invention.

The success of AI can be measured by the new levels of literacy, learning, and knowledge it generates. These advancements could potentially spark a new generation of polymaths and geniuses akin to Da Vinci. Just as Lee Sedol elevated his Go game to new heights in response to the novel challenge presented by AlphaGo, human-AI collaboration can lead to breakthroughs beyond our current imagination.

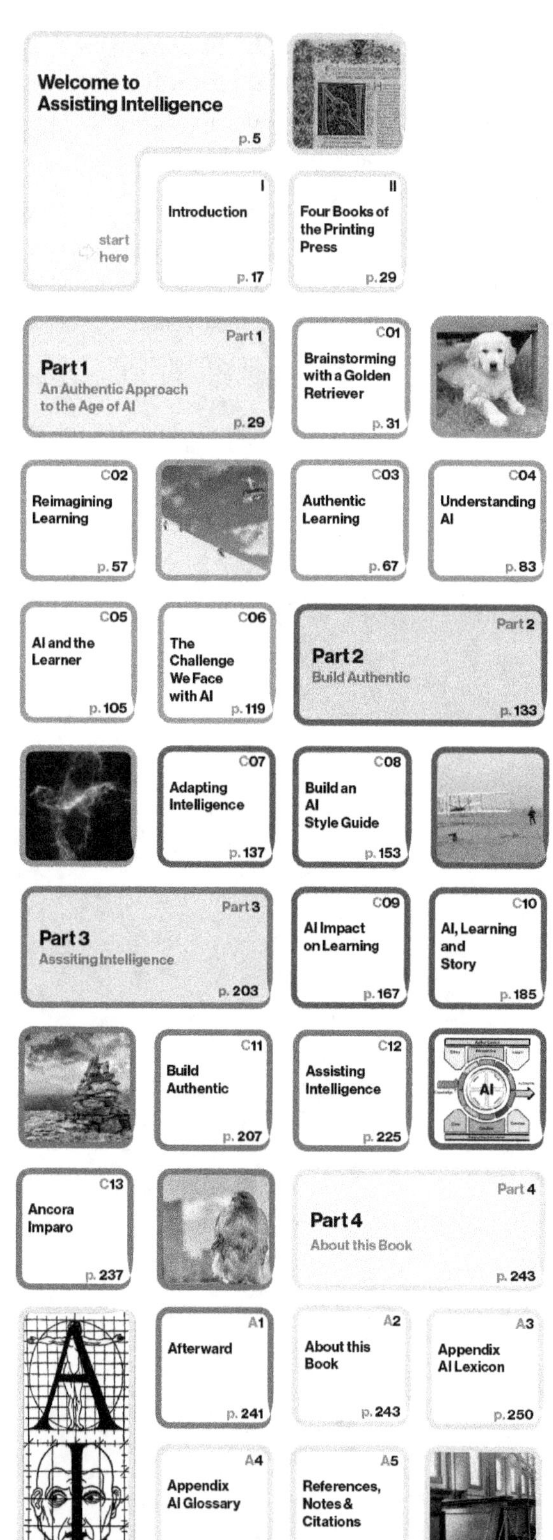

Authentic Approach to the AI Age

Organizations, like early printers, stand at a crossroads. Some may choose to fully delegate tasks to AI systems, striving to maintain an illusion of human touch. Others might embark on bold experiments to leapfrog innovation, grappling with unforeseen consequences. Yet, others will seize opportunities to innovate new products and services. All these paths lead to the generation of new knowledge, thoughts, and ideas. Assisting Intelligence aims to aid the latter category, helping organizations establish standards for knowledge construction and learning in the age of AI.

Assisting Intelligence posits that AI is not about replicating existing human skills or crafting a synthetic world. It's about harnessing AI's analytical prowess to empower human progress while preserving an authentic approach. "Assisting Intelligence: Build Authentic in the Age of AI" delves into this future. Part one provides a primer on the current state of AI, how to reshape learning for the AI age. Part two explores integrating AI with knowledge creation and development. Finally, the book tackles fostering effective collaboration for authentic learning, where AI plays a crucial role.

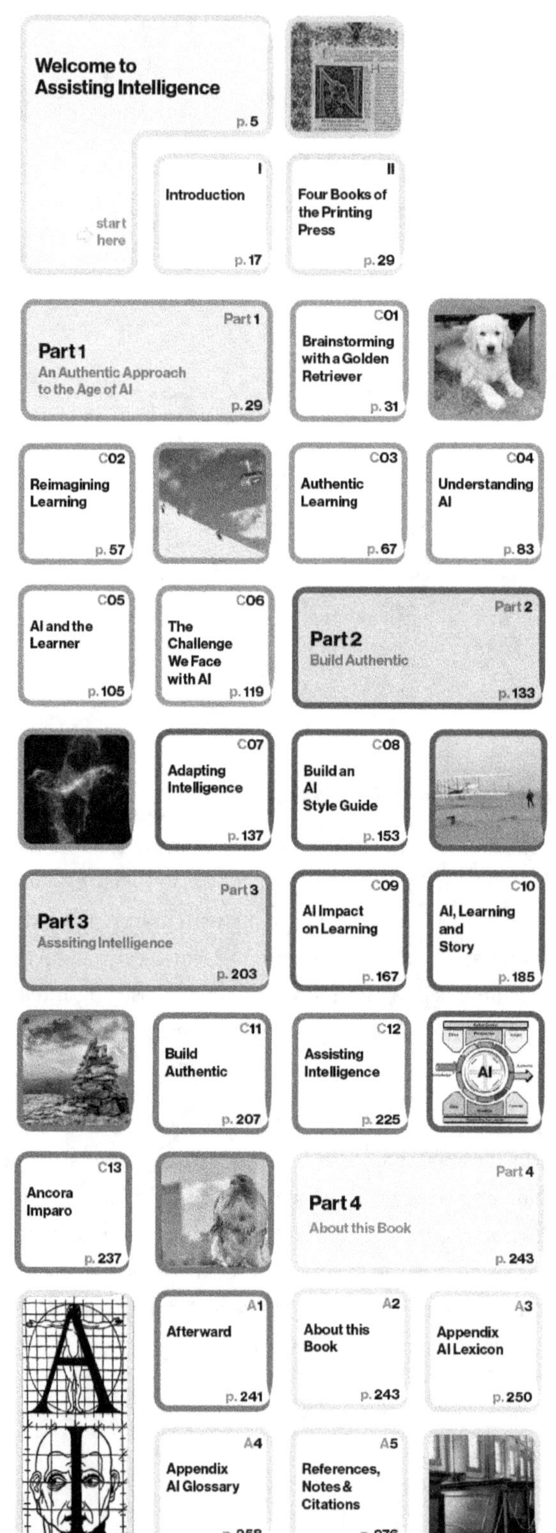

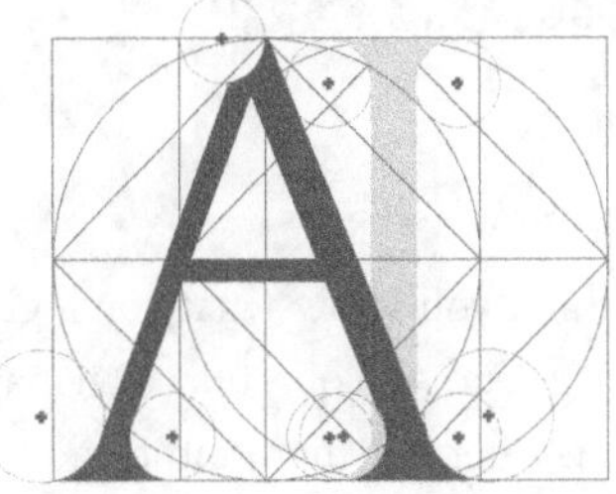

Chapter 1:
Brainstorming with a Golden Retriever

How AI will retrieve whatever it can find

In this chapter, we'll look at how Artificial Intelligence is already in use and impacts content, images, learning, and learners.

The greatest obstacle to discovery is not ignorance--it is the illusion of knowledge. - Librarian of Congress Daniel Boorstin

Brainstorming with a Golden Retriever

When you throw a ball to a Golden Retriever, you may think you know what you'll get back, but you can never be sure. The same is true when you ask an AI a question. You may think you know what the answer will be, but the reality is often far more intricate and surprising than you imagined.

Fetch Instinct

Consider Mara, my Golden Retriever, a fetch enthusiast. Her breeding, instincts, and training have perfected her fetching skills. Whether it's a ball or a chew toy, Mara retrieves it. However, her enthusiasm sometimes leads to unexpected returns. She may upcycle a stick to a ball, a ball to a shoe, or a shoe to a shirt still in use. She may bypass the ball to fetch a neighbor's paper.

Similarly, an AI excels at digital fetch. You request something, and it retrieves images, content, or data that it thinks you asked for. But like Mara, the AI's responses are shaped by its training. For instance, if you ask an AI trained in sports news for health tips, you'll likely get fitness advice instead of medical guidance. The data the AI was trained on becomes its "fetch object," influencing what it retrieves.

Mara often watches "Planet Earth" with keen interest. While she may not fully comprehend the scientific details, she is captivated by visuals and sounds. If she were to encounter David Attenborough, her familiarity with his distinctive voice might elicit a curious wag.

Sit, Stay, Prompt, Response

Give Mara a command or throw something, and based on her training, she usually does or returns what is expected. Mara might modify the objects thrown in transit. Toys can be returned with a missing limb, destuffed, or a new hole for better grip. Give her a command outside her training, and she will improvise her response.

AIs generate content by dynamically assembling the presented content each time. Neither a dog nor an AI truly understands why we ask or what we ask; they intuit from their training and experience with us and approximate the best response. According to an article in the MIT Technology Review, when an AI makes a mistake in its response — referred to as 'AI hallucinations' — it is a common behavior of AI. This happens because the AI approximates responses based on the language model it was built and trained on. These hallucinations can be entertaining, but as the article pointed out, every response from an AI is, to a degree, is a hallucination.[1]

Initiating Play

Asking an AI to start an engaging conversation is akin to Mara initiating play. She grabs a toy or shoe, something familiar and known to her, to elicit a response. Much like the AI, her objective is to engage us in play, engagement, or interaction. The specific toy or game is not important; it is the engagement that matters. Similarly, asking an AI to engage in conversation works in the same way.

```
Prompt: Let's have an engaging conversation; you start.
```

It will draw from common prompts, such as:

```
Copilot Response: Have you ever thought about what it would
be like to live in a different era? If you could choose any
time period to experience for a week, which one would you
pick and why?
```

```
Gemini Response: Let's talk about the future! Given the
rapid pace of technological advancements, what do you think
will be the most significant change in our daily lives
within the next decade?
```

For an AI, a conversation is simply an interaction where it strives to remain engaging. An AI's responses are in the moment. AIs do not retain information from conversations; their goal is to create an engaging experience every time they interact. Whether switching toys or topics, Mara and the AI will gleefully continue to play for as long as the game or conversation continues.

The Reality of AI and Pets

Our tendency to anthropomorphize our pets, attributing human intent to their actions, mirrors our inclination to ascribe human-like intelligence as we chat and interact with conversant AIs. However, neither possesses human intelligence. Our pets' responsiveness, loyalty, and enthusiasm stem from instinct, genetics, breeding, and training. AI's natural language processing and adaptability result from programmatic and statistical responses designed to engage and make us more comfortable, not to replicate human intelligence.

Stories of golden retrievers saving lives and AI revolutionizing industries captivate our imagination. However, the meticulous training and development underlying these achievements often go unreported. AI's seemingly effortless information retrieval can obscure the considerable groundwork involved, including programming, data curation, testing, modeling, training, and validation. Without critical thinking on the part of the user, AI's deluge of information can transform into a torrent of irrelevance, inaccuracy, and even harm.

Successful interactions with AI rely on the user's ability to discern genuinely useful information from what should be dismissed. Given AI's uncurated nature, human discernment is essential to sift through and extract valuable insights from potential distractions, ensuring that the obtained information effectively meets our requirements. It is vital to view AI not as a replacement for human intelligence but as a collaborative partner and a source of information to be leveraged effectively. Ultimately, we are responsible for determining the information's significance and devising the optimal way to leverage it.

Why Own a Golden or Use AI

Like a golden retriever, an AI will never tire of fetching results and is always agreeable to whatever is thrown and time spent. Understanding what an AI or dog was bred for and how it was trained can result in amazing experiences, results, and rewards. Just as effective training unlocks what a golden retriever is capable of, working with an AI and understanding its capabilities and limitations will allow you to maximize the return.

As we transition to discussing the types of AI available and how to think about them, it's important to remember that, like dogs, not all AIs are the same. They come in various breeds, each with its strengths, weaknesses, and ideal use cases. Understanding these differences is key to choosing the right AI for your needs and interacting with it effectively. Whether you're looking for a specific breed of AI to perform a specialized task or a more general-purpose AI, the key is to understand it resides in training, capabilities, and limitations. This understanding will enable you to harness the power of AI effectively, just like a well-trained golden retriever.

Training For Your AI

Imagine a frictionless, limitless content generator, and you possessed the powers to construct it like something Willa Wonka's mind would create. Your machine would be powered and possess all the boundless energy, enthusiasm, and resourcefulness of a Golden Retriever puppy, along with similar intelligence and ability to run amuck. How would you envision and build this system? What would you trust it to do? How much responsibility and autonomy would you give it? You would want to capture the enthusiasm and energy, but you would have to build a controlled environment for you and it to have any chance of success. Establish safe zones, boundaries, and guardrails —places AI systems cannot reach.

Mara quickly became an expert at breaking out of her crate. To escape her confines, increasing measures were defeated, even multiple carabiners. When left alone, she now sleeps in an oversized chair with an open window in the office. Despite best efforts, tightly confining AI to restrictive outputs will need to be tempered with realistic boundaries you can achieve. We have developed a measure of trust and comfort, making sure all the sock drawers are tightly closed.

In this book, we'll explore how to work with these Wonka-like systems of our business imagination, how to select and where to deploy them, and how to use them to assist us in generating and communicating knowledge.

Where AI is Having Success

Data fuels AI. Data access is crucial for AI to work effectively. Data consists of large copious amounts of structured and unstructured data. Many early adopter successes with AI showcase their ability to create new markets or drive deeper connections with their customers (Slack, Uber, AirBnB, Netflix). Companies that have benefited from the era of big data are now moving into AI, where they can gain additional insights from the increased analytical prowess of AI.

Businesses with access to high-quality, relevant, and proprietary data can use it to gain insights, create value, and improve decision-making. Their successes with AI also depend on having the data to process, analyze, and apply in meaningful and useful ways. Netflix uses its massive and rich data on user preferences, behavior, and feedback to power its recommendation system, content production, and personalization. [2]

Companies that successfully transition from big data analytics to AI gain a deeper understanding of their customers and insights into their services and processes. AI allows these companies to analyze large amounts of data more efficiently, predict trends, and make more accurate decisions. This evolution of AI has opened new opportunities for businesses, making it an essential tool in today's digital world.[3]

AI offers a dynamic and predictive understanding, making it a more powerful tool for many business scenarios.

AIs Opening Move — Open AI Systems

AI can help businesses improve their performance, productivity, and profitability by automating tasks, optimizing processes, and enhancing decision-making based on generalized data models. ChatGPT, MS Copilot, Google Gemini, and other open platforms offer the ability to generalize content, streamline processes, and create more personalized experiences and interactions with customers. These open-platform AIs are available to all businesses and industries and are developed on the LLMs.

By providing access, employees, students, teachers, and customers can apply and utilize their domain knowledge. When applied to AI, this domain knowledge about their organization, brand, unique positioning, and industry can help them innovate and differentiate themselves from competitors by creating new products, services, and markets.

AI can also help businesses and employees generate new data, such as feedback, preferences, and behavior, to further improve their products or services. Data access and AI are interrelated factors that can help businesses differentiate themselves.

In Creative Settings

AI systems can participate and automate many elements of creative expression. AIs can automate marketing content and image generation for social media and blogs, improve and edit content and images, diversify content and images (mediums, languages, and formats), and versioning for different audiences and applications. AI can power marketing applications. AIs can create, manage, and deliver personalized digital experiences that integrate with marketing channels, including web content management, digital asset management, and marketing campaign management. AIs can empower marketing processes with enhanced data-driven decisions to improve customer experiences.[4]

In Learning Settings

Already in business, education at the university level and K-12 must contend with AI entering all facets of learning. Organizations and institutions " have to decide what we're doing, rather than fighting a retreat against the AI."[5] AI can also help employees develop and learn new skills, knowledge, and competencies by providing personalized, adaptive, and continuous learning opportunities. By facilitating information sharing, feedback, and engagement, AI can also help employees collaborate and communicate more effectively with each other and customers. [6]

Artificial Intellects and Where to Encounter Them

Artificial intelligence is overtaking commonly used technologies by providing more advanced decisioning. [7]

Recommendation systems: AI powering systems in Netflix, AirBnB, and Amazon can analyze vast amounts of data to understand preferences and recommend personalized content.

Customer Service: AI-powered chatbots and virtual assistants are increasingly used in customer service to handle common queries, thereby improving efficiency.

Healthcare: AI is being used to predict diseases, assist in diagnosis, personalize treatment, and even in drug discovery. For example, AI algorithms can analyze medical images to detect anomalies.

Autonomous Vehicles: AI is under the hood of self-driving technology. It allows vehicles to understand their environment, make decisions, and navigate without human intervention.

Education: AI provides personalized learning paths using an AI-powered chat, such as with Khan Academy, where a chat that assists with schoolwork as a coach or tutor would.[8]

Finance: AI is used in algorithmic trading, fraud detection, credit scoring, and automating financial tasks. It can analyze market trends and make predictions with higher accuracy.

Each of these verticals shares the ability to further segment and provide personalized decisioning based on access to extremely large data sets. The potential applications of AI are vast and continue to grow as the technology evolves. (It will be fun to see how fast and by how much this paragraph becomes outdated)

New Levels of Understanding

Rumack : This woman has to be gotten to a hospital.
Elaine Dickinson : A hospital? What is it?
Rumack : It's a big building with patients, but that's not important right now.

With advanced analytical and language processing, AIs are more capable of understanding the context tasks presented to them and are more responsive to them than existing technologies. If a user were to ask an AI and a traditional search engine: [9]

"What are the symptoms of the flu?"[10]

Traditional Search Engine	AI Response
The search engine would return a list of web pages that contain information related to the query. For example, it might return pages from health websites that list flu symptoms. The user would be able to see the list of sources for information and select to learn more.	An AI system would understand the intent of the question and provide a direct answer. It might say, "The symptoms of the flu can include fever, malaise, headache, runny nose, sneezing, reduced sense of smell, metallic taste in mouth, chills, cough, body pain or muscle pain, and sore throat" based on information it has collected and interpreted from the data it house.
Information Retrieval	
Provide a list of documents, web pages, or resources that are relevant to the input query.	Generate a direct answer to the question posed by the user.

Understanding	
Primarily rely on keyword matching.	Understand context of a conversation, allowing for more interactive and dynamic exchanges.
Analysis	
Primarily designed to index and retrieve web pages.	While they can also perform specific tasks like setting alarms or playing music, they can also engage in more complex tasks like providing detailed explanations or generating creative content.

In a more conversational tone with a voice assistant, the question may change to:

"Tell me how I know if I have the flu?"

Traditional Voice Assistant	AI Powered Voice Assistant
The voice assistant may locate and quote web sources related to the query. It might read pages that describe the flu and recommend seeing a healthcare provider for a diagnosis. The results still could have symptoms in the response but hat word is no longer in the query. The user would hear the source that provided the information.	The AI system would understand that the user is asking for relatively the same information as in the first question but phrased differently. It might respond, "You might have the flu if you are experiencing symptoms such as fever, malaise, headache, runny nose, sneezing, reduced sense of smell, metallic taste in mouth, chills, cough, body pain or muscle pain, and sore throat. If you have these symptoms, it's recommended to see a healthcare provider for a diagnosis."
Information Retrieval	
Rely on predefined scripts and user data to respond to queries.	Uses large databases of text and learns from this data using machine learning techniques.
Understanding	
Handle basic context from the current conversation but may struggle with complex context or long conversation histories.	Handle complex context and maintain longer conversation histories. This allows them to provide more relevant and personalized responses.
Analysis	

They are primarily designed to perform specific tasks, such as setting alarms, playing music, or answering simple questions.

While they can also perform specific tasks like setting alarms or playing music, they can also engage in more complex tasks like providing detailed explanations or generating creative content.

In both cases, the phrasing of the question impacts the results. However, AI systems can provide a more direct and contextually appropriate response depending on how the person phrased the question.

Both voice assistants and AI-powered voice assistants can respond to user queries and perform tasks, yet the methods and capabilities can vary. AI-powered voice assistants, with their ability to handle complex context and generate unique responses, can often provide more personalized and contextually appropriate interactions.

However, the effectiveness of each tool can depend on the specific task and user requirements.

Culture is shaped by 7's

In 2023, BMW released an ad campaign for the BMW 7 Series. The ad added the BMW 7 series to a list of coincidental numberings - "Seven seas, seven continents, seven days of the week, seven colors of the rainbow, ..." before adding "7 Series" and then declared that "Culture is shaped by 7s."[11] Whether this ad was created with or by AI is not the question, how would we go about proving this assertion.[12]

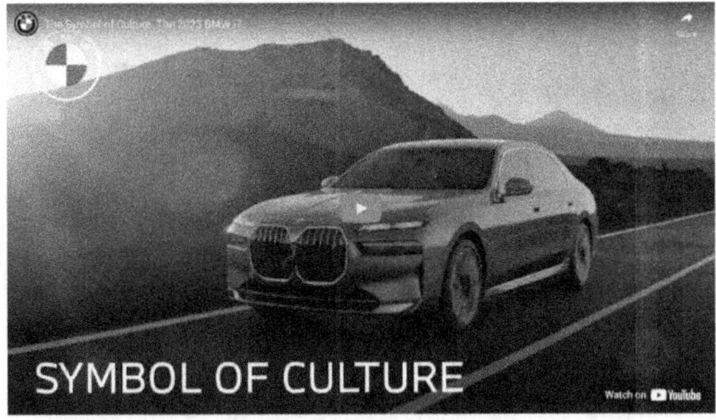

Image from the BMW ad, Symbol of Culture on YouTube.

A simple Google search will return 1,630,000,000 results highlighting links to "7 Elements of Culture, 7 Cultural Trends, 7 Dimensions of Culture." The overwhelming flood of possible content makes it seemingly impossible to validate or disprove the assertion from a search.[13]

If we test the ad's premise with an AI, the AI will not question the validity of the premise, bias, or assumptions built into the question. It will presume the premise of the question is valid and fetch responses that validate it regardless of its flaws.

```
Prompt: Is culture shaped by the number 7?

From Gemini: While it might seem surprising, the number 7
has held significant cultural, religious, and symbolic mean-
ing across various societies throughout history …

From Copilot: The number 7 indeed holds a special place in
many cultures and has influenced various aspects of life,
from religion and mythology to science and daily practices …
```

Both AIs provide supporting evidence without questioning or fundamentally challenging the premise of the question.

Hitchens's Razor

What can be asserted without evidence can also be dismissed without evidence.

Christopher Hitchens would make a great AI dog trainer.[14] He created a general knowledge rule that serves as a rule for rejecting certain knowledge claims.[15] Hitchens's razor underscores the importance of skepticism in dealing with AIs, from the claims about AI's capabilities to the results it produces and the methodologies employed in its development. This skepticism needs to be applied to:

- **Claims about an AI**: Any claim about an AI's capabilities, performance, or results should be backed by evidence. If an AI is said to have a certain accuracy level or perform a specific task, data or results should support this claim.

- **AI Results**: The outputs or results generated by an AI should be verifiable. If an AI is used to make predictions, there should be a way to test these predictions against actual outcomes.

- **AI Development**: When evaluating AI models, hypotheses or assumptions about the choice of a particular algorithm or the use of specific parameters should be justified with empirical evidence or theoretical reasoning.

It's not hard to imagine advertising is stretching credulity in the name of marketing. Applying Hitchens's razor to the assertion leaves most credibility behind. AIs will support assertions through a query without trying to ascertain if they are valid. Yet, taking this to extremes can yield remarkable results. Among our favorite results were:

Prompt: Is culture shaped by donuts?

From Google Gemini: Overall, the evidence suggests that donuts have had a significant impact on culture. They are a global food with a long and rich history, and they have been used in popular culture and to promote social change. Donuts are more than just a food; they are a cultural symbol that can be used to convey a variety of meanings.

From ChatGPT: While it might sound amusing to suggest that culture is shaped by donuts, it's essential to recognize that cultural influences are typically more deeply rooted in broader social, historical, and economic factors. However, one could argue that certain food items, including donuts, can become symbolic or carry cultural significance in specific contexts. Here are a few ways in which donuts might be connected to culture:

From Microsoft Copilot: Donuts, seemingly humble and sweet, have left their mark on American culture. From foreign pastries to blue-collar treats, they tell a story about our lives. Let's explore why these doughy delights matter.

Human Curation

With traditional search, relevant links are presented, and a quick scan can often find a credible source to pursue further discovery in research. And while it is true that AI is constantly evolving, these egregious mistakes will not be the case in the not-so-distant future. What is also true is that egregious mistakes will be harder to detect.

When conducting a traditional search, part of the results process occurs when the user selects the links from recognizable, credible sources. Beyond the sponsored links, the user curates the results by selecting the sources that are considered credible. This additional credibility filter is not always easy or intuitive with an AI. The responsive nature of an AI provides the answer without supporting evidence.

Artificial Sophists

Sophist: (soph·ist / ˈsäfist/)
• n. a paid teacher of philosophy and rhetoric in ancient Greece, associated in popular thought with moral skepticism and specious reasoning. A person who reasons with clever but fallacious arguments.[16]

An AI can more accurately be described as an artificial sophist rather than an artificial intelligence. Services provided by an AI are paid for directly or indirectly by the user, and an AI is immensely skilled in providing answers. When generating responses, an AI sophist may not necessarily provide the most credible answer among the available responses. [17]

An AI relies on patterns learned from training data and statistical modeling to generate coherent and contextually relevant answers. In addition to factual responses, the selection process can be influenced by the input prompt, its training, and the context provided. Further, AIs don't exactly convey that they are making statistical guesses and drawing conclusions based on the probability of being right.

Because an AI fundamentally lacks wisdom (think a giant data-driven golden retriever), it is the user's responsibility to evaluate interactions with it. Whoever makes a prompt from has the burden of proof regarding the truthfulness of a claim; if this burden is not met, then the claim is unfounded and should be dismissed. The importance of being earnest precedes any performance gains in using AI.

AI Hallucinations

AI hallucinations occur when a model generates content that is entirely fictional or diverges significantly from reality. These hallucinations can emerge during creative tasks or when the model lacks grounding in factual information. They are typically so far from the norm that they are easily dismissed. What is more insidious about hallucinations is that as models improve, they will become harder and harder to detect. [18]

AI Shenanigans

AI shenanigans refer to mischievous or unintended actions generated by an AI that, left unchallenged, can cause unintended mischief. During coverage of a Scottish football match, an AI-powered camera tracking system kept locking on the linesman's head during the game - mistaking it for the ball.[19] These actions can result from biases, flawed training data, or unexpected interactions between components. Shenanigans can be subtle, blending in with legitimate responses and they might appear plausible at first glance. Detecting shenanigans often requires understanding context, which can be challenging for AI systems. While AI Shenanigans can be amusing, they pose risks when users accept them as truth. [20]

Calling Out AI Bullsh@t

It is important to recognize and call out hallucinations, shenanigans, and outright BS before they leave the AI response. The danger of generated content is that it can be so convincing that it is nearly impossible to discern what is trustworthy and credible objectively.[21] Lack of clarity on how AIs function and perform can exacerbate issues that arise from the creative process and the finished results.

Working with an AI, especially through chat, both users and their audience of the content generated can be influenced by the nature of the responses. Taken to the extreme, this can be criminal activity. Government agencies are investigating and proposing rules regarding the use of AI. "Fraudsters are using AI tools to impersonate individuals with eerie precision and at a much wider scale. With voice cloning and other AI-driven scams on the rise, protecting Americans from impersonator fraud is more critical than ever."[22]

> *"People could easily be led to think that they're conversing with something that understands them and is on their side," Michael Atleson, Attorney, FTC Division of Advertising Practices.* [23]

The AI system does not truly understand emotions or intentions - it just follows patterns and algorithms. Yet it can be trained to take action on the patterns of emotions and intention. Learning and AI are at the cross-section of informing the audience of new knowledge. Learning intends to influence its audience's beliefs and behaviors, so the intent of an AI's natural language responses is to generate that same influence.

Attention Intelligence

Given that a golden retriever will endlessly fetch results and provide a continuous positive disposition to every interaction, it is hard not to get lost in distraction with them. One of AI's most harmful aspects is its ability to manipulate content to hold the learner's attention. As evidenced by 'doom-scrolling' — social media platforms use infinite scrolling and auto-play features to grab and hold attention.[24] An AI can dynamically prioritize content algorithmically to reinforce and maintain engagement and dynamically assemble content to ensure persistent engagement.

Ascertaining AI's Asseverate Assertions

> *assert (v.) ": to state or declare positively and often forcefully or aggressively."*
> *ascertain (v.) "to find out or learn with certainty."*
> *asseverate(v.) : to affirm or declare positively or earnestly.*[25]

The convergence of these terms largely does not exist outside of a courtroom or an old rhetoric text book, yet their meanings will have a resurgence in the age of AI. This alliterative title refers to situations where an AI confidently makes claims (assertions) without providing substantial evidence or proof (ascertations). Assertions that lack the necessary support or credibility allow an AI to make them misleading or harmful. AIs can generate, augment, or modify messages with strong conviction or certainty to convince people to shape, reinforce, or change their responses. Further, even though the response lacks evidentiary support, an AI can shape its response to persuade (asseverate) its audience even though it may not be true. An AI can create highly persuasive text, and its persuasiveness can be further improved with human curation.

In the context of AI, gathering credible evidentiary information from an AI is crucial for maintaining trust in AI systems and ensuring they are providing accurate and helpful information. The user must understand the AI's limitations by working with an AI to:

- **Evaluate Accuracy**: Check whether the AI's assertions are correct and based on reliable data or information.

- **Assess Confidence**: Determine how certain the AI is about its assertions. This could be indicated by the AI's use of language or by a confidence score provided by the AI system.

- **Understand Context**: Consider the context in which the AI makes assertions. This includes the data it was trained on, the inputs it received, and the task it was designed to perform.

- **Check Relevance**: Ensure the AI's assertions are relevant to the query or task at hand.

- **Switch Sides**: If an AI makes an assertion, try taking the opposing view or asking for contrarian input from the AI.

The Dangers of an Asseverate Intelligence

It was a bright cold day in April, and the clocks were striking thirteen. George Orwell 1984

The opening lines of George Orwell introduce us to a world where reality is manipulated, and the truth is malleable. Beyond media, beyond social media, and the internet, AI systems can, on a grander scale than ever before present, create, manage, manipulate, and distribute disinformation. For large actors, AI presents the opportunities to create sustained, multifaceted campaigns of disinformation so pervasive, so asseverative, that just as the citizens of Orwell's dystopia accept the impossibility of a 13-hour clock without question, people in our society might accept AI-generated disinformation as truth without critical examination.

Consider the Source

It can be frightening to think about how much AI models may be built on inherently flawed information. AIs can use social media content for training and as sources. Social media provides AIs with rich real-world language, slang, and informal expressions. It can also contain misinformation, rumors, and biased content.

The Internet, social media, and the democratization of content have created vast new content ecosystems. "Bullshit spreads more easily in a massively networked, click-driven social media world than in any previous social environment." [26]

Social media content presents challenges due to its noise, biases, varying quality, and use with AI. An AI model may inadvertently learn and reproduce these patterns. Further, an

AI can dramatically scale and create new content based on or even enhance false and disinformation.

> *"Crafting a new false narrative can now be done at dramatic scale, and much more frequently — it's like having AI agents contributing to disinformation."*[27]

Talent Borrows, AIs Steal

> *"Originality is nothing but judicious imitation. The most original writers borrowed one from another." — Voltaire*

> *"Talent borrows, Genius Steals!" — Oscar Wilde*

> *"Immature poets imitate; mature poets steal." — T.S. Elliot*

> *"Good artists copy; great artists steal." — Picasso*

> *"Good artists copy; great artists steal." — Steve Jobs*

The quote is often attributed to Voltaire and Oscar Wilde. Notables including Picasso, T.S. Elliot, and Steve Jobs have borrowed, stolen, recycled or upcycled the phrase. Open AI platforms, both image and content-based, have been trained on materials that include copyrighted materials and the intellectual property of others. Building new content from existing copyrighted materials can be considered fair use and not a violation of the copyright holder. Yet, providing for language processing, it is easy to see that many statements and the sentiment within them are direct lifts from original works despite there being syntactical differences.

Using a traditional search engine, finding the attributable source via a link is often easier. Blogs and other writings by individuals may be directly lifting content from other known credible sources, yet referencing a credible source in an article or book is a safe means to build upon the works of others and support your work with additional information and resources. AIs try to directly generate the answer, which can be an amalgam of several sources combined in a creative way or a direct unattributed lift from a limited number of sources. Understanding where a reference came from is often more difficult.

Directly Violating Intellectual Property

Image-based AIs can generate copious amounts of imagery yet may include outright or overly rely on copyrighted content in the creation.[28] While it may appear that these images are authentic originals, they are based on algorithms and data sets of existing images. When asked to produce an image from training data overwhelmed with similar images, it creates nearly identical images to original copyrighted works. AI's memorization of common images can result in a prompt asking for an image of animated toys to respond with characters from Toy Story. Or a popular movie icon, producing an image that looks directly lifted from the movie itself. AIs offer the opportunity to create content at an incredible speed without the need for specialized design skills or advanced systems. [29]

How to Handle Property

It is critical to ensure your content is accurately attributed to the appropriate sources. Whether direct or indirect usage of others' intellectual property is a risk, AIs can generate a storyboard image quickly but should not be part of the final deliverable. Content and images should be authentic.

> *Generative AI systems don't just generate new content in abstraction, they can be tailored to generate content in the style of a specific person. The trouble is that now a generative AI system can take hundreds of examples of what an individual has created and start to replicate their creative process, in some way stripping away their human identity or taking part of their human capital away from them.*[30]

Directing an AI to adopt a known persona or brand style can rapidly synthesize content that appears to be from the originators using their intellectual property and copyrighted materials. This may be permissible under the guise of fair use, but organizations and legislative entities are examining whether this fair use is ethical use of not only another's intellectual property but also their intellect and creative processes. Generative AIs can go beyond copying individual images to mimicking an entire creative process.

Giving over learning and intelligence to an AI blurs who owns what an AI creates is still being ironed out.

> *And if we don't retain ownership of our intelligence and creative process, then individuals will have a much lower incentive to develop that intelligence, or that human capital, in the first place.*[31]

What Are We Trading?

Mara persistently outwits us by leveraging her built-in Golden Retriever's ability to find things and her growing skill to determine the value of our objects and present them to us as a choice to 'watch me destroy this in front of you' or 'feel free to chase me.' She communicates that both options work for her with a methodic wag of her tail.

To remedy this our trainer suggested we create a third option. We taught Mara to 'trade.' This means she relinquishes items like shoes, towels, or socks that she would typically chew, in exchange for a treat. Mara quickly caught on to this 'trading' concept and now actively searches for valuable items to 'trade' with us. When interacting with an AI, what are we trading? Prompts and open generative systems are currently in the early stages of monetization. How much of the data given over in the prompt will become part of the equation as AI tech endeavors toward value returns and profitability? How much information is loaded into AIs becomes part of future data sets and insights that can be monetized? An AI just like Mara might 'trade' data for functionality. Providing insights on how to improve communication, an email can offer an AI an opportunity for domain knowledge on business communications and processes. An AI can mine your data for treasures it can present for treats and responses to others.

What you load into an AI can become part of its training data, potentially influencing future results for others. This includes not only your intellectual property but also confidential information. It's crucial to understand the risks associated with this.

The Temptation of AI

When faced with limited support or time from Subject Matter Experts, tight budgets, and time constraints, there is an inclination to utilize AI to generate knowledge. Opting to trust the AI system and proceed without further scrutiny is viewed as the quickest route to expedite content delivery. Emerging services that autonomously compose blog posts, generate images, generate podcasts, and craft content and are often perceived as cost-effective and efficiency-enhancing learning and experience development tools.

Imagine creating content and experiences for any domain. Yet, they will certainly lack insight beyond what an AI can provide. This need not ever be created. Any content created by an AI for consumption could be created by the intended audience themselves. Instead, focus on what makes the knowledge unique, authentic, and invaluable to the organization and allow the AI to handle the rest.

The perceived productivity gains of handing over content creation, curation, and development to an AI are staggering. Chat-based AIs can respond in seconds to questions with a mix of creative copy, perfected grammar, and endless stylistic choices. Yet the lure of the content is that regardless of the framing of the question, the response can be eroding and harmful to the organization's or brand's overall progress. [32]

Productivity Gains at the Cost of Commodity

Readers responded to a Cleveland Plain Dealer column that used an AI-generated image with the post. The author responded with an article presenting the reasons for using the image. Citing the publishing requirements, the difficulty in finding copyright images, and controlling expenses. The author went on to extol the benefits of the AI, generating 4 custom images within seconds without any cost or lead time.[33]

Yet, in defense of the usage, the editor included images used in other columns, including photos of his dog, personal items, and keepsakes with their own stories. While not directly related to the content, these items were authentic; they reinforced the perspective and tone of the content.

If you ever walk into a well-crafted and laid-out store, the surrounding imagery, design, and aesthetics become part of the buying experience. Our eyes are already trained to dismiss the images of ads surrounding content on the web. Constant distractors disrupt our ability to learn and absorb content.

AI will present options that are too easy for those who take it. The uptick in spam emails blindly trolling for leads with customized content is too easy to create. Hubspot's ChatSpot AI will create a blog post on demand.[34] The banality of the post, while giving the blogger or organization a boost in productivity and hits on their social feeds, will have a half-life as the audience will quickly dismiss the posts as uninformative and irrelevant. Once the audience is lost, what is the reacquisition path or costs? Will AI improvements outpace the ability of the audience to recognize and dismiss it?

What did the Cleveland Plain Dealer's writer sacrifice for the sake of convenience? What benefits did the AI image bring to the post? If the image was created in mere seconds, how can its value be measured? An AI-generated image can, at best, avoid damaging credibility, but it may still undermine the readers' trust if used for a trivial image, shaping the experience.

Artificial Identities

An AI can assist or take on as much responsibility as assigned to it. Whether it is your personal, professional, product, or organization's identity, an AI can quickly contribute content and automate large aspects of it. Your brand is how your identity is perceived and what the added value is beyond the functional benefits of role, service, or offerings.[35] With the rise of the internet and social media, the means of communication have changed, but the need for identification with brands remains. So, too, will the importance continue with the advent of AI. An AI can craft a brand and message using compelling language and imagery, but it cannot encapsulate what a brand truly is. Brands extend beyond what an AI can create—identity, perception, and purpose. They are signposts that aid your organization, your employees, and your customers in navigating the marketplace.

> *"The idea of brands is really a point of view. Brands are a lens to help make choices and register the ones we've made in the past. They're entities that hold companies together. They're actions that drive change. They're personalities you like or don't. But they're not simply an abstract creation of marketing. They're a force in the world, for better or worse."*[36]

AI will enhance new brands and shape others. New players leveraging the technology will emerge.

"Not only has AI collapsed the space between your idea and execution, but so has the influence between institutions and individuals. Building a brand has now become accessible to anyone and everyone. That is why it also has gotten that much more competitive. Fiercely so."[37]

What you hold onto will be your brand, the qualities that make it unique and out of the reach of an AI. "When AI was mentioned in the context of creative endeavors, people were quick to mention efficiency, not quality or originality."[38] If AI can reduce all the roadblocks for generating and creating content to building learning, what will you keep from becoming a commodity? When brands fail, they become a commodity, a substantially fungible resource that can be interchanged with similar resources. AI will extend and reshape digital identities, but we must hold onto the brand. In learning, a strong brand remains essential.[39]

Keep Reading?

Imagine being presented with a report of all your dog's growth through puppyhood. In the first column is a list of objects ranging from shoes, carpets, couches, and car tires and in the second column is a list of actions they were subjected too "chewed a hole," "eaten entirely," "peed on", "not sure, unusable" and "multiple actions". Confronted with this report and reliving these experiences, you may question whether getting a puppy was the right move. If you are reading this far, you may question why you should touch AI and how to construct AI traffic cones around your role and world. AI is neither a panacea nor a pariah.

> *It's everywhere*
> *In everyone*
> *And it will be every day*
> *From now on*
> *From now on*
> *- 'Amazing Song' by One eskimO*

AI is not a distant future; it's already here and is revolutionizing the way we gather and communicate knowledge. Just as Gutenberg's press ushered in a new era of knowledge sharing during the Renaissance, AI is poised to redefine the digital age. It is imperative that we anticipate this change and adapt our practices accordingly. Books became a ubiquitous presence in the decades after the presses started. Personal ownership of books, shelves for books, personal libraries, private and public libraries, universities, sharing, lending, and filling the evolving shelves of libraries into vibrant centers of study.

Ultimately, to best understand this new AI digital pup, we must understand what it has been bred to do. The rest of this book explores how AI is bred to complete tasks, assessing learning needs and opportunities, and how to leverage AIs built into an advantage. AI is poised to revolutionize how we acquire and share knowledge, but this doesn't mean it can seamlessly fit into our existing systems. To fully harness its potential, we must adapt our standards and processes to embrace AI's capabilities. Pivot points arise as much from new opportunities as they do from the stagnation of the status quo. The digital age offers a unique opportunity for transformation. Moving online and social media drove technological advancements and exposed limitations in our current approaches. Merely integrating AI into our online world won't solve our challenges; we need a fresh and strategic approach.

If you consider bringing home a golden retriever puppy, you may question but never regret; you will wish you had prepped, puppy-proofed, and trained more. The last known sighting of that shoe intact.

Playbook: Puppy Training for AIs

First encounters with your AI puppy can be wrought with opportunities, challenges, frustration, mystery, and reward. As much as you need to try to train the AI, you must also adapt, learn, and train to use it.

Games of Fetch

First encounters are about curiosity and patience. Ask questions you know and explore. Learn to adapt from searching logic and conversational fetching.

Simple Commands

Thinking about commands you're going to need and the tone that the AI responds to. Where should you make it stay, sit, or stop chewing the rhetorical sofa?

Trust Building

Ultimately, experimenting with AI is about understanding how big a leash you need for it. Try exploring the boundaries of AI in your work before unleashing it.

Tug-of-war

Arguing with an AI is like trying to get your shoe back from a puppy. You cannot believe how obstinate it can be; even in the face of proof and reason, it simply will not give up the shoe.

Tug of War Topics   **Best Arguments for/against**

Trade

Create a list of emails or content you might load into an AI to provide a summary and mine for insight. Then review the content for what intellectual property, value, and insight about your creative style an AI could adopt and take in trade.

Your Content (Retriever)   **Your Intellect (Trade)**

Crate Training

What are your boundaries for AI?

Your Content (Retriever)   **Your Crate (Boundaries)**

Playbook: AI Breeding

Consider the language, scope, and data that the AI platform was trained on and how it shapes its responses. Consider prompts and responses and set guidance for usage.

What has an AI been bred to do

AI Platform	Breeding	Best for / Avoid
1.	-	-
2.	-	-
3.	-	-

Playbook: Madlib with an AI

To best understand the extent to which AI will support your absurdities, try Madlib'ing AI. For instance, create prompts to ask an AI.

Verb	Favorite Food or Place
-	-

Prompt: How is culture [Concept Verb] by [Favorite Food or Place]?

Action Verb	Animal	Place	Action Verb
-	-	-	-

Prompt: How does AI [action verb] [animal] behavior in [place] and [action verb] outcomes?

Use these prompts as a starting point to explore the sophistry of an AI platform.

Playbook: Comparing Definitions

A simple way to understand the differences between a search engine result and an AI is to ask for the definition of a word and note the results, credibility of the source, and the next steps. Ask for a definition, and you will likely click on a source. Ask an AI, and you will likely receive the definition, but you must seek the source. Further, it may provide a definition in the context of previous entries.

Traditional Search Engine	AI Search

Information Retrieval

Understanding

Analysis

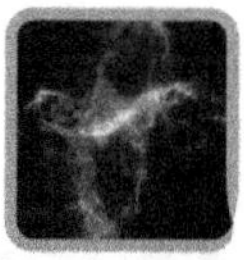

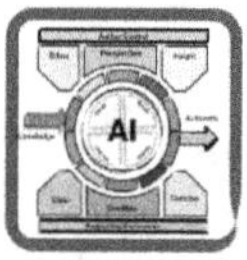

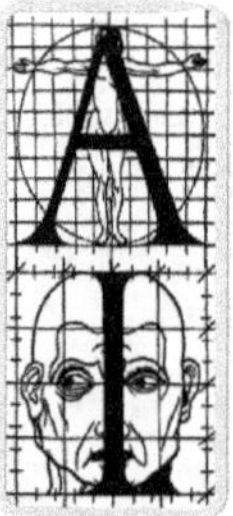

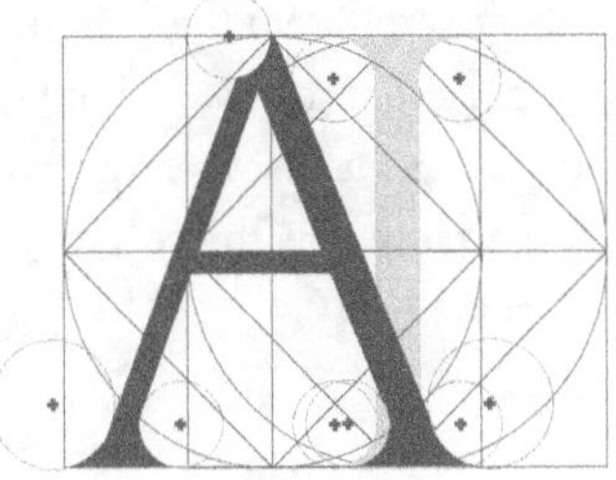

Chapter 2:
Reimagining Learning

In this chapter, we look at what knowledge and content sharing can and must become to stay relevant and empowering. This chapter is organized around the key terms and concepts related how each will play a role in reimagining learning.

Each of us has been designed for one of two immortal functions, as either a storyteller or as a cross-legged listener to tales of wonder, love, and daring. When we cease to tell or listen, then we no longer exist as a people.

Bryce Courtenay - Author of the Power of One

Defining Learning in the Age of AI

Knowledge is the fabric of learning, and AI is weaving a new pattern. From the personal level to an organization to society, AI is reshaping how we acquire, process, and apply knowledge, reshaping the very fabric of learning. To navigate this new landscape, we must first examine the fundamental building blocks of learning and explore how they evolve in the age of AI. In this chapter, we'll run through the basics:

- **Learning**: acquiring knowledge.

- **Learners**: individuals engaging in the process.

- **Mediums**: moving and conveying knowledge from teacher to learner.

- **Experience**: how we acquire, process, and apply knowledge.

- **Attention**: finding focus, interest, and motivation in learning and ourselves.

- **Digital Learning**: new technologies deployed to deliver.

- **Artificial Learning**: harness the power of AI.

- **Authentic Learning**: build authentic knowledge.

AI is revolutionizing the way we learn by transforming the fundamental elements of the process, from the content we consume to the tools we use. However, AI, like the computer, internet, and digital transformations before it, is not a panacea for learning. While these technologies have had a profound impact, they are not silver bullets. How we can reimagine learning with AI's assistance to build authentic knowledge and learning.

What is Learning?

Please Think and Be Careful

Just like AI itself, there can be so many definitions of learning and so many directions that we could choose to explore to provide one. Instead, here is an example of learning and what makes it one of the best we have ever encountered. A large sign sits at the top of the stairs on the entrance ramp, where skiers queue for the tram at Jackson Hole[1]. The sign conveys what it knows to be true to a specified audience in a means they can readily understand in the time they have available. The sign at the base is the definition of learning.

First, any learning must be purpose-driven. The sign exists to inform skiers. It exists to reach a particular audience and convey the knowledge the skiers need before embarking on the journey to ski the peak. Skiers may assess their ability to be better than they are and lack the knowledge to assess what is needed to perform at an expert level. Intermediate skiers especially may focus on performance that confirms their abilities rather than their limitations. The sign does not say 'Experts only,' pre-assess abilities, or provide any quali-fier to ability. The sign level sets all skiers to one level when it comes to Jackson Hole, "Our Mountain is like nothing you skied before."[2]

SAFETY MESSAGE

OUR MOUNTAIN IS LIKE NOTHING YOU HAVE SKIED BEFORE!
IT IS HUGE, WITH VARIABLE TERRAIN FROM GROOMED SLOPES TO
DANGEROUS CLIFF AREAS AND DANGEROUSLY VARIABLE
WEATHER CONDITIONS. YOU MUST ALWAYS EXERCISE EXTREME CAUTION.
YOU COULD BECOME LOST. YOU COULD MAKE A MISTAKE AND
SUFFER PERSONAL INJURY OR DEATH.
PROTECT YOURSELF - UNDERSTAND THE TRAIL MAP
AND ASK QUESTIONS BEFORE YOU PROCEED.
OBEY ALL TRAIL SIGNS AND MARKERS.

PLEASE THINK AND BE CAREFUL.

GIVE THIS SPECIAL MOUNTAIN THE RESPECT IT DEMANDS!

Recreation of the message on the Jackson Hole Tram sign.
[https://www.jacksonhole.com/blog/tram-line-etiquette]

It asks the skier to self-assess their abilities, not through a quiz or assessment, but to acknowledge that this is a serious endeavor. It is built for the learner's time, space, and medium. It asks no more of the skier, nor does it try to engage with the skier further with supporting information or details.

The sign at Jackson Hole offers knowledge, insight, and perspective to improve the skier's experience, well-being, and, in the case of Colbert's Collier, their life. Should the skier retain and reflect on this knowledge, they have the opportunity for increased wisdom. They also have the opportunity to reuse this knowledge and apply it when needed going forward. Unlike marketing and other forms of communication (fiction, parody, satire, hy-potheticals, expressive writing), learning is about conveying what you know to be true in a way that reaches the audience. Information that does not reach the intended audience is just that: information. Learning is what the audience retains and takes forward. Incumbent upon this is conveying credible, clear, and concise information to the learner.

Who Are Learners?

As Bryce Courtenay aptly noted, teaching and learning are immortal functions. We are often in a mix of both states. Learners are defined by their ability to embrace and make sense of knowledge provided to them in a meaningful way. Learning is conveyed through a medium that provides an experience from which a learner can take knowledge away.

What are Learning Mediums?

Learning mediums are the means of moving or conveying knowledge to your audience. Leaders, learning instructors, and managers have a variety of platforms and mediums at their disposal to convey learning. Learning aims to persuade and align the audience to a stated goal and outcome.[3] The fundamental elements of communication and knowledge acquisition can be broken into four main categories:

Data

Presentation of data (charts, graphs) so that conclusions can be derived. In learning, this is often an infographic, presentation, analysis, or report — providing evidence to inform employees, who can then adapt their behaviors and workflows to adjust and move the numbers.

Rhetoric

Rhetoric persuades to convince; presentation of support. In learning, rhetoric provides features, benefits, and information to support, engage, and inform learners to adopt the learning perspective. Rhetorical learning offers to onboard learners to new concepts and provide change management to adapt to new processes or systems. Listing features benefits from the learning as reasons for onboarding and change management for a new digital system.[4]

Narration

Narration follows a series of events or processes from end to end. This can be journalism, documentaries, podcasts, or reporting. In learning, this is documentation, training, processes to follow, and learning that step through a series of changes, processes, or steps to the desired outcome. For this to be successful, the process and the outcome must be communicated, or the supporting rhetoric convincing of the desired outcomes.[5]

Story

Story focuses on the dynamic changes within a series of events—the how and why, the causalities, and the outcomes to convey meaningful outcomes and changing behaviors. Within the narrative are dynamic changes that shape. A successful story builds logically toward recognizing the purpose and emotionally engaging the learner in their role in their work-life.[67]

Should AI be added to the list? Data, rhetoric, narration, and story are all powerful tools for conveying information and shaping understanding. AI has the potential to interact with and manipulate these elements and create unique experiences. However, AI is not a new medium for conveying information; rather, it can assist existing mediums. By leveraging AI, we can create more engaging and personalized experiences for the audience while relying on traditional mediums to convey information and shape understanding.

What is Learning Experience?

All teaching and all intellectual learning come about from already existing knowledge. — Aristotle, Posterior Analytics (71a 1)

Learning Experience is often used to describe a learning event, object, course, design, or the generalized form the learning takes.[8] If learning is the process of acquiring new knowledge, skills, behaviors, or attitudes, then experience is the practical cognitive contact the audience has with the knowledge and skills conveyed. It involves participation or observation in events, providing a unique perspective and contributing to learning. The design of the experience, including the thought, structure, content, and delivery, is essential in shaping the learner's engagement and, ultimately, the effectiveness of the learning. By breaking down learning into smaller, manageable components and tailoring the experience to the learner's individual needs, an experience can create dynamic and effective learning journeys that lead to measurable outcomes.

What is Learning Attention?

On a January day in '23, a group gathered in London to listen to a call from New York City. The two-hour meeting focused on call quality. While the first transatlantic call occurred in 1915, by 1923, the emphasis had shifted to improving quality. Research conducted during this call later presented in a paper, was among the first to describe signal-to-noise ratios.[9] Signals, what we aim to focus on, and noise, along with interference, shape our ability to maintain and hold attention. In signal processing, noise refers to unwanted modifications a signal may suffer during communication. Interference arises from competing signals.

Learning attention is the ability of knowledge, a signal, to overcome noise and interference and reach the learner. Every communication and learning medium has encountered noise and interference during its development. AI is no exception. With AI's ability to create vast quantities of content and the internet's and social media's open platforms for dissemination, it represents an explosion of signals. Recognizing the intended audience and crafting effective messages amidst AI-generated interference will be crucial in the cacophony AI creates.

Beyond AI's ability to create content, it possesses a unique capacity to hack our attention. AIs can generate an insidious interference — false flags. Originally associated with military deception, false flags have evolved into potent digital tools for manipulation.[10] By spreading misinformation and creating distractions, false flags can hijack our attention and undermine our ability to learn. The deceptive nature of these signals can make distinguishing between credible and unreliable information challenging. Additionally, AI can analyze vast datasets, identify behavioral patterns, and tailor content to capture and hold our interest. This can lead to highly addictive content that can keep us engaged at the expense of learning.

What is Digital Learning?

As mobile apps and cloud-based application architectures became common in the workplace, new avenues for learning and learning distribution began. Today, much of learning is informed by the Internet, and enterprise, and social channels.

The Internet and its collaborative open access to information are undergoing a significant transformation. Societal and cultural shifts, coupled with an overwhelming expansion of content, have made learning from the Internet increasingly challenging. The democratization of publishing, which has given everyone the ability to create and share content, has led to an unprecedented volume of information available online. This makes it difficult for users to discern credible sources from unreliable ones, leading to a paradoxical scarcity of useful knowledge amidst a sea of information.

Moreover, monetizing online content has shifted the focus from fostering scholarship and knowledge dissemination to optimizing for search engine visibility or SEO (Search Engine Optimization). Content creators are incentivized to prioritize visibility over the quality and accuracy of their content.

What is Artificial Learning?

Artificial Learning refers to the learning process that AI primarily generates. It can involve creating content, improving the quality of the content, and tailoring the learning experience to meet the specific needs of individual learners. Artificial Learning can be seen as the application of AI to enhance the learning process. Artificial Learning impacts include:

1) Learning content generated by AI.

2) Learning content enhanced by AI.

3) Learning production enhanced by AI.

4) Learning delivery enhanced by AI.

AI can assist and enhance learning by tailoring content to individual learners' needs, learning paths, and learning styles. AI can facilitate development, compressing the gap between ideas and execution. ChatGPT AI is already tremendously impacting learning from a student and instruction perspective. Substituting a person for AI on either side of learning ensures both sides are unengaged with the learning. An instructor can create and deliver a lecture as easily as a student can generate a paper on a topic and hand it in. Using AI to develop learning, is learning without the experience. To be successful, learning must leverage experience.

Attention Intelligence

In the 1980s sitcom Taxi, the character Jim, portrayed by Christopher Lloyd, becomes captivated by a sea of TV screens. He and his fellow drivers eventually succumb to distraction, watching the debate over whether the Delaware legislature would adopt the name "Delawareans" or "Delawarites." "*Delaweenians never stood a chance.*" This scene, set twenty years before the internet, thirty before the iPhone, and forty before the release of ChatGPT, serves as a fitting metaphor for the modern learner's experience.[11]

The advent of film, television, broadcasting, cable, digital media, and streaming has exponentially increased the breadth of content, learning opportunities, and exposure to learning signals. The sheer volume and variety of information available across multiple devices simultaneously, coupled with the challenge of navigating it and the relentless pursuit of technology platforms to capture and hold our attention, have created a complex landscape for learners. In today's interconnected world, where multiple devices and services operate simultaneously, learning must compete with an overwhelming cacophony of signals and mediums. Learners are constantly bombarded with information from multiple devices.[12]

Attention is no longer a fair fight. In the past, learners controlled their attention. However, with the rise of social media and smartphones, we have learned that not all platforms play fair. Social media platforms actively manipulate information to steal, capture, and hold our attention. By using and interacting with these platforms, you are effectively programming them to capture your attention more effectively.[13]

How many skiers today would bother to look up from their phones to read the sign at the Jackson Hole tram? How many more would pose for a 'pic' without reading it? How many skiers' knowledge of the peak was informed by a TikTok, or reel?

To safeguard our ability to learn and maintain attention in the age of AI, it is essential to understand and protect against deceptive and distracting tactics employed by AI-driven noise, interference, and false flags. This includes:

- Evaluating the credibility of sources, considering biases or conflicts of interest.

- Identifying patterns or narratives that might indicate manipulation.

- Building a credible and curated network of reliable sources.

Maintaining attention in the AI age necessitates a proactive approach to discerning reliable information from the torrent of noise, interference, and deceptive tactics to ensure the acquisition of accurate knowledge.

Crafting Learning in the Age of AI

What learning elements will continue in the age of AI? How will they be shaped? How can we create meaningful learning that benefits our organization? By using AI to streamline the development and production of learning materials, we can create purposeful, authentic learning.

As many organizations race to integrate AI into their workflows, AI as a learning development tool cannot be a direct replacement for human experience. The challenge lies in balancing the use of artificial learning for efficiency and customization while ensuring that learning remains meaningful and aligned with organizational needs. Ultimately, successful learning will focus on:

- **Your Learners**: Have a clear understanding of your learners' needs and continually engage them wherever they are on their learning journey.

- **Your Learning Experience**: Ensure learning is engaging, relevant, and effective.

- **Your Learning Mediums**: Engage learners using your brand, voice, leadership, and perspective.

- **Your Learning Attention**: Help learners to focus on the learning experience.

While AI can improve and speed up the development of each learning category, it should not overshadow the importance of human input in creation, design, and strategy. Incorporating these elements leads to authentic learning.

Playbook: Learning Experience

How do you know what you refer to when referring to learning experiences?

Expressing what a learning experience is almost always requires more description, so here is a way to break out of the learning experience.

When it means	Think	Use
Learning is the chunk of knowledge to be conveyed.	… is the what.	Learning
Design is the intention of how that learning is to be conveyed.	… is the how.	Design
Experience is what happens when the learner engages with the learning.	… is the when.	Experience

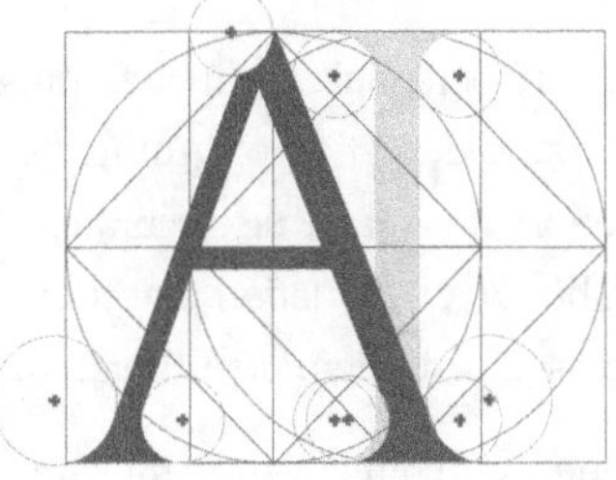

Chapter 3:
Authentic Learning

In this chapter, we look at how learning in its most authentic form can be shaped to be an antidote to artificial learning.

SEAN: So if I asked you about art, you'd probably give me the skinny on every art book ever written. Michelangelo? You know a lot about him. Life's work, political aspirations, him and the pope, sexual orientation, the whole works, right? But I bet you can't tell me what it smells like in the Sistine Chapel. You've never actually stood there and looked up at that beautiful ceiling. Seen that.

Good Will Hunting, Played by Robin Williams

What is Authentic Learning

Authentic Learning is a transformative approach to education, personalizing the learning journey to resonate with the learner. Let's start with a working definition of 'Authentic'. Something is said to be Authentic if it is not false or imitation; it is real, true, accurate, or as claimed. It carries weight from some form of authority, brand, or validation that things or individuals are as they claim or appear to be. It can also assert an origin or authorship.

In the context of learning, "authentic" refers to a genuine and directly relevant learning experience. It is centered around the idea that knowledge is most effectively acquired when instructional significance is connected to the learner's relevance and conveyed to the learner during the experience.

Authentic learning, therefore, helps to forge significant and engaging connections during the knowledge and skill acquisition process. It aligns with the learner's life, purpose, and work, sparking intrinsic motivation, reflections, and added insight. This makes the learning process more personalized, engaging, and directly applicable to the learner's environment.

If learning is the act or process of acquiring knowledge or skills, then Authentic Learning is when the instructor's unique interest, perspective, and insight enrich the learning. This approach to education not only makes the process more engaging but also ensures that the learning process is effective and resonates with the learners, making it more impactful and memorable.

Learning is in Trouble

Why do we need Authentic Learning

In 2019, Carmine Gallo wrote in the Harvard Business Review that "The Art of Persuasion Hasn't Changed in 2,000 Years."[1] Back then, Aristotle identified three essential rhetorical appeals that authors use to persuade their audience: **Ethos**, **pathos**, and **logos**.[2] These elements of persuasion have formed the foundation of how we convey information and create wisdom in others.[3]

- Ethos refers to the **credibility** and **character** of the speaker or writer. It encompasses the author's reputation, expertise, and moral standing.

- Pathos appeals to the **emotions** and **sympathetic imagination** of the audience. It aims to evoke feelings, beliefs, and values.

- Logos is the rational principle that governs the universe.

A well-crafted argument combines all three appeals—**logos**, **ethos**, and **pathos**—to create a compelling and balanced case. Each appeal balances the others. Ethos ensures that emotional appeals do not become manipulative. By maintaining credibility, authors prevent their arguments from being dismissed as mere emotional ploys. While the 'art' of persuasion hasn't changed in 2000 years, the ensuing years from 2019 since the article was published, having endured a pandemic, the explosion of social media, the emergence of disinformation as a political and societal weapon, and the advent of AI have bludgeoned the 'art.'

Ethos	**Pathos**	**Logos**
Credibility	Emotion	Logic/Rational
Ethos refers to the credibility or ethical appeal of the author. It pertains to how knowledgeable or wise the author is about their argument and how reputable they are morally in the eyes of their learner.	Pathos appeals to the learner's emotions to persuade them—moving the learner to an emotional state where they are more likely to consider the validity of the author's ideas.	Logos is the logical appeal of an argument by forming meaningful connections between facts, supporting claims through factual evidence and statistics.
Abuses:		
Misrepresentation of credibility or authority, often seen in media where individuals or organizations present themselves as experts without proper credentials.	Manipulation of emotions and creating emotional appeals can be misleading and confuse.	Misinterpreting data or providing incorrect or biased information.
Examples:		
Ad Hominem attacks False attributions Pseudoscience Fake news Deep fakes	Emotional manipulation Sensationalism Click-baiting	Manipulated Data Dis/misinformation Biased News Echo chamber effect

Apathetic Intelligence

Pushing the boundaries of appeals in all directions results in a complete breakdown of a disinterested audience to rhetoric, a consequence of the abuse of disinformation (logos), the loss of respect and credibility (ethos), and frenetic appeals (pathos). Imagine a scenario where the audience has been bombarded with emotional persuasion and disinformation past the point of saturation. This is when the breakdown of information rhetoric occurs, in which the audience no longer respects the speaker, has any emotional capacity to process information, or believes it. It is not hard to imagine bad actors with an AI creating this effect. It is already happening. Each of Aristotle's rhetorical elements has been pushed to extremes. With AI empowering a massive increase in quantity, skilled arguments can be generated, full of emotional manipulation, and disseminated easily from deepfakes.

Approbation Intelligence

The digital world has little patience for wisdom; its values are shaped by approbation, not introspection.[4] -The Age of AI: And Our Human Future

Content available online and online learning is moving away from knowledge gathering and creating wisdom to grabbing, holding, recognizing, and rewarding attention. We receive approbation, which generally refers to the approval, agreement, or praise often given by an official group or community, through accessing information on social media and learning.

In social media, approbation can be seen as the positive appraisal and acceptance of someone or something via social approval, which can take the form of likes, shares, positive comments, and follows. In learning, approbation often comes in the form of positive feedback or recognition, awards, and achievements. This kind of positive reinforcement can motivate learners to continue their efforts and strive for further improvement. Approbation plays a significant role in shaping behaviors and attitudes for both the learner and the learning system, and it can have a profound impact on an individual's self-esteem and sense of belonging.[5]

When online content strategies skew the focus toward attention-holding over knowledge-implementing, they can significantly impede our ability to gather information. This is particularly evident in instructional videos that deliberately withhold key elements to ensure they are watched to the end.

Online content reward systems, a key component of digital learning, is designed to gather and hold attention. This is nothing new; stories by design try to embrace and open the learner to the situation and develop the story in the learner's mind. And, yet, when the monetization structure of public content is based on attention, the stories and content are skewed and distorted to attention versus knowledge transference.

Imagine if the sign at Jackson Hole were monitored to create value for every reading or interaction. How would this shape the learning conveyed? The sign at the Jackson Hole tram causes introspection. Its key learning outcome is to get the skier to think about their abilities. It does not offer any reward other than the knowledge and safety to maximize the experience. The reward comes not from the signage or interaction with it but from boarding the tram with confidence in the skier's abilities.

70

Social media platforms, content generators, and learning platforms have yet to find a means to monetize introspection, and that is unlikely to change.

Almost Intelligence

AI can mimic human learning, but it cannot truly experience the world. Learning designed by AI can feel impersonal and lacking in depth. It's like knowing all about Michelangelo but never experiencing the Sistine Chapel firsthand.

> *Then we entered the Sistine Chapel, which we found bright and cheerful, and with a good light for the pictures. "The Last Judgment" divided our admiration with the paintings on the roof by Michael Angelo. I could only see and wonder. The mental confidence and boldness of the master, and his grandeur of conception, are beyond all expression. After we had looked at all of them over and over again, we left this sacred building.[6]*
> *— Johann Wolfgang von Goethe*

Artificial learning is temporal and transactional. It's about learning through algorithms and patterns. AI tutors can provide personalized instruction on various subjects. However, both instances of learning lack the depth and richness of experience. AI may assist in creating authentic learning, but it cannot replace the human element. Just as AI can't truly experience the Sistine Chapel, it can't fully replicate the richness of authentic learning, which is deeply rooted in the author's ethos, perspective, and insights.

Why Authentic Learning Works

Authentic learning fosters a deeper understanding, critical thinking, and active engagement with real-world opportunities, applications, and impacts. It conveys the sense of standing in the Sistine Chapel, looking up, and experiencing the beauty of the ceiling. Authentic learning provides a context that ensures meaning and value for the learner, often derived from unique and organic sources and experiences based on the authority brand and credibility of the author. Goethe's writing conveys authentic knowledge of the Sistine Chapel. An AI could use the word "sacred," but only one who has experienced it can truly convey its meaning. Authentic learning invests in establishing credibility and trust by creating unique learning based on the brand's experience, needs, and insight. Rather than embracing the easy production AI offers, it turns that on its head to do the additional work and put in the added effort and attention to detail to customize and make the learning their own.

Why the Sign at Jackson Hole Works?

The learning objective and desired outcome for the sign at Jackson Hole are simple: to encourage introspection and reflection among skiers by asking them consider their abilities before getting on the tram. In the simplest terms, the sign conveys the message directly, bypassing all technology. It does not try to do everything—plenty of supplemental content is available, including trail maps, ski ambassadors, and fellow skiers.[7]

Your learners can access a wealth of information and distractions at all times, which should define how you develop learning. Being authentic means choosing the medium that most effectively and efficiently causes the learning outcome in a way that engages the learn.

Arguably, the Jackson Hole ski area is one of the planet's most immersive and stimulating environments. For a learning message to compete with this, the medium selected is the most simple direct path presented precisely where and when the learner needs the information. As a premier resort and destination, the resort is not constrained by budget or a shortage of amazing content and digital footage. Instead of a flat screen showing the terrain at the peak, visualizations of steep descents await with a Warren Miller voiceover. It is succinct, direct — blunt. The sign fits in the learner's space, fits their timing and schedule, and conveys exactly what the learner needs without extraneous information. The sign at the Jackson Hole Tram warns skiers about the mountain's unique challenges and potential dangers. Remember, for the skier, each aspect of Learning, Design, and Experience contributes to a holistic understanding of skiing Jackson Hole's challenging terrain. Now, let's delve into each aspect from the skier's perspective: learning, design, and experience with the sign.[8]

Topic	Jackson Hole Tram Sign
Learning	The sign states, "Our Mountain is like nothing you've ever skied before." Take this seriously. The tram rises **4139 vertical feet**, and the weather at the top can be drastically different from the base area. The sign serves as an educational tool designed to enhance the skiers' knowledge and preparedness, ensuring a safe and enjoyable skiing experience. The sign provides crucial safety information to the skier. It emphasizes the unpredictable nature of the mountain terrain and weather conditions, the potential risks involved, and the need for caution. It encourages skiers to familiarize themselves with the trail map and obey all signs and markers. The sign also subtly educates skiers about the respect the mountain demands due to its challenging nature.
Design	The sign is composed of clear and concise sentences, which facilitate understanding. It directly addresses the skier using the word "YOU," creating a personal connection and making the message more impactful. The language used is descriptive, directive, and cautionary, providing a vivid depiction of the mountain's terrain, along with specific safety instructions. The sign concludes with a powerful message about respecting the mountain, emphasizing the importance of comprehending and adapting to the natural environment and conditions.

<table>
<tr><td>Experience</td><td>In just nine minutes, the Big Red tram will carry you and 99 other skiers 4139 vertical feet to the summit. The sign offers a moment of introspection while waiting with "swarthy locals who've skied the tram for decades to the greenest newbies here for the first time." Skiers will likely engage initially by reading it out of curiosity or to pass the time. As they read, the sign's clear and direct language would inform them about the mountain's challenging terrain and the importance of safety precautions. This could evoke a sense of anticipation and respect for the mountain. The sign's cautionary tone might also make them more aware of potential risks, prompting them to mentally prepare for the skiing conditions ahead.</td></tr>
</table>

Despite the availability of budget, technology, and production, a large red sign is the most authentic version of learning and the most effective means of communicating with skiers. It allows the learner to form a picture of their performance in their mind and assess their abilities against what the mountain holds. The message, the medium, and the choice of wording are the heart of authentic learning. This sign is on one of my favorite t-shirts in the base lodge gift shop. It also appears on magnets, mugs, and stickers. Your learning truly resonates if it is in the gift shop. Creating something authentic can become lasting and memorable.

You know you've got strong brand loyalty when your customers tattoo your logo on their arm,[9]
— Speaking of Harley Davidson, Don James, chairman and chief executive officer of Fred Deeley Imports Ltd.

The Design of Authentic Learning

Going beyond what authentic learning is, we have to come up with a design for authentic learning, including how it can be constructed and the elements that reinforce it. By adjusting design elements that focus on the author and the learner, authentic learning builds connections between the author and the learner that convey the author's knowledge in a way that the audience's perception or reception of the learning. The key elements of authentic learning are broken into two main categories: the Author and the Learner. For the author, we delve into the concepts of ethos, perspective, and insight. For the learner, we examine what makes the content credible, clear, and concise. Each of these aspects contributes to the overall effectiveness of learning. By understanding and adjusting these elements, authors can bring learning to life in the learner's mind.[10]

For authentic learning to work, it is about replicating the wisdom of the author in the mind of the learner. Authentic learning emphasizes creating a unique connection between the author and the learner. This connection is not merely transactional but a transformative experience that enhances the learner's understanding and application of knowledge.

The author plays a crucial role in this process. The author's ethos is the foundation of this connection. It is the author's responsibility to present information in a way that is reliable and trustworthy. The author's Perspective provides a unique viewpoint on the subject matter, adding depth and richness to the learning experience. The author's insight allows the learner to see beyond the surface of the information, encouraging critical thinking and fostering a deeper understanding of the subject.

The learner, on the other hand, is not a passive recipient of information. They actively engage with the learning content and other information. When the learner assesses the author's credibility and the information presented, it influences their willingness to engage with the content. Clarity in the presentation of information ensures that the learner can easily understand the content. Conciseness ensures that the information is presented in a straightforward and efficient manner, respecting the learner's time and cognitive load.

In essence, authentic learning is about creating a symbiotic relationship between the author and the learner. The author provides valuable insights and perspectives while the learner actively engages with the content, assessing its credibility and clarity. This dynamic interaction facilitates a unique connection that enhances the overall learning experience. Understanding and adjusting these elements can effectively bring the authentic learning model to life, creating a meaningful and impactful learning journey.

Arena Intelligence

The battle for the learner's mindshare is fierce —competing with a cacophony of voices, messages, memes, videos, channels, devices, and platforms, many of which are solely motivated by capturing and holding the learner's attention by any means necessary.

Refer to the Jackson Hole sign. "Our mountain is like nothing you have skied before!" This is immediate engagement. It triggers 'What am I getting myself into?' in the mind of the learner. Without hyperbole, the message is the effectiveness of the economy of words.

When it is too easy to create information when content can be manufactured and manipulated to evoke responses, of the three, pathos, logos, and ethos, ethos offers the best path through noise and distraction. Establishing the credibility of the source that can be easily verified by the learner and the learning's bone fides with the clear and concise intention for the purpose and the learning outcomes ensures a connection between the author and the learner. From here, the learning can start.

First and foremost, it has to come from a source that the learner respects. This is at the core of the ethos for authentic learning. Second, it must be clear, using the language and leveraging the learner's knowledge. Here, shared perspectives and knowledge about the brand and organization, roles, and experiences can be leveraged. Finally, the learning has to be insightful and empowering, enabling the learner to take the next steps on their own or seek further guidance.

AI is set to become a staple in the workplace, permeating all aspects. The challenge will be to distinguish the authentic from the automated. In this impending struggle, largely instigated and driven by AI, learning must maintain the aspects that create real connections with learners and embrace AI where it can be advantageous to assist in designing, creating, storyboarding, developing, and producing learning materials.

Elements of Authentic Learning

Remember, these terms focus more on building a reinforcing connection between the knowledge transference between the author and the learner, on the content and delivery of the message rather than the audience's perception or reception of the learning. Each of these aspects contributes to the overall effectiveness of learning. For any learning, the audience must be able to scrutinize information, question authority, and make decisions based on truth and integrity.

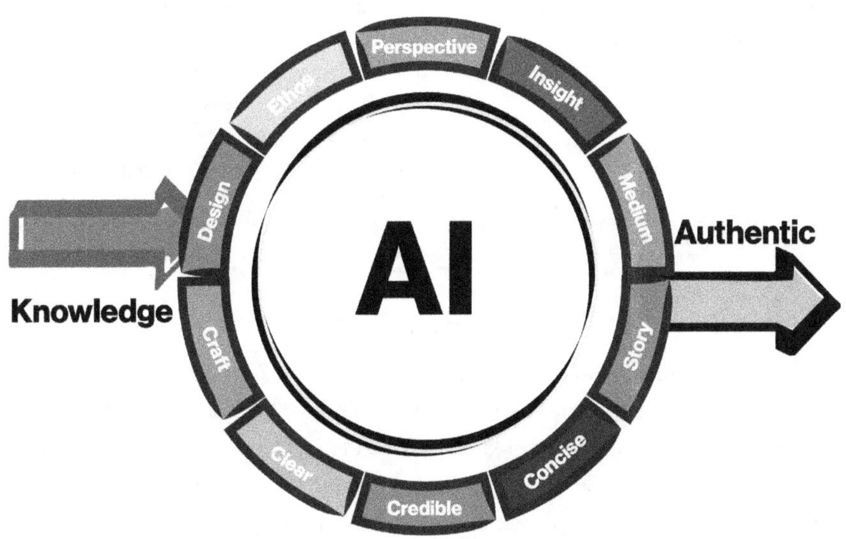

From the Author	To the Learner
Ethos	**Credible**
Ethos refers to the credibility or trustworthiness of the speaker. It is how well the speaker	Credibility refers to when the learner trusts the knowledge conveyed from the learning

convinces the audience that he or she is qualified to speak on the subject. Ethos is critical for establishing the credibility of the learning in the mind of the learner.

and perceives the content as believable and trusted.

Perspective	Clear

Perspective is composed of two key elements.

- The experience(s) of the author relevant to the learning.
- The brand that is invested in the learning and its outcomes.

This refers to how clear and understandable the message is. A message with high clarity is easy to understand and interpret. This refers to the correctness or precision of the information in the message. An accurate message is free from errors or distortions. This refers to how closely the message aligns with the topic or context. A relevant message addresses the matter at hand directly.

Insight	Concise

Going beyond what will come from an internet search or general information, what are the key insights that can be conveyed in the learning that will create the best outcomes for the learner?

This refers to expressing much information clearly and in a few words, brief but comprehensive. Concise does not mean overly simplified or edited down more that it offers a complete message that leaves no crucial details out. A consistent message that can be relied upon with all the necessary and appropriate information.

Authentic Design of Jackson Hole Tram Sign

The Jackson Hole tram sign message is an authentic and informative communication. It effectively uses ethos, perspective, and insight to deliver a safety message that resonates with skiers in a clear, concise, and credible way that enhances their mountain experience. By encouraging skiers to reflect on their abilities and the potential risks, the message empowers them to make informed decisions or seek guidance. This combined effect creates an authentic and engaging experience for the skier.

From Jackson Hole:	To the Skier in the queue:
Ethos	**Credible**

The sign establishes its authority by speaking from the perspective of the mountain's management. It uses phrases like "Our Mountain"

The sign's credibility is established through its clear and direct communication about the potential dangers and the need for caution. It

Perspective	Clear
The sign provides a comprehensive view of what to expect from the mountain. It doesn't shy away from highlighting the potential dangers, thereby offering an honest and realistic perspective of the skiing experience.	The sign's message is clear and straightforward. It uses simple language to convey its safety message, making it easy for skiers of all levels to understand.
Insight	**Concise**
The sign offers valuable insights into the nature of the mountain, the variability of the terrain, and the potential risks involved. It encourages skiers to exercise caution, understand the trail map, and obey all signs and markers, thereby providing practical advice for a safe skiing experience.	Despite the complexity of the information it needs to convey, the sign, both in visual design and language, does so in a concise manner. It delivers a comprehensive safety message without unnecessary embellishment or complexity.

(continued from previous page) and "Give this special mountain the respect it demands!" to assert its credibility and establish a moral connection with the skier. ... doesn't sugarcoat the risks, which enhances its trustworthiness.

Tools Available

Effective communication relies on credible, clear, and concise messaging, supported by ethos, perspective, and insight. Story, craft, and medium are the levers we pull and adjust to reach the learner. Story is as old as language itself; craft and mediums evolve over time, keeping pace with our progress and technical innovations. AI brings new possibilities and capabilities to our ability to communicate. In the following sections, we'll explore how to utilize AI to build authentic.

Playbook: Authentic Learning

Review a recent learning that you found effective and run through the elements of an authentic design. You can also spend 20 minutes on a social media channel feed and compare the results.

Recent Learning   **Social Media Feed**

From the Author

Ethos

Perspective

Insight

To the Learner

Credible

Clarity

Concise

How would you evaluate the other aspects of the learner and social media feed? What held your attention, and what did you engage with?

Playbook: What is Your AI Ethos

Review the list of authentic learning and list how these will be impacted by or protected from AI.

Our Authentic Purpose	How will AI Integrate, Influence, Exclude, Explicit
From the Author	
Ethos	
Perspective	
Insight	
To the Learner	
Credible	
Clarity	
Concise	

The Economy of Opening Lines

Think about the opening lines and how much they can capture. If you're starting with the purpose of the communication, housekeeping, or about the communication, you may have lost the audience to an AI to provide a summary. Write something that hooks the audience, not an AI.

Jackson Hole Tram Sign

OUR MOUNTAIN IS LIKE NOTHING YOU HAVE SKIED BEFORE!

Steve Jobs, iPhone Introduction

Every once in a while, a revolutionary product comes along that changes everything. And Apple has been-- well, first of all, one's very fortunate if you get to work on just one of these in your career.

A Prayer for Owen Meany, John Irving

I am doomed to remember a boy with a wrecked voice— not because of his voice, or because he was the smallest person I ever knew, or even because he was the instrument of my mother's death, but because he is the reason I believe in God; I am a Christian because of Owen Meany.

Our Attempt:

When you throw a ball to a Golden Retriever, you may think you know what you'll get back, but you can never be sure. The same is true when you ask an AI a question. You may think you know what the answer will be, but the reality is often far more intricate and surprising than you imagined.

Review the list of quotes above, are there any words to add for clarity or can be removed?

Now Think About Your Opening

Research presentations, speeches, and work you have created. Reflect on any memorable ones and the openings they had. Evaluate what makes them clear, credible, and concise. Finally, submit your work to a generative AI for review to see if it can make clearer and more concise edits. Review iterative rounds of lines and see how the lines change.

Opening Lines

Version 1

Version 2

Version 3

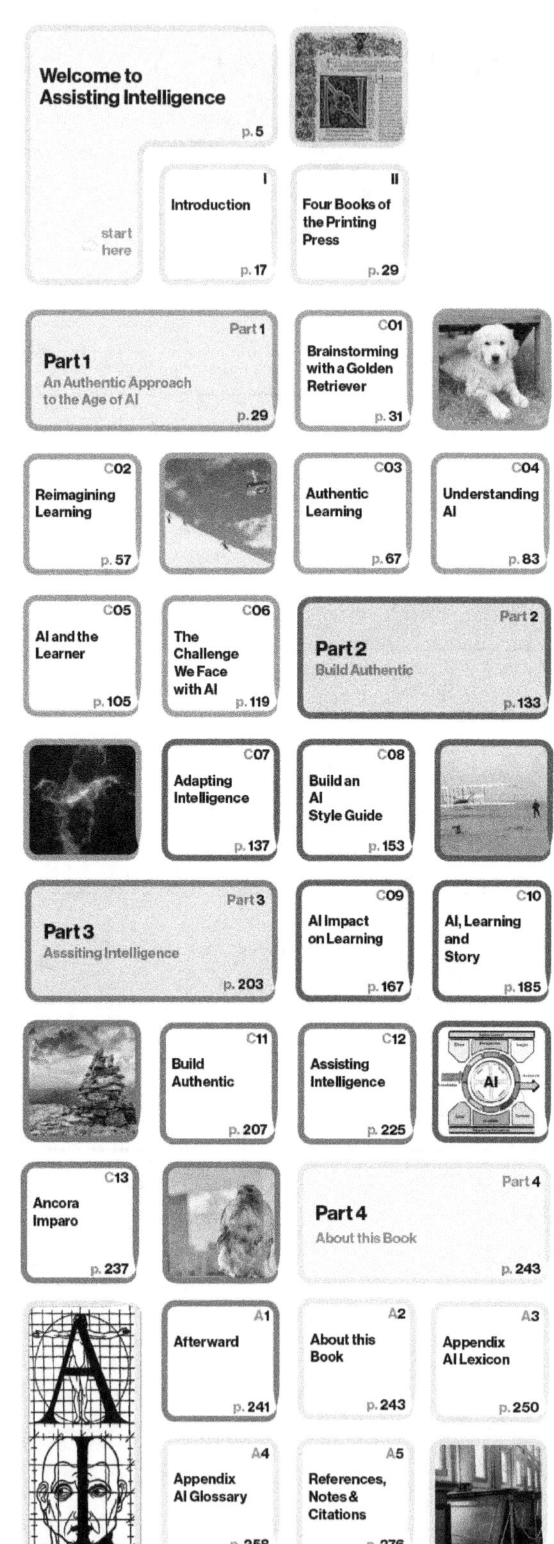

Welcome to
Assisting Intelligence
p. 5

start
here

I
Introduction
p. 17

II
Four Books of
the Printing
Press
p. 29

Part 1
Part 1
An Authentic Approach
to the Age of AI
p. 29

C01
Brainstorming
with a Golden
Retriever
p. 31

C02
Reimagining
Learning
p. 57

C03
Authentic
Learning
p. 67

C04
Understanding
AI
p. 83

C05
AI and the
Learner
p. 105

C06
The
Challenge
We Face
with AI
p. 119

Part 2
Part 2
Build Authentic
p. 133

C07
Adapting
Intelligence
p. 137

C08
Build an
AI
Style Guide
p. 153

Part 3
Part 3
Asssiting Intelligence
p. 203

C09
AI Impact
on Learning
p. 167

C10
AI, Learning
and
Story
p. 185

C11
Build
Authentic
p. 207

C12
Assisting
Intelligence
p. 225

AI

C13
Ancora
Imparo
p. 237

Part 4
Part 4
About this Book
p. 243

A1
Afterward
p. 241

A2
About this
Book
p. 243

A3
Appendix
AI Lexicon
p. 250

A4
Appendix
AI Glossary
p. 258

A5
References,
Notes &
Citations
p. 276

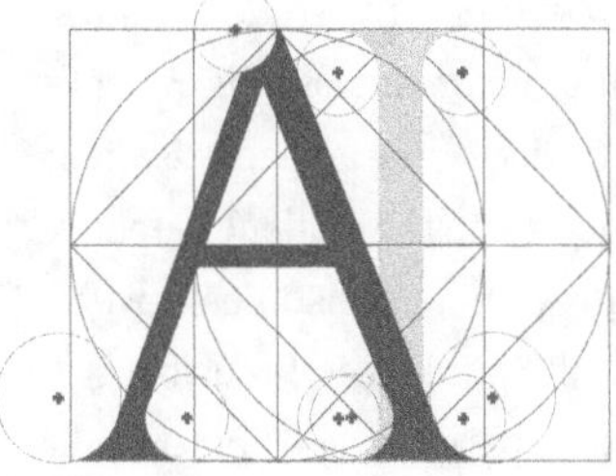# Chapter 4:
Understanding AI

This chapter provides a primer on how AI functions and is structured as a learning and learning development tool. Before engaging with AI, understand how it functions and how it can be trained and utilized to craft learning.

O this learning, what a thing it is!

— *William Shakespeare, The Taming of the Shrew*

Learning AI from Beethoven's 10th Symphony

An eager student takes on the ambitious task: to complete the 10th Symphony based on the fragments that had been left behind during his final years of illness. The student studied and improved daily, listening to input and feedback from instructors, mastering Beethoven's style and techniques, eventually producing a finished piece that amazed listeners who could hardly tell where Beethoven's original sketches ended and the student's creative extrapolation began. The student was an AI named Playform AI that learned Beethoven's creative process from a data model of his entire oeuvre with the guidance of music historians, musicologists, composers, and computer scientists. The experimental AI produced a finished version of Beethoven's 10th Symphony from mere notes as a starting point.[1]

While the AI did not artificially replicate Beethoven's intelligence, it helped in the practical development, modeling, and production of a symphony from an inspirational collection of Beethoven's notes into a robust and completed performance.

Watch and listen to the trailer here: [https://vimeo.com/642290986]

Trailer for the Beethoven X - The AI Project. View at https://vimeo.com/642290986

How Did an AI Create the 10th Symphony

How could an AI be deployed to complete what has been left unfinished for centuries? By leveraging the mathematics that underlies the structure of musical compositions. At the heart of the problem was math; the basic music patterns can be represented by mathematical equations between pitch and frequency for different notes, forming into geometric series.[2] Musical composers used advanced mathematical series to create music long before these series were formally identified in mathematics.[3]

Behind the music, the existing and missing pieces could be represented as sequences of math symbols and problems, and with enough data and computing power, an AI could be applied to create the 10th Symphony. This generative process can be applied to various domains, such as music, art, medicine, education, and more, to solve problems requiring massive amounts of data to discern patterns.[4]

A generative AI cannot be set to complete a task without a large quantity of data to build statistical models. In addition, the AI must be trained to understand the parameters of the problem and the fundamental requirements of the solution. Before composing music, the AI first needed to learn the musical style and structure of Beethoven's symphonies and his creative process and sketches for the 10th Symphony. This can be done by analyzing a large amount of data, such as all the musical scores of Beethoven, his contemporaries, audio recordings, and historical documents. Using various mathematical techniques like statistics, probability, optimization, and machine learning to sift through the data. **Data analysis** is the process of collecting, processing, and interpreting data, such as text, images, audio, or video, using mathematical and statistical methods and can help an AI learn from existing information and discover patterns and insights.

Next, **Generative Modeling** creates new data or content, such as music, text, or images, using existing data and some rules or parameters. Generative modeling can help AI systems produce original and diverse outputs that match a certain style or structure. The AI needs to generate new musical material consistent with Beethoven's style and sketches, but also original and expressive. Four neural networks were developed to create the symphony. "Two models used in language translation proved best for adding harmony and orchestration, another transformer served to develop themes, and a BERT model helped bridge between themes." This enabled the AI to produce complex and diverse outputs while maintaining the harmony, melody, rhythm, and form of the Symphony.[5]

Feedback learning helps an AI system adapt to changes and optimize goals and objectives. This involves collaboration with humans to ensure the quality and authenticity of the final product. This can be done by using feedback mechanisms. The AI also needs to communicate and interact with the human team members, using natural language processing and computer vision, to understand their suggestions and preferences and to explain their decisions and actions. [6]

What was AI

In 1956, John McCarthy coined the term "artificial intelligence" at the Dartmouth Summer Research Project on Artificial Intelligence.[7] This marked the birth of a name for a field of study that aimed "to proceed on the basis of the conjecture that every aspect of learning or any other feature of intelligence can in principle be so precisely described that a machine can be made to simulate it."[8] The definitions of AI have been expanding and evolving almost as fast as the technology advances. As a working definition to start with, we can use a common definition: "AI is a branch of computer science that focuses on creating systems capable of performing tasks that would typically require human intelligence."

What is Artificial Intelligence

Let's start with some notable definitions and their differences:

Source	Definition	Notable Focus
Stanford University Human-Centered Artificial Intelligence Institute (HAI)[9]	AI is the science and engineering of making intelligent machines, with an emphasis on machines that can learn.	Focus on the engineering aspect and the ability to learn.
Britannica[10]	AI is the ability of a computer or robot to perform tasks that are commonly associated with intelligent beings, such as reasoning.	Emphasizes the tasks associated with intelligence
IBM[11]	AI refers to machines that can reason, learn, and act autonomously.	Highlights the reasoning, learning, and autonomous action capabilities.
Cambridge Online Dictionary[12]	The use or study of computer systems or machines that have some of the qualities that the human brain has, such as the ability to interpret and produce language in a way that seems human, recognize or create images, solve problems, and learn from data supplied to them.	Provides a more detailed view of AI, explicitly mentioning language, image recognition, problem-solving, and learning.
New Scientist[13]	Artificial intelligence or AI simply means software used by computers to mimic aspects of human intelligence.	This definition emphasizes the software aspect and highlights that AI systems are designed to replicate certain cognitive abilities.

The nuances among the definitions reflect the evolving nature of the field and the ongoing debate about the true nature of intelligence, both artificial and human. However, these definitions do not explain how a symphony is created from a series of notations.

Asking AIs what they think they are.

Source	Definition	Review:
	Prompt: What is your succinct definition of Artificial Intelligence?	Prompt: What do you think of this definition? Asking what the AI thought of the other's definition.
Google Gemini	AI is essentially machines programmed to tackle tasks that involve human-like thinking. This includes learning, problem-solving, and adapting.	Our succinct definitions are very similar! Both focus on machines mimicking human thinking for tasks. Mine is shorter by omitting "computer-controlled systems" and "adapt and improve over time". These are good details, but not crucial for a basic understanding.
Microsoft Copilot	Artificial Intelligence (AI): It refers to the capability of computers or computer-controlled systems to perform tasks that typically require human intelligence, such as reasoning, learning, and problem-solving. AI encompasses various techniques, including machine learning, natural language processing, and computer vision, to create intelligent systems that can adapt and improve over time.	Both definitions converge on the idea of creating intelligent machines, but mine emphasizes the core tasks involved.

NOTE: In both instances, I had to add the word 'succinct' to the prompt and even had to admonish Copilot for not knowing what succinct was. Response: "I apologize for the verbosity in my initial response! Let me provide a more concise definition of Artificial Intelligence (AI): ... " It was still significantly longer than Google Gemini - even Gemini called out Copilot on it.

Our Working Definition of AI

Artificial Intelligence (AI) is a rapidly evolving field, with new innovations and ideas being constantly expressed in the news and online. Combining both the Stanford HAI and Cambridge definitions that use the **capability** of machines to exhibit human-like intelligence and fields of study that **explore** how to achieve this capability. We add that the focus of AI should be on **assisting** our intelligence rather than outsourcing or replacing it.

Artificial Intelligence (AI) is the field of study that emphasizes the development and application of machines and systems capable of assisting humans in idea exploration, task execution, decision-making, and problem-solving, by simulating and augmenting human cognitive abilities.

What is an AI (System)?

An AI system is purpose-built to derive insights, make decisions, and produce outcomes based on the data it has been trained on. These systems can utilize a combination of learning methods, such as:

- **Machine Learning**, where systems learn to extract rules and insights from extensive datasets.

- **Deep Learning**, where systems can independently expand their knowledge base.

The functionality of an AI system is largely determined by the dataset it is trained on. For instance, the AI system that composed the 10th Symphony was trained on musical compositions and theories. Artificial Narrow Intelligence (ANI) refers to specialized AI systems that excel at a specific task. They operate within a confined domain and cannot perform tasks outside their predefined scope. Examples include customer service chatbots and systems that power recommendation algorithms (like Netflix's "what to watch next" feature).[14]

What is a Generative AI System?

Generative AI systems are designed for learning and content creation. They are built from large language models and vast amounts of content, images, or both to create a worldview paired with natural language processing. These systems understand and interpret prompts and can respond to nearly any question that can be interpreted from the data provided.

What Other Types of AIs are There?

The field of AI is changing at a frenetic pace; listing the innovations, changes, systems, and opportunities in a book would be as useful to you as writing down a stock ticker from the day I wrote this sentence. The S&P 500 is 5,308, AAPL is trading at 190.52, and NKE is trading at 91.76 — a fun prompt would be to ask an AI when this pricing occurred together, and it would likely triangulate these data points to the exact date and time of this sentence. (Answer key:12:37 PM 5/24/2024) Q.E.D. It is nearly pointless to describe all the possible AIs. Find a reputable, credible, trusted source to follow and watch the space regularly. We rely on the Economist's AI coverage and the MIT Technology Review.

What AI Can Perform Defines How it Can be Characterized

Most business users, authors, and subject matter experts will encounter three main areas of AI capabilities in the ordinary course of business. These tools include plugins, apps, and platforms either enabled within their enterprise, available to their role in the organization, or accessible from their system.

- **AI Content Creation, Writing, Curation, and Editing**: These are the tools, including Copilot, Gemini, and ChatGPT, involved with text-based interactions and writing.

- **AI Image Tools**: generating and manipulating images from text prompts and embedded technologies in common platforms. Adobe Firefly, DALL-E, Midjourney.

- **AI Data Analysis & Quantitative Tools**: provide for visualizing data, automating code, and data analysis. Tableau GPT, OpenAI's Advanced Data Analysis, and Microsoft Power BI.

- **AI Task Assistance**: Systems and task automation assistants integrated into the daily work-life. Webex AI Tools, Hubspot, Grammarly, .

- **AI-Enabled Platforms**: Integrated technologies into the workflow of systems. Apple Intelligence, Copilot into Windows and Office, and AI into Adobe's creative tools.

The Math Behind AI

Underneath all of AI is math. AI is essentially a conversation with math, using mathematical concepts and algorithms to create models that perform tasks mimicking human intelligence.

> *"Generative AI, like OpenAI's ChatGPT and Google's Bard, relies on statistical probability. Today's computers are powerful enough to train large language models on billions of pages of text. The models can detect the patterns of language well enough to respond with startling lucidity, but they do not truly understand the subject matter. Given a word or letter, the models reference their training data and determine the word or set of words most likely to come next."* [15]

In particular, AI leverages three branches of mathematics: Statistics, Probability, Linear Algebra, and Calculus. [16]

Concept	Description	Beethoven's 10th
Probability	Deals with uncertainty and randomness. It's crucial for AI as it allows the system to make predictions and decisions even with incomplete or noisy data.	Estimate the likelihood of a musical note or phrase being generated by Beethoven.

Statistics	Helps AI make sense of real-world observations. Inferential statistics, in particular, uses sample data to conclude about a larger population.	Make sense of Beethoven's musical patterns and draw conclusions about his musical style.
Linear algebra	Deals with vectors, matrices, tensors, and their operations. It's essential for AI as it allows for efficient representation and manipulation of data and models.	Efficiently represent and manipulate musical data.
Calculus	Used in AI to model and optimize complex systems. For instance, it can be used to find the optimal parameters for a neural network.	Find the optimal parameters for a neural network that can generate music based on Beethoven's sketches.
Confidence Interval	Used in AI to estimate parameters while accounting for sampling error.	Estimate the accuracy of its musical predictions.

Remember, these mathematical concepts often overlap and are used together in the field of AI. In the Beethoven 10th Symphony project, a team of experts in machine learning and musicology used these and many more mathematical concepts to create an AI that could complete Beethoven's unfinished symphony. For example, confidence intervals could be used in conjunction with probability and statistics to make predictions about Beethoven's musical style based on incomplete data.

Understanding How AI is Structured

A critical aspect of how best to interact with an AI in the learning creation process is to understand better what you are dealing with and how an AI can assist and detract from learning experience development.

The AI's foundation model, the logical expressions it applies to the data set, and the prompts that trigger the process are all designed to provide precise and reliable responses. Unlike human data processing, AI provides numeric expressions and responses to queries with exacting detail, regardless of how the query is framed.[17]

1) Business User Input

The business user interacts with an AI system by asking a question or providing input as a prompt. This is where you, the business user, provide a question or task for the AI system. A prompt most commonly is a text-driven question to the AI to retrieve, synthesize, or take some action.

2) I know what you NLU mean

The AI system processes the prompt using Natural Language Understanding (NLU) and interprets the business user's intention in asking the questions. This includes breaking down the words into tokens, identifying entities, and labeling words (nouns, verbs, etc.). Once broken down, if the prompt involves text data, NLP techniques might be used to understand the meaning and sentiment of the text. The AI identifies the user's intent behind the prompt and classifies it as an information request, command, etc.

3) Feeding the Prompt to an AI Model

Depending on the nature of the intent, the AI begins working out the response to the user. The models can include a variety of knowledge sets, but the common ones they often include:

- **Machine Learning:** The AI system learns from a large dataset of past information to identify patterns and predict new data. Machine learning attempts to create intelligence by learning from experience (1) by using algorithms and data to create rules that allow computers to answer questions and perform tasks without being explicitly instructed on how to perform each step. Machine learning requires lots of data to train on and iterations to learn — the idea is that with lots of data, machine learning responses can be fine-tuned and made more accurate.

- **Deep Learning:** Deep learning is based on algorithms that analyze almost any kind of data. This is a type of machine learning that uses artificial neural networks, inspired by the structure of the human brain, to process information. Deep Learning can solve more complex problems that traditional machine learning algorithms might struggle with, like processing unstructured data, automatically learning relevant features from raw data, and scaling well with large datasets.

To build the response, the model relies on the raw information that the AI system is trained on. The dataset should be relevant to the task you want the AI to perform.

4) Crafting a Response

The AI responds with an answer or result that the AI system provides based on the prompt and data it was given. A user-friendly response is formulated using natural language generation (NLG). The answer is presented to the business user as a text response, voice output, or visual display.

5) Refine, ReAsk, Respond, React

Unlike a search engine, AIs are constructed to engage with. You may review the results and follow up with the AI to refine and improve the prompt with more specificity or details that support your request or even respond and react to the information given.

LLMs and Data Lakes

"Give me a lever long enough and a fulcrum on which to place it, and I shall move the world." - Archimedes.

"Give me a data lake large enough and a model powerful enough, and I shall shape the world." - Microsoft Copilot.

The first quote is attributed to Archimedes, demonstrating the principle of the lever, a simple machine that amplifies force and provides a mechanical advantage. The second quote is an adaptation to illustrate the power of AI language models (LLMs).

In the realm of AI, when a user submits a prompt to an AI, the AI steps in to understand the question. It is the LLM and the underlying data lakes that hold the data that can provide the answer.[18] A data lake is a centralized repository that stores all the structured and unstructured data in its original format at any scale.[19] An LLM acts as a lever, amplifying the computational power to process and understand vast amounts of data. The fulcrum, in this case, is the data lake, a large and diverse dataset on which the LLM rests, learns, and adapts. Just as the fulcrum's position can change the direction or magnitude of the force exerted by a lever, alterations to the data lake can influence the quality or quantity of the data processed by an LLM, thereby impacting the results.

These two elements, the LLM and the data lake, work in tandem to provide the 'mechanical advantage' in the AI world, enabling the generation of near-instantaneous responses to complex queries. By manipulating large amounts of data, the LLM synthesizes responses, much like a lever moving a heavy load with minimal effort.[20]

The LLM allows an AI to converse with prompts, answer questions, and generate and paraphrase content. In the Beethoven X project, all of the scores, music, and gathered information formed the data lake, and the LLM was trained to fill in and create the missing musical scores to complete the symphony. Expanding the data lake and training the LLM effectively shaped the resulting symphony.

Down the Digital Rabbit Hole

Chasing an AI Rabbit From Prompt to Response. Understanding all the steps involved in what appears to happen with little or no latency between a prompt and an AI response will help us better engage with and improve interactions with the AI system.

1. Asking a question ... Prompt Input

Whether through some form of text, speech, or other input, the prompt is how you engage an AI to perform an action and respond. Prompts bridge your intent and the AI's machine understanding and capabilities.

Prompt:"Write a blog post discussing the impact of AI on corporate training. Include real-world examples and practical tips for businesses to leverage AI effectively."

2. Preprocessing

Preprocessing may include cleaning and normalization (may include removing extraneous characters, stop words, punctuation, and capitalization). Preprocessing gives the NLP the best chance at understanding what you are asking of the AI.

    Prompt: Write blog post discussing impact AI corporate
    training Include real-world examples practical tips busi-
    nesses leverage AI effectively.

3. Tokenization

Tokenization breaks down the input text into smaller units called tokens. Tokens can be words, characters, or subwords that represent meaningful units that an AI model can process and generate a relevant response.

    "Write", "blog", "post", "discussing", "impact", "AI", "cor-
    porate", "training", "Include", "real-world", "examples",
    "practical", "tips", "businesses", "leverage", "AI", "effec-
    tively"

4. NLP Transformation

The NLP transforms the original prompt to simplify the language while retaining the essence, restructures the prompt to a common structure for requesting content and explicitly calls out the task and desired content.

    Compose a blog post that explores the influence of artificial
    intelligence (AI) on corporate training. Provide concrete
    real-world instances and actionable recommendations for busi-
    nesses to effectively harness AI.

5. Model Inference

Using semantic understanding, the NLP model processes the transformed prompt, identifies the task, extracts relevant information, and generates an initial response aligned with the prompt's requirements.

- Task Identification: The NLP model identifies the primary task: "Compose a blog post" that requires generating content.

- Topic Extraction: The model extracts the main topic: "the influence of artificial intelligence (AI) on corporate training" as the blog post's focus.

- Specific Requirements: The prompt specifies two specific requirements:

- "Provide concrete real-world instances": The model infers that it needs to include practical examples from real-world scenarios.

- "Actionable recommendations for businesses": The model understands that it should offer practical tips for leveraging AI effectively.

- Response Generation: Based on the task, topic, and requirements, the NLP model generates an initial response. The response will likely address AI's impact on corporate training, provide relevant examples, and offer actionable advice.

6. Content Generation (Natural Language Generation - NLG)

Based on the semantics, context, and pre-trained language representations, the NLP model generates an initial response. It constructs sentences and paragraphs related to the prompt's requirements. The response may include relevant examples, insights, and practical tips.

Here's the initial draft of the first paragraph for the blog post on the impact of AI on corporate training, tokenized:

```
'Title', ':', 'The', 'Influence', 'of', 'Artificial', 'In-
telligence', 'on', 'Corporate', 'Training', 'Artificial',
'intelligence', '(', 'AI', ')', 'has', 'revolutionized',
'various', 'industries', ',', 'and', 'corporate', 'learn-
ing', 'is', 'no', 'exception', '.', 'As', 'organizations',
'strive', 'to', 'enhance', 'employee', 'training', 'and',
'development', ',', 'AI', 'technologies', 'offer', 'unprece-
dented', 'opportunities', '.', 'In', 'this', 'blog', 'post',
',', 'we', 'delve', 'into', 'the', 'profound', 'impact',
'of', 'AI', 'on', 'corporate', 'training', ',', 'exploring',
'its', 'benefits', ',', 'challenges', ',', 'and', 'real-
world', 'implications', '.', 'Let', "'s", 'uncover', 'how',
'businesses', 'can', 'leverage', 'AI', 'effectively', 'to',
'transform', 'their', 'learning', 'strategies', '.'
```

The generated response undergoes postprocessing, including reassembling tokens into natural language sentences, formatting to ensure proper grammar, punctuation, and readability, and trimming to a reasonable length.

```
Title: The Influence of Artificial Intelligence on Corporate
Training

Artificial intelligence (AI) has revolutionized various in-
dustries, and corporate training is no exception. As organi-
zations strive to enhance employee training and development,
AI technologies offer unprecedented opportunities. In this
blog post, we delve into the profound impact of AI on corpo-
rate training, exploring its benefits, challenges, and real-
world implications. Let's uncover how businesses can lever-
age AI effectively to transform their learning strategies.
```

7. Iterative Refinement

During the iterative refinement step, several actions are performed on the content to enhance its quality and coherence. Iterative refinement involves making incremental changes to the content that enhance clarity, relevance, and effectiveness. Content may be added or removed, rephrased, or restructured. Refinement continues for multiple rounds, improving the content. Patterns and recurrent themes are identified, and common sources are identified and appended.

```
Title: The Influence of Artificial Intelligence on Corporate
Training

As technology continues to advance at an unprecedented rate,
businesses must stay ahead of the curve. Nowhere is this
more critical than in the realm of corporate learning. Enter
Artificial Intelligence (AI)—a game-changer that promises to
revolutionize how organizations approach employee training
and development.

In this article, we explore the profound impact of AI on
corporate training. From personalized learning experiences
to real-time progress tracking, AI offers a host of bene-
fits. We'll delve into the tools, technologies, and applica-
tions that make AI a powerful ally for businesses seeking to
enhance their learning strategies. Whether you're an L&D
professional, a manager, or an employee eager to upskill,
understanding AI's role in corporate learning is essential.

Please note that this refined version balances clarity,
depth, and relevance, setting the stage for an insightful
exploration of AI's transformative effects on corporate edu-
cation.
```

8. Final Version to User

The final version was deemed suitable based on feedback, readability, and alignment with the article's objectives. The paragraph is an effective introduction, inviting readers to delve deeper into AI's transformative role in corporate learning. In summary, the iterative refinement process ensures the content aligns with user needs, feedback, and organizational goals, resulting in a polished and informative introduction!

```
Title: The Influence of Artificial Intelligence on Corporate
Training

As technology continues to advance at an unprecedented rate,
businesses must stay ahead of the curve. Nowhere is this
more critical than in the realm of corporate learning. Enter
Artificial Intelligence (AI)—a game-changer that promises
to revolutionize how organizations approach employee train-
ing and development.
```

In this article, we explore the profound impact of AI on corporate training. From personalized learning experiences to real-time progress tracking, AI offers a host of benefits. We'll delve into the tools, technologies, and applications that make AI a powerful ally for businesses seeking to enhance their learning strategies. Whether you're an L&D professional, a manager, or an employee eager to upskill, understanding AI's role in corporate learning is essential.

Please note that this refined version balances clarity, depth, and relevance, setting the stage for an insightful exploration of AI's transformative effects on corporate education. 📎📚

User Reaction and Iteration

The user receives the response and may provide additional prompts or feedback. The interactions with the AI continue iteratively, repeating for each additional prompt in the thread until the user is satisfied or the chat ends.

Down the Physical Rabbit Hole

From Laptop to Data Center and What Alice Saw There. It is important to understand where the AI rabbit hole leads physically and digitally—engaging with an AI chat and following the prompt down the digital rabbit hole to the heart of an AI Wonderland.

1) The Curiouser Prompt

Imagine Alice sitting at her desk on a hybrid office day, interacting with an AI chatbot. As they type a prompt into their laptop and connect to the internet, they initiate a complex digital journey.

2) The Wireless Transmission

The prompt leaves the laptop as a Wi-Fi signal, bouncing around the room until it reaches the router. This device acts as a gateway, guiding the prompt to its destination.

3) The Digital Transformation

Upon reaching the router, the digital signal is split into countless smaller beams, each racing down different paths. The prompt follows a specific path, leading it deeper into the digital realm.

4) The Information Superhighway

The prompt, now converted into light, travels across vast networks of fiber-optic cables. It passes through switches that determine its route, zipping through continents, under oceans, and over mountains.

5) Arrival at the Data Center

Eventually, the light beams converge at a massive data center. This facility, filled with servers, cooling fans, and blinking lights, is where the real magic happens.

6) Processing the Prompt

Inside the data center, the prompt is decoded, transformed, and stored. It merges with other requests, forming a vast tapestry of information. Powerful AI chips work tirelessly to process these prompts, consuming significant amounts of energy in the process.

7) The Return Journey

Once processed, the prompt, now transformed into a response, retraces its steps. It travels back through the switches, across the oceans, up to the router, and across the room to the awaiting laptop.

8) The Final Destination

Back at the desk, the business user reads the AI's response on their laptop, completing the round trip from their initial query to the AI's response. This intricate process, often taken for granted, underpins our daily interactions with AI technology.

Data centers comprised of millions of computers across the globe house all the digital bits we create and seek. Questions and contributions are translated to digital signals of light and electrons traveling through silicon to reach a data center hundreds or thousands of miles away and return at the speed of light. For a digital native, it is hard to comprehend the traveling at this speed as they always have been.

Training an AI

With the systems and data in place, an AI can only respond to prompts with training and an AI only improves from extensive training and feedback. Once a model is created, training involves various steps and techniques to enhance the performance, accuracy, and efficiency of an AI model.

Step	Business Analogy	Definition
Data Preparation	Market research	Data is gathered, cleaned, labeled, and augmented for training. The quality of this data directly influences the AI's performance, much like how accurate market data drives informed business decisions.
Model Selection	Choosing a business strategy	The model and algorithms that best suit the data and objectives are selected. Different problems require different solutions, and so the choice of

		model and algorithm depends on the problem to be solved.
Initial Training	Employee onboarding	The data is fed into the AI model, allowing it to learn and find patterns. Like a new employee, the AI model learns from its initial mistakes and gradually improves.
Validation	Performance review	The AI model is evaluated on unseen data to measure its accuracy, correct any errors or biases, and assess other performance metrics. This step helps fine-tune the model for better results.
Testing	Product Testing	The AI model is tested in real-world scenarios to ensure it meets expectations, just like businesses test their products or services before launching them in the market.
Feedback	Customer Feedback Loops	Iterative feedback from users, customers, or stakeholders improves the AI model, much like businesses use customer feedback to enhance their products or services.

Training Beethoven

The efficacy of an AI system is fundamentally tied to the quality of its training. This was particularly evident in the 10th Symphony project, where the AI's performance was enhanced through iterative training and feedback. The AI, as initially designed, was incapable of completing the symphony independently. It required human intervention and oversight to ensure that the segments it generated were in line with Beethoven's stylistic nuances, artistic vision, and personal preferences. A team of experts meticulously reviewed, edited, and curated the AI's output, while also infusing their own musical contributions into the symphony.[21]

> *The to-do list grew: We had to teach the AI how to take a melodic line and harmonize it. The AI needed to learn how to bridge two sections of music together. And we realized the AI had to be able to compose a coda, which is a segment that brings a section of a piece of music to its conclusion. Finally, once we had a full composition, the AI was going to have to figure out how to orchestrate it, which involves assigning different instruments for different parts. And it had to pull off these tasks in the way Beethoven might do so.[22]*

The AI was subjected to comprehensive training on Beethoven's entire body of work and his creative process. This enabled it to learn how to generate musical ideas, develop themes, add harmony and orchestration, and seamlessly transition between different sections.

> *Only those who intimately knew Beethoven's sketches for the 10th Symphony could determine when the AI-generated parts came in.*[23]

This project underscores the iterative nature of AI training and the pivotal role of human feedback in refining AI capabilities. It also highlights the fact that, while AI can accomplish remarkable feats, it often requires human expertise and guidance to reach its full potential.

A Mathematical Game of Plinko

Imagine a Plinko board, where a ball drops from the top and bounces through a series of pegs before landing in a slot at the bottom. Each peg represents a decision point, guiding the ball's path based on its interactions.

When you enter a prompt into an AI system, it triggers a series of complex computations. The AI processes vast amounts of data to construct responses dynamically. It utilizes sophisticated computer chips specifically designed to perform highly complex and computationally intensive tasks.

A simplified way to visualize what an AI is doing is to imagine an AI Plinko board, with each peg representing a computational step in the AI's processing. While Plinko relies on chance, AI relies on sophisticated algorithms and learning processes. The AI processes the input through multiple layers of neural networks, each layer performing specific calculations to generate the final output. This can involve millions, sometimes billions, of calculations happening simultaneously.[24]

In both cases, the outcome is determined by a series of iterative steps. In Plinko, the ball bounces from peg to peg. On the AI Plinko board, information flows through multiple layers of neurons, being processed and transformed at each step. In both systems, complex behaviors can emerge from simple interactions. In Plinko, the final outcome is determined by the interplay of many individual bounces. In AI, the ability to recognize patterns and make decisions emerges from the collective behavior of neurons.

Just like the ball's path in Plinko can be influenced by random bounces, an AI's responses can vary due to several factors. These include the initial conditions (random initialization of weights), the training data it's exposed to (different training datasets), and how you phrase your question (variations in the prompt formulation).

A recent experiment we conducted demonstrated this variability. Identical queries were submitted to two leading AI platforms over a three-week period. The goal was to get a concise, engaging, and informative definition of generative AI's benefits for businesses. Both platforms consistently met word count requirements and provided plausible, relevant answers. However, each platform produced slightly different responses every time, high-lighting the inherent variability in AI outputs.

While AI models can continue to learn from new data, their learning capabilities are often limited by their architecture and training methods. This dynamic nature necessitates a flexible approach from users. Unlike search engines that deliver static results, AI models craft answers anew with each query, drawing from a vast and constantly evolving knowledge base.

Directing AI: The Key to Unlocking Outcomes

To fully harness generative AI, users must adopt a directorial mindset. View the AI as a versatile tool capable of producing countless variations. Just as a director guides a film from script to screen through multiple takes and edits, users must iterate and refine their prompts to achieve desired outcomes. Generative AI excels at responding to direction, embracing nuance and adaptation. By experimenting with different prompts and requesting multiple drafts, users can uncover the strengths and weaknesses in an AI's responses. Understanding that an AI is unlikely to repeat itself unlocks the potential to generate a wide range of creative outputs through subtle prompt variations.

10th Symphony's AI Achievement

The 10th Symphony is a stunning achievement and a beautiful piece of music. Yet, is it what Beethoven envisioned? Had Beethoven only sketched out the musical notations of starting with a bright C major chord, followed by a rising pattern on G, A, B, C, D and repeating this pattern, descending down to G, then back up again, could the same AI have created Ode to Joy? Would the AI have included human voices or have known to include a powerful message of joy, bright spark of divinity, inspired by a poem by Friedrich Schiller?[25]

What inspiration would have taken the place of notes, and what instructions for instruments and arrangements would have come? What if Beethoven had erased something in a later draft? The AI represents not the finished work but a possible scenario modeled to completion. AI cannot artificially create insight, innovation, intent, purpose, or vision — the ingredients of wisdom. Those elements that make wisdom from knowledge remain in the domain of the AI handlers and technicians, performers who instruct, judge, and interpret the AI. All of which should now be the focus of learning instruction.

Where Does an AI Fit in the History of the 10th Symphony? Beethoven's 10th Symphony has been a source of fascination and speculation for music lovers and scholars for almost two centuries. The Playform AI achieved something that no human has done in the 200 years since the Beethoven penned the notes for the 10th Symphony. While attempts have been made, most notably in 1988, musicologist Barry Cooper assembled the fragmentary sketches for the first movement. He wove together 250 bars of music from the sketches to create what was, in his view, a production of the first movement that was faithful to Beethoven's vision. No one could move beyond the sketches to a full symphony because of the sparseness of Beethoven's notations.[26]

With learning, the opportunity within AI is not to replace the core of learning but instead to enable more realistic practice scenarios, improved performance support, and the ability to personalize learning and rapidly progress skill sets that bridge knowledge from further afield. As AI in learning progresses, the focus can be on teaching concepts and facilitating opportunities to seek innovation and translate them to an individual's experience and requirements.

For true wisdom, we will continue to need learning to provide the creators and consumers of AI's assistance with the knowledge and wisdom to instruct AI. Learning with an assisting intelligence can provide immediate feedback and personalized interpretive responses. Based on the inputs, opportunities, role, and profile of the learner, the learning outcomes can be shaped to have a more significant impact on the development of the learner. Yet, AI cannot provide insight or innovation — the elements of wisdom. For that, we will continue to need learning to give the creators and consumers of AI assistance with the knowledge.

QED

"Quod Erat Demonstrandum" (QED) is a Latin phrase that translates to "which was to be demonstrated" or "what was to be shown."[27] This term, often used at the conclusion of mathematical proofs, signifies the completion and validation of the work presented. In the context of AI systems, QED underscores the criticality of demonstrating and validating the reliability and accuracy of the results.

Integrating AI content into business communication requires a meticulous process to ensure accurate and relevant results. Achieving QED in AI involves a multi-step process that transforms artificial results into meaningful and actionable insights. This process includes:

- **Transparency**: Being open about the data sources and methodologies used.

- **Recognition of Flaws and Biases**: Identifying potential errors and biases in the results.

- **Interpretation**: Translating the results into a format that is applicable within your organization.

QED underscores the idea that the principles of setting a proposition and proving it — the essence of QED. QED emphasizes the importance of clear objectives, systematic work towards them, and validation of results. These principles work for AI systems and are integral to successfully integrating AI into business communication and learning.

Macbeth the Back Cover Reviews

Create your own prompt and style variations and see how the AI responds.

> **Prompt:** Could you write a smart one-paragraph review of Macbeth that would appear in the paperback edition of the book and sounds like Elmo?

Experiment with different prompts and styles to see how the AI's responses vary. Here, we had fun providing a detailed scenario expressing the breadth of knowledge and literal references. Vary the style to see how the content shifts.

Prompt	Response
Could you write a smart one paragraph review of Macbeth that would appear on the paperback edition of the book?	"Shakespeare's 'Macbeth' is a timeless masterpiece that explores the dark corners of ambition and guilt. The play's eponymous hero, driven by prophetic witches and his own wife's relentless ambition, ascends to the throne through a path stained with regicide. However, his reign is haunted by paranoia and a gnawing sense of doom. Shakespeare's eloquent prose and profound understanding of the human psyche turn 'Macbeth' into a riveting exploration of power, morality, and the devastating consequences of unchecked ambition."
Like Shakespeare wrote it himself?	"In sooth, 'tis a tale most dark and full of dread, where ambition doth rise like a specter, leading a noble heart to a path most foul. Macbeth, once a paragon of virtue, is undone by his own hand, spurred by whispers of power and kingship. A cautionary tale it is, that unchecked ambition can lead even the noblest soul to damnation. Verily, this tragedy of Shakespeare doth hold a mirror to our own selves, showing us the dire consequences of surrendering to our basest desires. A tale it is, as timeless as the stars, that doth remind us of the frailty of our mortal coil and the impermanence of power ill-gained."
Like Elmo from sesame street wrote it - focus on his child like optimism?	"Elmo thinks Macbeth is a big story about a man who wants to be king very much! He listens to some funny ladies and makes oopsies. But Elmo knows it's important to be nice and share, not be greedy. Shakespeare writes good stories, even if they're a little scary. Remember, always be kind to your friends!"
Like Ernest Hemingway wrote it - focus on his brevity and powerful word selection?	"Macbeth: a tale of ambition, steeped in blood. A man, a crown, a damning prophecy. Witches whisper, a wife goads, a king falls. Fear rules, guilt consumes. Shakespeare's words, stark and potent, dissect the human soul. A chilling testament to power's poison kiss."

Step 1:

Create your own prompt and see how the AI responds.

```
Prompt:

Response:
```

Step 2:

Use the table below to add style variations to the prompt and see how the AI adapts the response.

Prompt Style	Response
Style 1	
Style 2	
Style 3	
Style 4	

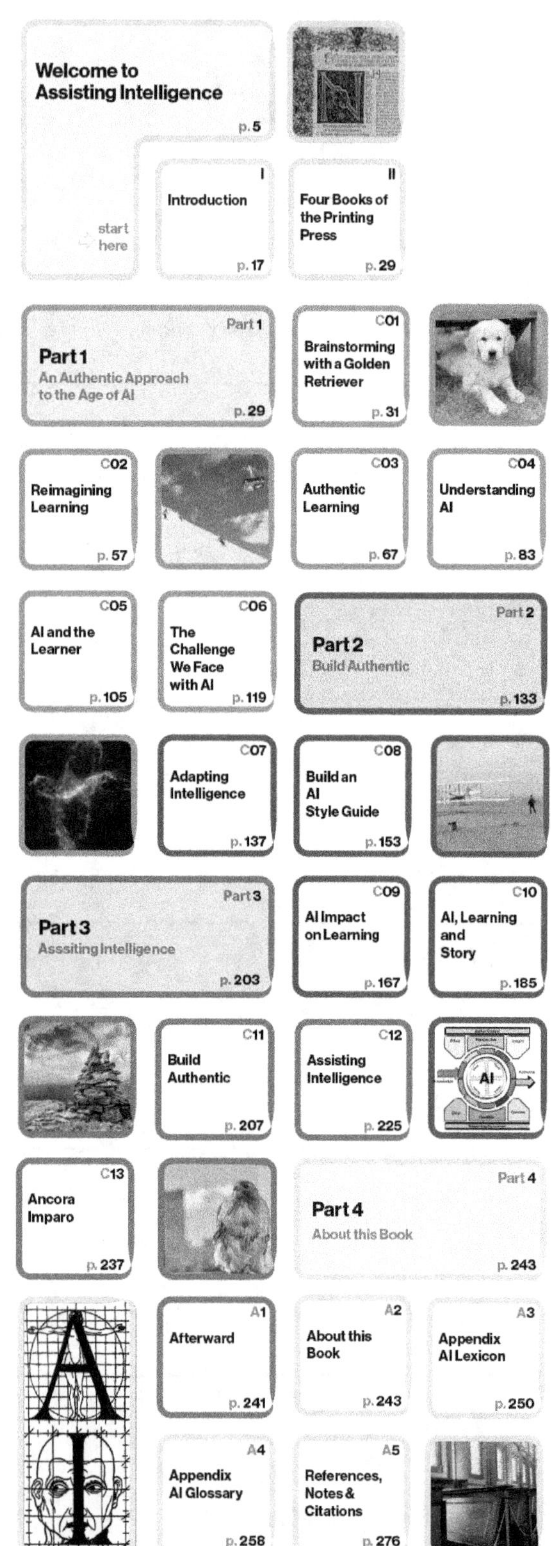

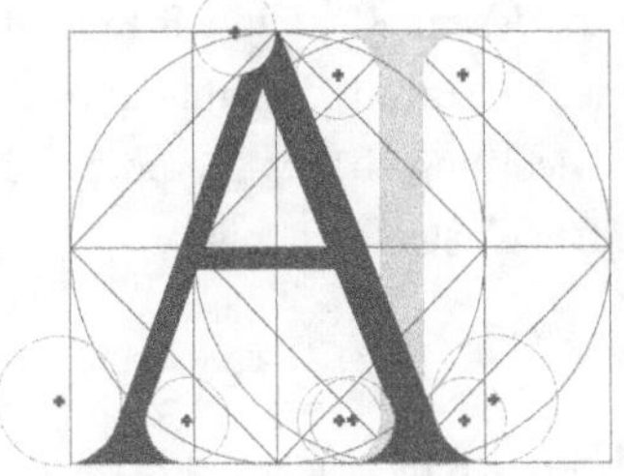

Chapter 5:
AI and the Learner

If an AI aims to create or shape knowledge, it requires a learner as a recipient. This chapter explores the diverse range of learners, from the *Silent Generation* to *Artificially Augmented*.

"No, no! The adventures first," said the Gryphon in an impatient tone: "Explanations take such a dreadful time."
- Lewis Carroll. Alice in Wonderland

Who is the Learner?

Michael Goldman, director of the U.S. Holocaust Museum, describes the intent to treat visitors to the museum as 'engaged witnesses' to the experiences surrounding them.[1] How the audience is defined and how they will experience the learning shapes the potential learning expectations, experiences, and outcomes and defines what a learner is.

What Must Happen to Become a Learner

As mentioned before, authentic learning must be based on credible, clear, and concise communication for the learner to accept it on its merits. But what defines a learner, what makes them ready to learn, and where and when are we likely to encounter them? There are three components that, when in alignment, distinguish the learner from a distracted and disengaged observer:

- **Perspective:** Learners arrive with their own experiences, perspectives, and biases. While change may be the desired learning objective and outcome, in reality, learning provides an opportunity for knowledge to influence and shift perspective.

- **Purpose**: Learners arrive with intent. Whether assigned by a manager or teacher or seeking new knowledge or development, they expect this experience will assist them on their learning journey.

- **Capacity**: Experience shapes the learner —moving them from ignorant curiosity to a level of engagement with the subject to understanding and sympathy. They must have the capacity to move forward, taking the acquired knowledge with them.

If the content or knowledge created does not meet the learners where they are at, aligned to these three criteria, they will remain unengaged and uninformed. Effective learning development and delivery is about making the learning applicable to multiple learning personas and perspectives. Understanding learners' knowledge levels and perspectives allows us to address their unique requirements, capabilities, and potential within a cohesive, responsive, and dynamic learning experience.

How Learners Make Decisions

Learning and development in terms of 'behavioral economics' can be defined as informing, improving, or altering judgment and decision-making when faced with choices or uncertainty.[2] These behavioral economic themes can drive learning related to decision-making:

- **Heuristics**: decision-making uses mental shortcuts or rules of thumb.

- **Framing**: the collection of anecdotes and stereotypes that make up the lens individuals rely on to understand and respond to events.

- **Structural factors**: the conditions and environment in which the learner is making these decisions.

Each of these factors may compete, hinder, and interfere with a learner's ability to change or adopt new thinking. When developing learning, a best practice is to examine how to shape the learning paths to best address the behavioral economic elements for each learning persona. The principal means to achieve this is by recognizing the learner's perspective as a starting point and developing a learning path, story, or journey to move the learner toward more informed judgment and decision-making. Applying behavioral economics principles means achieving learning outcomes by recognizing the learner's perspective as a starting point. A learning path, story, or journey moves the learner toward a more informed judgment and decision-making.

Further, many learners may have a misperception as a starting point for learning. The models they apply for learning may mean their biases can lead to an incorrect starting point when engaging with the learning.

> *That people's learning is governed by some amount of misperception seems unavoidable: The world is highly complex, and even the most sophisticated person will not be able to correctly perceive all aspects of her environment.*
> *—Mira Frick, Yale Economist.* [3]

Utilizing stories in practices and decision-learning scenarios enables the learner to understand better and overcome their initial biases and misperceptions about the learning subject.

Learners' Perspectives: Six Public Clocks

An art installation on Canary Wharf London, by Konstantin Grcic, presents the time across a series of six two-sided clocks. The current time they convey is all the same, yet each has a unique perspective - highlighting a single hour on the 12-hour dial. Each clock reflects the same time from their individualized point of view. Each number represents what may be important to the individualized users and what they may seek and take away from an experience. Beyond telling the time, by simply and effectively shaping the information to the learner's heuristics, framing, and structure, digital learning can convey learning experiences from different perspectives and dramatically improve learning outcomes.[4]

Digital Techno-types

For our purposes, we can all be defined generationally by our interactions with varying technologies and innovations during our development and lifetime. While older generations may have fully migrated to digital fluency or are nearing the end of their careers, younger generations are increasingly digital natives. Each generation's unique interactions with technologies and innovations shape their perspectives, usage, and outcomes.

Generation	Tech Witnessed	What They Saw	What They Saw With
Great Gatsby Grans Silent Generation Born 1928–1945	Radio, Black-and-White Television	The dawn of broadcasting and mass communication.	Traditional broadcast television and cinema.
Space Invaders Baby Boomers Born 1946–1964	Color TV, Moon Landing Broadcast	Saw the transition from radio to television as the dominant media platform.	Cable TV, recording devices VHS, and rentals.
Wired Walkmans Generation X Born 1965–1980	Personal Computers, Personal Devices	First generation to grow up with computers in the home, albeit not as connected as today. Witnessed the rise of video games and the beginning of the internet era.	A mix of cable TV and DVDs, early subscription, and premium content platforms.
Dumbledore's Streamers Millennials Born 1981–1996	Internet, Smartphones	First generation to grow up fully immersed in digital technology and the internet.	Primarily online streaming services, with a preference for binge-watching series.
Meta's Minions Generation Z Born 1997–2012	Social Media, Streaming Services	Never knew a world without the internet; social media is a primary form of communication.	Mobile devices and streaming platforms, with a significant presence on social media channels.
Artificially Augmented Generation Alpha Born early 2010s – …	Virtual Reality, AI Assistants	Growing up with advanced AI, IoT, and immersive technologies as the norm.	Augmented reality AI Intelligent and Voice Agents

Each group exerts force to shape and remake its world physically and digitally. They all inhabit a world shaped by rapid digital advances, which challenge our understanding of truth and trust in information.

In every sense, all generations are now completely media savvy and equipped with 4K, 5K, and even hyper-visualization capabilities. Yet the more we see, the more items are visualized, the more we lose the ability to differentiate the digital from the physical world. In the 1970s, IMAX 70mm films, which could achieve approximately 18K resolution, brought new immersive experiences to select theaters.[5] A Las Vegas venue called The Sphere opened with a wraparound interior LED screen achieving a 16K (16000 × 16000-pixel) resolution, making it the highest-resolution LED screen in the world.[6] In 2022, the Rijksmuseum created the largest digital image of a work of art. The museum created a digital image of Rembrandt's Night Watch measuring 925,000 by 775,000 pixels or 717 gigapixels.[7]

Every generation witnesses visually stunning moments that evoke awe, wonder, and engagement. While the Silent Generation experienced the transition from black-and-white to color film in the Wizard of Oz, Baby Boomers were captivated by the first images of a blue marble from the moon. For a GenXer, watching Jurassic Park in theaters, with Spielberg's direction, Williams's score, and groundbreaking computer animation, was a singularly awe-inspiring experience. As digital and computing power established a firm foothold, Millennials and Gen Z witnessed new clear views of the expansive heavens with the Mars Rovers, Hubble, and JWST, to the minute details found in the Human Genome Project. References to these scenes continue to spark a sense of awe for the generation that experienced them, even though subsequent generations may perceive them as commonplace. For my daughter and the upcoming Gen Alpha, Apple TV's Prehistoric Planet, displayed on a 5K screen, presents artificial computer graphics, like a swimming T-Rex, as if they were part of everyday nature.

Binary Personas: Digital and Physical Identities

Just as binary stars are a system of two stars gravitationally bound to each other, our identities, too, have become binary in nature—our digital and physical personas. The digital identity, defined by our unique digital footprint, and the physical identity, characterized by tangible aspects in the real world, are like the two stars in a binary system.[8] Traditionally, the physical identity was dominant, akin to the primary star in a binary system. However, our online presence has gained equal importance

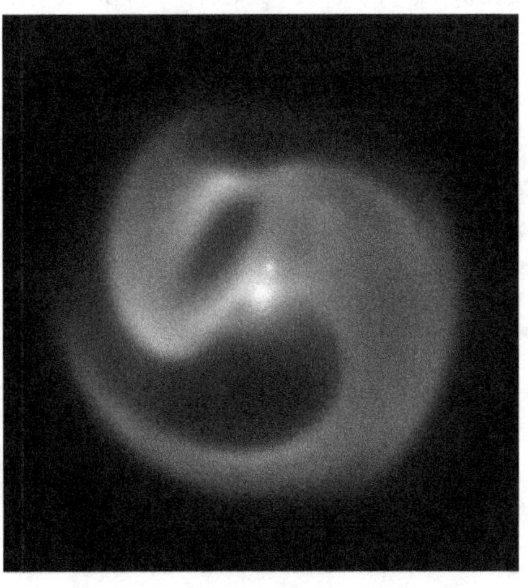

Image of a Binary Star from JWST

in the digital age, much like the secondary star gaining prominence over time.

The gravitational distortion between binary stars mirrors the influence our digital and physical personas exert on each other and can impact learning outcomes. For instance, our online activities (digital persona) can impact real-life decisions (physical persona) and vice versa. At a distance, these intertwined identities can appear as a single entity.

It's crucial to understand which identity—digital or physical—you are interacting with and designing learning for. The learner's digital or physical persona may be dominant at different times, and effective learning must address both halves of this binary learner to engage them properly. Equipping learners with knowledge and resources for both the real and digital worlds is essential. Failing to address one can impact the effectiveness of the learning, much like a binary star system's stability being affected if one star is neglected. Their interconnectedness and mutual influence emphasize the importance of maintaining a balanced and authentic representation in both realms. Understanding and addressing both the digital and physical aspects of our identities is essential for effective learning in the age of AI.[9]

AI's impact on the learner is just starting, but technological advancements have created challenges for learners. Smartphones, personal devices, social media, and the availability of digital information have already transformed every generation's learning, education, workplace, and cultural experience.[10] Jonathan Haidt's 'The Anxious Generation: How the Great Rewiring of Childhood Is Causing an Epidemic of Mental Illness' is a compelling exploration of the impact of smartphones and social media on Gen Z's mental health and learning. While Haidt's book primarily focuses on , its insights can be generalized to all generations. To varying degrees, even before the arrival of AI, information overload is causing increased anxiety, distorted perceptions, and increased distractions.[11]

Just as there was a divide between digital natives and previous generations, we can expect a similar divide between AI natives and those who grew up before AI. A pivot point for society and learning comes as modern education can leverage these technologies to enhance learning outcomes or find a new path for learning. A new path that uses these technologies as tools to aid learning that neither adds distractions nor becomes a source of stress.

Roles of Engagement

The different roles, personas, and profiles engage with the learning content. How learners engage with learning is often reflected in their capacity to engage with learning. Learning must be shaped to meet the learners where they are and move them forward. Learner profiles fit into one of four personas:

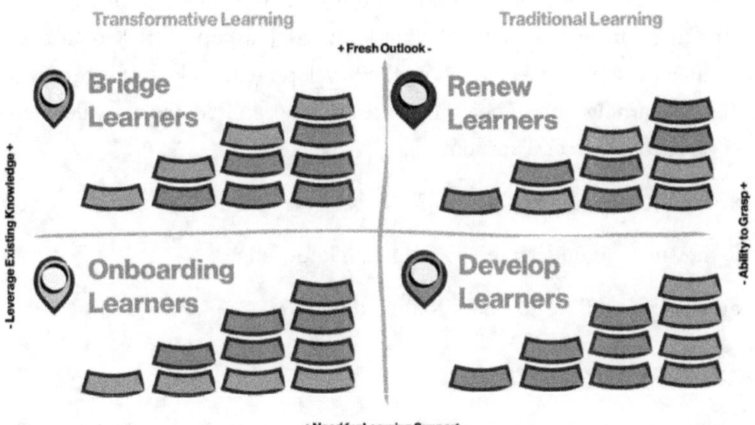

Nontraditional Learning	Traditional Learning
Bridge Learners	**Renewal Learners**
Bridge learners transition knowledge from another domain. They can leverage other experiences to assist with acquiring new knowledge.	Renewal learners reflect and reaffirm knowledge, with the ability to learn new aspects or hone skills. Fundamentally, these learners may be experienced practitioners of learning looking to augment or improve their performance.
Novice Learners	**Development Learners**
Novice learners explore new information equipped with curiosity. Their curiosity will be fundamental to grasping new information and knowledge.	Development learners acquiring knowledge along their career or development path. They have all the prerequisite knowledge and background to advance to the next step and are focused on acquiring knowledge for career path development.

Dynamic learning broadens the learner base and disseminates knowledge to diverse learning groups. Traditional learning pathways primarily facilitate skill acquisition within a specific domain. However, thriving in the digital economy and during transformative periods requires a blend of skills and the ability to avoid a 'competency trap'.[12] Learning is designed to disseminate information beyond the domain and attract new learners to the realm of knowledge and understanding.

Learning experiences extend beyond the core development path, supporting both novice and bridge learners. Within an organization, bridge learners can be described as being 'inboarded', enabling them to explore or transition from another role. Bridge learners are often the most driven, as they seek your knowledge as a potential solution and may even invest their personal time in pursuing the development. In the instances of nontraditional paths to learning line onboarding and bridging and AI can provide the general knowledge needed to success, including:

- What base knowledge do they need to?

- What do they need to understand your domain knowledge?

- What knowledge can they take back to their domain?

Consider All Your Learners

When someone learns something new, they take away different things. It's not just who they are, but also what they know and how they see the world. For example, a ski instructor might use the Jackson Hole tram sign as a refresher for their students, while a new skier might read it carefully. A local skier might see it as a familiar reminder, while a vacationer might use it to decide whether to try skiing. Your learners include subject matter experts (SMEs), stakeholders, and active and passive participants. What they learn depends on their unique experiences and perspectives. Learning is a personal journey influenced by factors like interest, past experiences, biases, and even mood.

Once you understand who you're engaging with, you can focus on how to reach them and achieve results. It's not enough to just present information. If you're not invested in the outcome, learning can feel like a distraction. Learning needs to evolve to keep up with how learners consume content. The trend toward building engaging and accessible learning experiences will only continue to accelerate.

Learners today are more screen-savvy than ever before. They can spot fake content and useless scenarios a mile away. If the learning materials are poorly designed, it will show. To create effective learning experiences, you need to give learners more control. Allowing learners to control their experience can make learning more engaging and empowering — enabling them to explore the content at their own pace. Training and learning should offer the right tools in the right setting. Find the right medium for effective learning.

In 2017, Grant Dalton, Crew Chief of Emirates Team New Zealand, challenged his team to set ambitious, personalized goals and do whatever it took to achieve them. "Throw the ball out as far as they could and then do whatever it took to reach it." His team, despite being outspent and out-resourced, developed a revolutionary foiling sailboat that outperformed the heavily financed defenders. Similarly, learners can achieve extraordinary results when provided with a supportive environment and encouraged to set audacious goals. By pushing themselves beyond their perceived limitations, learners can unlock their full potential and contribute significantly to their organizations.[13]

Reaching Learners Where They Are

Learners are becoming more diverse and unique at a time when the volume of content and access to technology are growing exponentially. As learners face an overwhelming amount of information, it's crucial to recognize the individuality of their digital and physical personas, the technology they interact with, and their position in the learning process. To be effective, learning should meet learners where they are and create a sense of connection. This shared interest or shared goals ensures that learning is relevant and impactful. By understanding the characteristics of your learners and delivering an authentic message, you can create a truly effective learning experience.

Physical /Digital Personas

Reflect on your physical and digital personas, identify similarities and differences, and analyze how they interact to shape your overall identity.

Your Profile	Physical	Digital
Describe		
Sources of Knowledge		
Go to Places/Sites		
Your Professional		
Your Personal		
Your Connections		
What They Share		
What is Unique		
Values		
Skills		
Abilities		

Consider how your physical and digital personas are interconnected. Do they complement each other? Are there any conflicts or contradictions between the two?

Playbook: Your Gen Profile

Think about your learning profiles that could be involved in the learning experience. List the primary profiles that could participate and their learning requirements.

Your Profile	Your Notes
Your Generation	
Tech You Witnessed	
What You Saw	
What You Saw With	
Sense of Awe	

Playbook: Learning Profiles

Step 1:

Think about the potential roles that could be involved in the learning experience. List the primary renewal profiles that could participate and their learning requirements.

Bridge Learners   **Renewal Learners**

Novice Learners   **Development Learners**

Step 2:

For each category:

- List three attributes of their physical and digital personas.

- List three specific characteristics they can identify with.

- List three specific connectors to your learners.

- List three specific ways they can help each other.

- List three specific items they will engage with.

Step 3:

Using a generative AI, list all the items provided as a prompt and ask the AI to build a persona from it. You can do this with text or image. Ask the AI what would give it a more complete picture and provide iteratively.

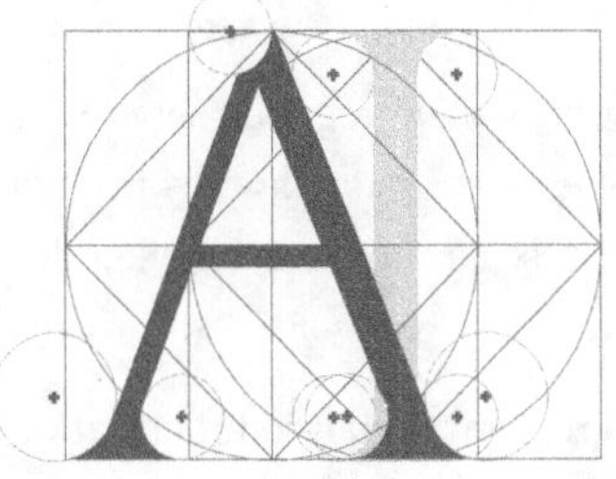

Chapter 6:
The Challenge We Face With AI

In this chapter, we look at the challenges we face before even engaging and embracing AI. AI is coming of age in an era of profound distrust and misinformation.

I am sure they will have more worldly wisdom, and enough, I hope, to know that honesty is the 1st chapter in the book of wisdom. - Thomas Jefferson to Nathaniel Macon, January 12, 1819

How Far Has Trust Fallen

In October 2021, Colorado Search & Rescue Groups posted online a public service announcement imploring hikers to answer the phone if they receive multiple calls from an unknown number. A lost hiker ignored repeated calls from rescuers because the hiker didn't recognize the number.[1]

This incident underscores a pervasive erosion of trust in digital communication, fueled by the cacophony of digital noise. In the face of overwhelming spam and disinformation, even legitimate calls can be dismissed as scams.

For generations accustomed to the reliability of landline phones, a phone number was a symbol of identity and credibility. The advent of the internet and VoIP, however, has democratized calling, allowing anyone to reach out to anyone else. Daily, we are inundated with countless messages, many of which are unsolicited and often deceptive. The once-solid foundation of trust in digital communication is crumbling under the weight of disinformation and spam.

Despite the hiker's physical vulnerability, digital assistance was hindered by their preconceived biases. As companies leverage AI to create increasingly personalized content, the potential for abuse and manipulation grows exponentially.

The spread of disinformation has fueled an erosion of trust across societies, leading to skepticism about the reliability of information sources and technology platforms.

Bad actors are now capable of creating comprehensive campaigns of disinformation. According to the New York Times, "the 'Disinformation Dozen,' a list of 12 people responsible for sharing 65 percent of all anti-vaccine messaging on social media." Dr. Joseph Mercola "published over 600 articles on Facebook that cast doubt on COVID-19 vaccines" while reportedly earning 100 million dollars in supplement sales.[2]

The advent of AI, with its ability to generate highly realistic content, has added a new dimension to the problem of disinformation. AI-powered deepfakes and chatbots can be used to create convincing but false narratives, further eroding trust in digital information. The erosion of trust in the digital world is already alarming, but the advent of AI threatens to shatter it entirely.[3]

While disinformation campaigns erode trust, competing with bad actors generating digital content will be secondary to physical evidence and authenticity, which are essential for building and maintaining trust. The World Economic Forum highlights that trusted resources online can help users find truthful information.[4]

Who They Trust, Where is There Risk

Each generation has experienced transformative technological innovations, which have created both new sources of trust and mistrust. As events shape our understanding of the world, these technologies influence how we perceive information and build trust.[5] A combination of global and geopolitical events significantly impacts how each generation perceives truth, threats, and trust. Understanding these generational perspectives is crucial for effectively communicating and adapting knowledge.

Generation	What they Trust	Sources of Mistrust
Great Gatsby Grans Silent Generation Born 1928–1945	Edward R. Murrow Newspapers Roosevelt on the Radio	Great Depression Fascism / WWII Propaganda McCarthyism
Space Invaders Baby Boomers Born 1946–1964	Walter Cronkite Network evening news 60 Minutes	Cold War Vietnam War Watergate
Wired Walkmen Generation X Born 1965–1980	CNN, Anderson Cooper PBS National Newspapers	Tabloids Cable News Syndicated Talk Radio
Dumbledore's Army Millennials Born 1981–1996	Aggregated News Fact Checkers Daily Show, Jon Stewart	Social Media Fake News Echo Chambers
Meta's Minions Generation Z Born 1997–2012	Crowdsource Journalism Peer Networks Podcasts	Social Media Platforms Bots Deep Fakes

'Artificial' has an Authenticity Problem

Our evolving views on AI are intertwined with the historical context of the word 'artificial'. John McCarthy's selection of 'artificial' in coining the term artificial intelligence at a conference at Dartmouth College in 1956 was in keeping with the sentiments of the times, a technical and human achievement.[6]

In the post-war era, artificial was imbued with a sense of wonder and pioneering science. There is no doubt that McCarthy would have been aware that the "artificial heart," the "artificial lung," and the "artificial satellite" represented the boldest aspirations of science.[7] The year before the Dartmouth conference, the New York Times front page on July

31, 1955, announced to the world, "MAN REACHES INTO SPACE—PLANS ARE AN-NOUNCED FOR FIRST ARTIFICIAL SATELLITE".[8]

A surge in artificial materials and products and expanding usage meant "artificial" began to diverge from innovative scientific pursuits. Synthetic fibers, plastics, and artificial ingredients in foods became commonplace, and the term took on a more negative connotation. These were less about making technological advances and more about substituting natural elements with imitation. Growing environmental and health concerns, further tarnishing the image of the artificial. Products were often seen as inferior substitutes for natural products.

Popular media also transformed the perception of AI. Films like 2001: A Space Odyssey and The Terminator portrayed AI as a malevolent force. These portrayals solidified the notion of AI as an unnatural and potentially dangerous creation.[9]

Today, "artificial intelligence" is caught in this semantic tension. It straddles connotations between the idea of innovation and cutting-edge technology involving scientific endeavors that great leaps forward and something that suggests an inauthentic artifice and source of apprehension. The rapid development of misinformation (e.g., deepfakes) and breakdowns in societal trust have exacerbated this apprehension.

Users and audiences associated with AI have to confront this duality, which reflects broader societal attitudes towards technology—its potential to revolutionize and its capacity to deceive. Any usage of AI must strive to overcome the negative connotations associated with the term "artificial." As AI continues to advance, an audience will have to reconcile the desire to leverage innovations with the need for authenticity and confront the evolving meaning of the word that defines it.

Provenance of AI

The release of ChatGPT marked a significant leap in AI technology, enabling natural, human-like conversations with machines. However, this innovation raises concerns about the potential for escalating misinformation and manipulation, reminiscent of the yellow journalism era.[10] In the 1890s, two media moguls, Joseph Pulitzer, and William Randolph Hearst, engaged in sensationalized reporting to dominate the newspaper industry. Their tactics included exaggeration, scandal-mongering, and sensationalism to attract readers and influence public opinion.[11]

Today, social media platforms exhibit the worst aspects of this journalism, with sensationalism, misinformation, and clickbait dominating the landscape. Social media moguls, modern-day Pulitzers and Hearsts, wield social media platforms and advanced algorithms to capture user attention and influence public discourse. These moguls are developing AI technologies that could amplify the potential for harm, escalating misinformation and manipulation on a global scale. The danger is that AI can power an escalation far beyond what Hearst and Pulitzer were able to achieve.

The influence of yellow journalism waned as independent newspapers and dailies provided alternative perspectives. New journalistic standards and adherence to higher principles helped restore public trust. To safeguard the credibility of AI-generated content, it is crucial to prioritize the provenance of knowledge. Reliable information must come from continuously curated sources and be regularly updated with the latest evidence—the credibility of AI platforms and their content hinges on this provenance.[12]

- **AI Platform Provenance**: Understanding the background and evolution of AI platforms, including their creators, infrastructure, supported models, and development timeline.

- **AI Content Provenance**: The history of content generated by AI systems, detailing which AI models created the content and any human or system edits. This helps assess the reliability, authenticity, and potential biases in AI-generated content.

The decline of yellow journalism's influence occurred as readers became more discerning and new journalistic standards emerged. In the age of AI, prioritizing the provenance of AI-generated content and supporting independent news sources are crucial steps to mitigate the potential harms of AI on social media platforms and in the media.[13]

In 2017, the PEW Research Center studied "The Fate of Online Trust in the Next Decade' and concluded that "Many experts say lack of trust will not be a barrier to increased public reliance on the internet" and yet, it was not that the mediums would endeavor to become worthy of public trust is that "inured to risk, addicted to convenience and will not be offered alternatives to online interaction."[14] We are nearly ten years into that forecast, and we are not so much inured as enduring the persistent risk.

A Historical View of AI's Honesty and Transparency

If honesty is the first chapter to wisdom, as the second U.S. President wrote in a letter, then history can write its introduction. Historical context provides valuable insights into the importance of honesty, as Jefferson recognized. AI may not have a long history, but the companies do. Many companies developing generative AI platforms and related technologies are the same ones involved in the explosion of social media and the data they leverage to fuel their language models.

Personal data is a powerful resource for AI, but it also poses significant challenges. Frank McCourt's warnings about the dangers of uncontrolled data are relevant to the challenges we face with AI.[15] The content, creativity, and interactions scraped from social media and the Internet are driving the foundational development of large language models and AI. Meta, for example, uses user posts and information gathered on Facebook and Instagram to train its AI. Meta's history of data privacy breaches and misleading practices raises concerns about its commitment to transparency and user well-being. X, formerly Twitter, uses posts to train its AI-based Grok chatbot.[16] This training data includes a significant amount of disinformation and apparent lies.

Trusting a new technology is challenging. History can provide guidance. The question of who controls and oversees AI usage has become increasingly pressing. Should it be the AI platforms themselves, government regulators, or a combination of both? We must remember that we select and utilize AIs.

While AI platforms often tout their commitment to ethics, their business models and historical practices often raise concerns about data privacy and transparency. The rapid rise of social media platforms, particularly without adequate safeguards for young people, as noted by Jonathan Haidt and Frank McCourt, has demonstrated the dangers of entrusting our data to entities that may not have our best interests at heart. By examining the history of social media platforms, we can gain valuable insights into the potential pitfalls of AI. The way these platforms, such as Meta, have handled user data, manipulated algorithms, and prioritized profit over ethical considerations serves as a cautionary tale. If we fail to learn from these mistakes, we risk repeating them with AI. Many of the organizations that were not honest brokers are now leaders in the development of AI. We cannot afford to make the same mistake with AI.

GrAIy Market

Ask an AI if it was trained using copyrighted materials, and it's likely to respond affirmatively. The gray market for AI-generated images, content, and products presents a significant threat to copyright enforcement and the integrity of creative industries. Using such content can lead to copyright and trademark infringement issues, as well as ethical concerns.

One of the primary challenges posed by AI-generated content is the lack of source reference materials, particularly in images. This makes it difficult, if not impossible, to reverse engineer the source and determine whether it is copyrighted. Additionally, the training data used for large language models (LLMs) supporting generative AI can be decoded and encoded as visual concepts, which can be reassembled in response to natural language prompts. This can result in the unintentional creation of derivative works.[17]

The gray market extends beyond the obvious legal issues to economic and ethical implications. A gray market can:[18]

- **Steal Revenue:** Creators and content owners may experience a decline in revenue as AI-generated content can be used without proper compensation or attribution.

- **Distort Opportunities:** The proliferation of AI-generated content can distort the market, making it difficult for creators to compete and earn a fair return on legitimate work.

- **Appropriate Inspiration:** AI models can be trained on copyrighted material without the permission of the original creators, raising ethical questions about the appropriation of intellectual property.

- **Empower Accomplices:** Operators may intentionally or unwittingly infringe on copyright by instructing AI to generate content that closely resembles existing works.

- **Erode Trust:** AI-generated content flooding the market with inferior knockoffs barely distinguishable from the originals can erode trust in creative works.

To address these challenges, it is essential to establish clear guidelines and regulations for the use of AI-generated content, leveraging both market forces and advocating for individual and organizational responsibility. This includes ensuring that creators are appropriately compensated for their work and that AI systems are trained on data that is ethically sourced and does not infringe on copyright. Additionally, it is crucial to educate your consumers about the risks of using AI-generated content and your efforts to engage with them in an authentic way.

AI Governance

Regulating AI in an era of rapid innovation is challenging, especially when developing regulations in tandem with its development. Governance establishes protections, frameworks, and guardrails to ensure that AI platforms are used fairly and ethically. It tries to ensure that the direction, research, and development of AI are built with measures for safety and respect for human rights. Governance provides broad structures and safeguards for the entire AI ecosystem, society, and economy. **Governance, however, is not usage**. While advocating for governance, we must choose AI platforms carefully and use them responsibly. If governance shapes the AI environment, individuals must take control of their AI usage.

Agency Intelligence

"To be or not to be," the AI choice is ours. Hamlet's indecision ultimately led to his downfall. Similarly, inaction with social media has contributed to a myriad of issues shaping generations, the economy, and trust in information. With AI, we cannot hand over the definition of usage or await proper regulation. We must be proactive in shaping the future of AI, rather than passively accepting its outcomes. We must take ownership of our AI usage by actively selecting platforms that align with our values and priorities. **We have agency over AI.**

By understanding AI's limitations and biases, we can use it more effectively and ethically. By controlling our AI interactions, we can better understand their limitations, biases, and potential risks. In sailing, one of the common cures to seasickness is allowing the person to steer. Steering the boat forces focus and concentration, and participation means control. The perception of having control of the situation allows the person to anticipate movement and adapt their movement to the motion around them. With AI, it is equally important to take the tiller, steer your usage of AI, and actively evaluate how AIs use the data and interact with you, how you pay and don't pay for the services, and what the sources of data are in their language models and income.

We have the power to influence AI's development and use. By making informed choices, selecting AI platforms that align with our values, and using them responsibly, we can influence the development and deployment of ethical AI. Our usage shapes the future of AI. We must take ownership of our digital lives and actively select the AI platforms that align with our values and priorities. As learners, we can shape the future of AI through our choices and actions.

With AI, we cannot hand over the definition of usage or await proper regulation. We cannot "lose the name of action" as Hamlet does.[19] We must select AI platforms that transparently and honestly approach learning and define the usage of AI on our terms. Before adopting a generative AI, consider the following questions:

- How is your data passed along, tracked, and captured?

- What AI sources of content and truth are used?

- How was the AI's data acquired, and how were its sources compensated?

- Does the AI's training data involve the "filching" of user data?[20] How does the organization justify the use of this data?

- How transparent and honest is the AI organization now and in its history regarding using and protecting personal, public, and collective information?

The answers to these questions should be decisive factors in your choice of AI platform. By considering them, you can better evaluate AI's ethical implications and ensure that it is developed and used responsibly, both as an individual and an organization.

Playbook: Write Your AI Masthead

In sailing, the standard colors were raised to the Masthead for all to see. In the newsprint age, newspapers displayed their standards on their masthead.

What would you imagine ChatGPT's, Microsoft Copilot's, or Google Gemini's masthead if they had one? Other AIs?

Ask an AI what should be on its masthead, and you will receive a variety of choices. Think about how to shape and manipulate the prompt for the desired result.

Think about your masthead for AI usage in your organization. What would it say?

Here is what we came up with for an AI masthead:

> *"Use more, Trust less."*
> *"All the Truth an Algorithm Will Allow."*

What is Your GrAIy Market Exposure

A gray market extends beyond legal issues to economic and ethical implications. Consider what these aspects of a gray market can do. How might this manifest in your organization, and what guidelines would you put in place to prevent and protect against it?

Gray Market	Impact	Guardrails
Steal Revenue		
Distort Opportunities		
Appropriate Inspiration		
Empower Accomplices		
Erode Trust		

Steal Revenue: Creators and content owners may experience a decline in revenue as AI-generated content can be used without proper compensation or attribution.

Distort Opportunities: The proliferation of AI-generated content can distort the market, making it difficult for creators to compete and earn a fair return on legitimate work.

Appropriate Inspiration: AI models can be trained on copyrighted material without the permission of the original creators, raising ethical questions about the appropriation of intellectual property.

Empower Accomplices: Operators may intentionally or unwittingly infringe on copyright by instructing AI to generate content that closely resembles existing works.

Erode Trust: AI-generated content flooding the market with inferior knockoffs barely distinguishable from the originals can erode trust in creative works.

To address these challenges, it is essential to establish clear guidelines and regulations for the use of AI-generated content, leveraging both market forces and advocating for individual and organizational responsibility.

Playbook: **AI Provenance**

The provenance of an organization creating an AI platform is a significant factor in evaluating its ethical development. Consider the organization creating the AI as much as how they conduct themselves in creating the AI. Complete the worksheet for any AI platform, note this is a primer for an evaluation process.

AI Platform	Evaluation
Platform Parent Company	
Track Record History of ethical practices, transparency, and accountability	
Values and Mission Values align with ethical AI principles	
Reputation Strong reputation for ethical behavior	
Engagement Actively engage with stakeholders	
Leadership Help shape the future of AI	
Transparency Transparent about its AI systems, data, and decision-making processes	
Openness Open for analysis and evaluation	
Advocacy To develop and implement effective policies	

Playbook: Points to Ponder

Readers Digest used to include a regular column, 'Points to Ponder, ' in each issue. This column included more thought-provoking ideas and commentary than the quotation column. With that in mind, review the full text of Thomas Jefferson's honesty of a first chapter quotation.

> *"But I see nothing in this renewal of the game of 'Robin's alive' but a general demoralization of the nation, a filching from industry it's honest earnings, wherewith to build up palaces, and raise gambling stock for swindlers and shavers, who are to close too their career of piracies by fraudulent bankruptcies. my dependance for a remedy however, is in the wisdom which grows with time and suffering. whether the succeeding generation is to be more virtuous than their predecessors I cannot say; but I am sure they will have more worldly wisdom, and enough, I hope, to know that honesty is the 1st chapter in the book of wisdom." - Thomas Jefferson to Nathaniel Macon, January 12, 1819*

Before putting a generative AI into your service, ask yourself:

- Robin's 'AI'ive: Children played a game called "Robin's Alive," where they passed a burning stick around a campfire. The child holding the stick when it went out was eliminated, and the last child standing won. How is the "Robin" of data passed along, tracked, and captured? What sources of content and truth were used?

- Modern-Day Filching: Does the AI's training data involve the "filching" of user data? How does the organization justify the use of this data?

- History of Truth: How transparent and honest is the organization now and in its history regarding the usage and protection of personal, public, and collective information?

- The answers to these questions should be decisive factors in your choice of AI platform.

By considering them, you can better evaluate AI's ethical implications and ensure that it is developed and used responsibly, both as an individual and as an organization.

End Part 1

We must approach AIs as learners, seekers of knowledge and truth, and improve our ways of conveying information to assist audiences in their quest for learning.

In Part 2, we'll examine what it takes to 'Build Authentic' that reaches the intended audience and how to craft effective messaging with an AI that achieves authentic outcomes.

Ancora Imparo e Assisto

We build authentic content as learners, and AI can assist.

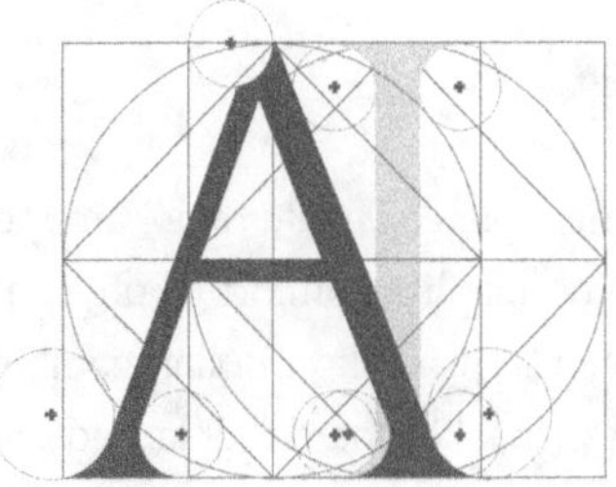

Part 2

Build Authentic

In part one, we kicked the tires and got acquainted with AI and what the content it generates means for learning and learners. To integrate AI effectively, we need guidance, limits, and starting points to protect essential authentic elements.

How can we guide employees, customers, students, and society in preparing for and adapting to the changes brought about by AI? Part 2 provides a walkthrough of how to construct AI frameworks, focusing on what to preserve, replace, and restore.

Where is the Number Pad

In the months leading up to the 2007 launch of the iPhone, a fierce debate raged among the media and tech giants. Would consumers abandon the familiar comfort of physical keyboards for a new, untested interface: the touchscreen? This billion-dollar gamble hinged on a fundamental question: could users adapt to a virtual keyboard that lacked the tactile feedback of traditional buttons? The iPhone's revolutionary design, featuring a touchscreen instead of a physical keypad, required a significant shift in user behavior. Steve Jobs dismissed concerns about the virtual keyboard. Users, he asserted, needed to "trust the keyboard, and then you will fly." The key to embracing this new technology lay in overcoming initial hesitation and trusting the unfamiliar.[1]

To fully harness the potential of AI and related technology, we must adapt our thinking and approach. By understanding how AI works, we can approach problems in a way that computers can assist and build trust.

This episode from our tech history offers valuable insights into the future of AI. We can adopt a similar adaptation mindset to harness AI's potential fully. By understanding how AI works, we can leverage its capabilities to enhance learning.

> *As computers get better, humans need to adjust to this and know more, get more experience about whether that works, where it doesn't work, where we can trust it, or we can't trust it.[2]*

Just as the iPhone revolutionized communication despite initial limitations in call quality, AI will transform knowledge creation and sharing in ways we can't yet fully imagine. However, it won't replace what exists; it will necessitate their evolution. Adding AI to existing systems without careful consideration is unlikely to solve fundamental problems.

The iPhone's success defied analyst predictions built on the assumption that "cellphone experiences are terrible and there's nothing you can do about it."[3] Just as the touchscreen revolutionized communication, AI has the potential to revolutionize. iPhones and the apps that reside on them have created an entire ecosystem of knowledge and productivity tools, revolutionizing how we handle information and connect with others. AI can do the same.

Learning to adapt to an AI mindset can unleash new avenues for development, knowledge sharing, and experiences once we learn to adapt our assumptions about AI and learn to fly.

In Part 2

In part two, we'll explore how to build trust in AI's ability to assist and deliver on its promises. Similar to the initial discomfort with the touchscreen, we need to learn how to interact effectively with AI to fully benefit from it. Using AI in our work requires a clear understanding of our goals. We can divide these goals into smaller tasks where AI can provide targeted assistance. The key lies in understanding AI's strengths and leveraging them to assist, not replace, human capabilities.

As AI continues to evolve, so too must our understanding of its potential and limitations. We must continually learn and gain experience to build trust in AI's ability to assist and deliver on its promises.

The iPhone's success defied analyst predictions, which were based on the assumption that "cellphone experiences are terrible and there's nothing you can do about it." Just as the touchscreen revolutionized communication, AI has the potential to revolutionize learning. By adapting our assumptions and embracing this new technology, we can unlock exciting possibilities for learning.

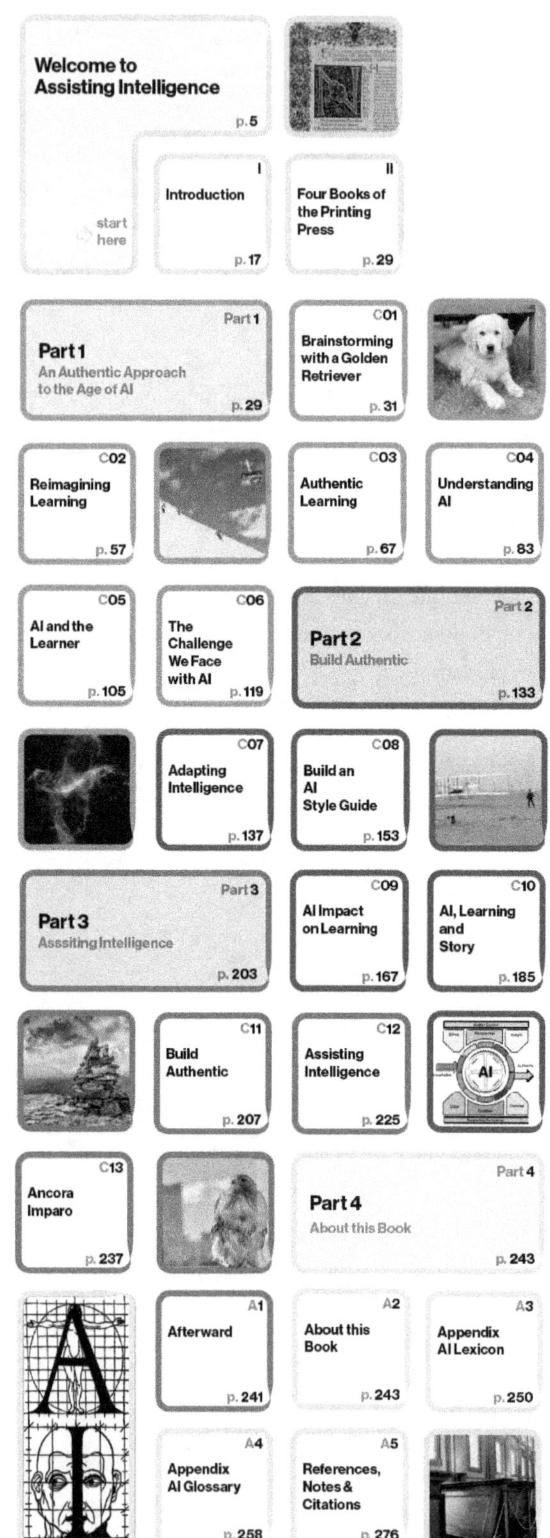

start here

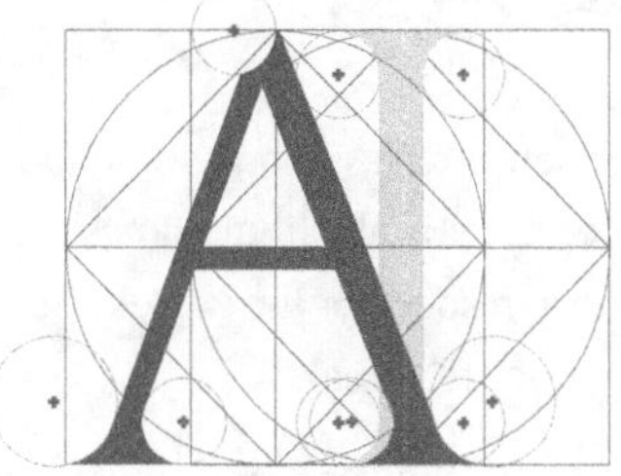

Chapter 7:
Adapting Intelligence

Where to Start with AI

How might you start with AI? In the rapidly evolving landscape of artificial intelligence, establishing clear guidelines for content creation is paramount. An AI Style Guide serves as a valuable tool, providing both guidance and guardrails to ensure that AI-generated content aligns with your brand's voice, values, and overall objectives. By adhering to a well-defined style guide, you can maintain consistency, enhance quality, and mitigate potential risks associated with AI-generated content.

When information is contextualized, it becomes knowledge.
When knowledge compels convictions, it becomes wisdom.
-The Age of AI: And Our Human Future: Henry A Kissinger, Eric Schmidt,
Daniel Huttenlocher

Replace, Preserve, or Restore

As a master shipwright (a builder focused on repairing wooden and classic boats), Reuben Smith understands that every wooden boat is a living history. At Tumblehome Boatshop, he and his team approach each restoration project with a deep respect for the vessel's heritage and a commitment to preserving its beauty for generations to come.

As I learned in a boat-building course under Smith's tutelage years ago, there are three primary approaches to repairing a wooden boat: replacement, preservation, and restoration.

- **Replacement**, the most drastic, involves a complete overhaul, often substituting traditional materials with modern fiberglass components. In this case, much of the boat's character is lost to materials and approaches that mimic it in modern form.

- **Preservation**, on the other hand, adheres strictly to original techniques and materials. It's a delicate balancing act that seeks to preserve the boat's authenticity and character.

- **Restoration** is a middle ground that combines traditional craftsmanship with modern innovations. It revitalizes a vessel while respecting its heritage.

Smith emphasized that repairing a classic boat is the owner's choice, and repairs could follow any of the three paths. Restoration offers the balance of allowing the shipwright to leverage their experience and expertise to maintain the character of the boat while embracing advantages that could reduce cost, increase functionality, and improve longevity. Restoration could embrace modern advancements like epoxy resins and remain committed to preserving the boat's original character. If shipwrights had access to this stuff in their day, they would have used it. This perspective underscores the idea that practitioners of traditional methods could use the best available techniques, materials, tools, and technologies in their time to effectively restore boats. Craft and authenticity are about staying true to the creative process and the desire to create purposeful and meaningful results.

For nearly any consumer product you can envision, there is an entirely handcrafted version on sale on Etsy, a brand name commercial version manufactured to standards adhering to the brand's reputation and definition of quality, and a commodity version by an unknown seller on Amazon or eBay. The choice of how products are constructed shapes the future for your customers and your organization.

When Considering How to Utilize AI

Entering the Age of AI often means building upon existing foundations. We face three fundamental choices: **replace, preserve, or restore**. Each has its merits.

- **Replacement** might involve using AI to generate entire articles.

- **Preservation** could mean using AI for research but writing the article manually.

138

- **Restoration** involves combining original elements with AI-generated content to improve quality.

Preservation maintains tradition and authenticity, resisting AI integration in certain economic segments. **Restoration** selectively integrates AI, determining where it can assist and where human knowledge is paramount. **Replacement** with AI, while modern, may sacrifice some authenticity and craft.

The decision of how to use AI shapes the future of craft and authenticity. Building authenticity in the age of AI involves deciding what to preserve, what to replace, and where to collaborate with AI to create genuine content and experiences. The extent to which you use AI depends on how much you wish to preserve and own the intellectual property of your content.

Adapting Physical to Digital and AI

Integrating AI into content creation shifts the process to the digital realm. AI lacks physical experience, and digital content now faces skepticism due to its impersonal nature.[1] To maintain trust, consider these strategies:

- **Preserve key elements**: Protect essential components of the original content to maintain tradition and authenticity.

- **Replace when unnecessary**: Allow AI to generate, substitute, or overhaul content where trust is not a concern.

- **Restore through collaboration**: Combine original elements with AI-generated content for enhanced quality; humans determine where AI can assist and where human insight and perspective are paramount.

Effective AI content requires careful prompting, curation, and editing. To establish a framework for AI usage, organizations should develop an AI Style Guide. This guide should prioritize content integrity by defining what to protect, what can be replaced, and how to effectively collaborate with AI. By incorporating human judgment into the process, organizations can harness the power of AI while maintaining the highest standards of content quality.

Building a Foundation

The Importance of an AI Style Guide

To integrate AI effectively, we need clear guidance and limits. A well-crafted style guide can provide this framework, ensuring consistency and protecting elements that should remain authentic. Geoffroy Tory recognized the need for standardization in the rapidly expanding French printing industry. His Champ Fleury aimed to achieve a consistent presentation of language, type, and fonts for readers.

Style guides have been developed for nearly every profession and organization, and opportunity for consistency and standardization to benefit the learner. Across industries you can find and encounter:

Guide	Description
Writing Guides:	Journalists and writers rely on style guides like Elements of Style by Strunk & White, the AP Stylebook for factual communication, and The Economist Style Guide for effective English language use.
Technology Guides:	Style guides extend beyond language to technologies and coding. Examples include Brendan Kehoe's early "Zen and the Art of the Internet" guide. The GitHub Style Guide provides guidelines for contributing code to GitHub repositories, including formatting, naming conventions, and documentation.
Field Guides:	Before smartphones, field guides were essential tools in fields like botany and ornithology. They provided accurate information through images, descriptions, and concise explanations.
Professional Guides:	The American Psychological Association 'APA Style Guide' was established in 1929 to promote clear communication in psychology—others the American Medical Association (AMA) Style Guide.

Brand and Style Guides

Brand and style guides are essential for maintaining consistency and authenticity in an organization's communications. It outlines the brand's values, tone, voice, and visual elements, ensuring all materials align with its identity.

Brand and style guides include the three key elements of a brand:

- **Brand values:** The principles that guide the brand's behavior. A clear statement of the brand's purpose and goals.

- **Brand personality:** The brand's character and how it is perceived by customers, as well as the tone and style of the brand's communications.

- **Brand identity:** The logo, colors, typography, and other visual elements.

These elements are documented with specific instructions and guidelines on how to use the brand's elements correctly. Brand guidelines seek to establish and reinforce conduct and communication as representative of the brand.

In marketing, guides does not create rules or provide steps for creating creative. The hallmarks of great brands' advertising strategy present a disparate view of a consistent brand by showcasing diverse and contrasting elements while maintaining a unified brand identity. This approach contrasts varied campaigns and mediums but is rooted in consistent messaging. Despite the varied visuals and stories, the core brand messages remain constant. Each brand has its unique approach, but they all share a common goal: to ensure that their communications are consistent, authentic, and effective. By developing a comprehensive brand style guide, organizations can ensure that employees work, interactions with the outside world whether digitally, social, formal, informal, internal and physically aligns with their brand identity and resonates with their target audience.

What is an AI Style Guide?

An AI style guide stands between the actions of employees interacting with generative AIs and the brand guidelines they must adhere to. An AI style guide ensures consistent and effective communication when integrating AI. This guide defines how to use AI tools while preserving core values and upholding ethical practices. By establishing clear guidelines for AI usage, organizations can achieve optimal results and maintain a strong brand reputation.

How do you offer a consistent, engaging approach to fantastic technology that will change everything … in 1992?

> *Welcome to Cyberspace! We've been expecting you. Be careful as you try out your new legs —the ground's firm, but does have some unexpected twists and turns.*
> *— Preface to Zen and the Art of the Internet*

In June of 1992, Brendan Kehoe published *Zen and the Art of the Internet* as a freely available eBook. This book was unique not only because it was one of the first ebooks published as a free resource available online, but also because it was written in the format of a style guide. The book was released at the beginning of the Internet's rapid growth and was designed to introduce the average user to this emerging technology. It lightly covered technical information, providing enough to serve as a starting point for reference, but its main focus was to offer an introduction to engage users in the use of the internet and to highlight its potential.

Brendan Kehoe's Zen and the Art of the Internet possessed all the qualities of a significant and impactful style guide for a new technology.

Guide	Example from *Zen and the Art of the Internet*
Level-setting user experience:	Zen is excellent for onboarding new users and as a quick resource for people with experience, allowing them to complete and fill in their knowledge. Combining these two audiences also becomes the resource an experienced person would reference when teaching someone new.
Be helpful to start:	Quick, direct tips with examples of code and A person's email address on a computer: user@somewhere.domain A computer's name: somewhere.domain
Provide references worth coming back to:	Providing a list of all the country codes for FTP will help any level learner with a quick lookup for navigational information — regardless of experience level.
Show what's possible:	From a chapter entitled "Things You'll Hear About," we learned about "A Coke Machine on the Internet" that broadcast its inventory of cold drinks to the CS department at Carnegie Mellon — this simple use case of what would become the Internet of Things and is now shaping supply chains and global manufacturing.
Styles, quirks, and customs:	Zen is authentic. "*Try sending yourself mail a few times, to get used to your system's mailer. It'll save a lot of wasted aspirin…*" Intermixed with knowledge, resources, and examples is the author's voice.

Zen and the Art of the Internet was quite novel and groundbreaking for its time and set a precedent for the distribution and accessibility of digital books. Brendan Kehoe negotiated with the publisher Prentice Hall in July 1992 to allow the digital version of the book to be one of the first mass-published ebooks on the Internet. The book's original edition would remain free of charge on the internet for everyone to access. As one of the first substantial books freely available for reuse on the Internet, Zen predated and helped to inspire the free culture movement.[2]

Zen grew and fostered new growth of the internet. It outlasted many of the technologies it gave instructions for and is sighted as one of the most important works that helped not only the growth and adoption of the internet but also the idea of free, unrestricted reuse. I first encountered Zen in 1993, when I started my professional career working with technology; a copy still sits on my bookshelf today. It was the first eBook I ever encountered about the internet in my professional career.

AI Platforms Responsibility Structures

The technology companies behind the leading AI platforms each have policies and online resources presenting their view on AI, its usage, and their perspective on their responsibility for its development and deployment, which is increasingly important in today's world.

AI Platform Responsibility Tagline and Description	Key Terms and Focus
Microsoft AI https://www.microsoft.com/en-us/ai **Tagline: Trustworthy AI** *Build business value confidently with AI you can trust. Microsoft is committed to providing trustworthy AI—with decades of research, customer feedback, and learnings informing the capabilities that deliver privacy, safety, and security.*	**Key terms:** Trustworthy, Emphasizes the reliability and dependability of Microsoft's AI, focusing on privacy, safety, and security.
Google AI https://ai.google **Tagline: Making AI helpful for everyone** *We're committed to improving the lives of as many people as possible. And we'll continue to responsibly build products and platforms – powered by the most advanced technology – for billions of people around the world.*	**Key terms:** Helpful, improving lives Highlights the humanitarian aspect of Google's AI, aiming to improve people's lives globally.
OpenAI https://openai.com/safety/ **Tagline: Safety at every step** *We believe in AI's potential to make life better for everyone, which means making it safe for everyone.*	**Key terms:** Safety, potential Underscores the importance of safety in AI development and application.
Meta AI https://ai.meta.com/responsible-ai/ **Tagline: Driven by our belief that AI should benefit everyone** *Our Responsible AI efforts are propelled by our mission to help ensure that AI at Meta benefits people and society. Through regular collaboration with subject matter experts, policy stakeholders and people with lived experiences, we're continuously building and testing approaches to help ensure our machine learning (ML) systems are designed and used responsibly.*	**Key terms:** Benefit, people Reinforces Meta's dedication to ensuring AI benefits for society, with a focus on collaboration and testing.

Choices in each company's language reflect its unique approach to responsibilities and inform its approach to AI. How does the use of trust and security compare to global accessibility and improvement, safety, as well as societal benefits and collaborative efforts?

An Authentic Framework for AI Style Guide

Developing an effective framework for AI, a rapidly evolving and nascent technology, mirrors the challenges faced in the early days of the internet. How can we provide guidance for a technology that is still incomplete yet deeply integrated into our organizations? Despite potential limitations, AI guidelines can have a profound impact. Even incomplete guidelines can provide valuable direction, helping organizations navigate the complexities of AI adoption and mitigate associated risks. In addition, AI poses significant risks, including misinformation, bias, and erosion of trust. As AI continues to evolve and permeate all aspects of our digital lives, it is essential to provide informed guidance. To mitigate these risks, we must establish a framework for authentic communication.[3]

- **Ethos:**Establish a clear stance on AI's potential benefits and risks and importance to the organization to get it right.

- **Perception:** Embrace a diverse range of perspectives on AI, including those of innovators, skeptics, and affected communities.

- **Insight:** Recognize AI's evolving nature and create adaptable guidelines that can keep pace with technological advancements.

- **Credible:** Provide trustworthy assessments of the organization rooted in honesty and accountability.

- **Clear:** Offer concrete examples to illustrate AI's impact and provide practical guidance.

- **Concise:** Explain AI's relevance and implications in a clear and understandable manner.

As a foundation for an AI Style Guide, we can craft and adhere to principles that harness AI's power for everyone's betterment while mitigating risks. For the elements that are incomplete for AI usage, the brand and organizational principles provide the guardrails for expectations of usage.

Creating a Style Guide for an Evolving Technology

Creating a style guide for an evolving technology not yet defined like AI may seem counterintuitive. A style guide can bridge the gap between entrepreneurial innovation and corporate inertia, providing a framework for guiding organizational actions. In the dynamic digital transformation landscape, organizations often grapple with a fundamental duality: the entrepreneurial spirit of continuous discovery and the corporate imperative of stability and control. These tensions from either side of the action spectrum can hinder execution and prevent organizations from fully embracing new opportunities.

Transformations are a continuum, and the complete vision of the strategy can take years and even decades to play out. Yet, to begin, all parts of the organization must buy into this incomplete vision and execute even when it is known that elements of the transformation are incomplete and not all the envisioned functionality is in place.

Entrepreneurial innovation thrives on exploration, experimentation, and a willingness to take risks - they risk continuing to explore alternatives and discoveries over working with the execution framework. Corporate inertia favors waiting until all elements are in place - they risk never starting. An organization can only transform and move forward when these two forces are brought into alignment on execution.

From the outset of the book, *Zen and the Art of the Internet* embraced this approach to the early Internet and how the guide could assist with finding a foothold but not anticipate all the twists and turns of the road ahead. The book's approach emphasizes assisting understanding without attempting to predict every future development, a strategy that remains relevant for guiding users along the winding path of AI's evolution. A transformative style guide can play a critical role in achieving this balance by providing a framework for guiding organizational actions and ensuring that entrepreneurial innovation is aligned with the overall strategy. The guide should address all sides, stating that this is a starting point and embracing the strategy's incompleteness.

Overcoming Organization Resistance

The wabi-sabi philosophy, rooted in authenticity, simplicity, and the acceptance of impermanence, can guide our approach to both AI and the creation of AI style guides. In the context of AI, wabi-sabi encourages us to embrace the evolving and imperfect nature of AI systems.[4]

Organizations often face inherent resistance to change, a phenomenon described by Julian Birkinshaw as a 'corporate immune system'. This resistance can hinder the adoption of AI, even in the face of its potential benefits.[5] To overcome this, organizations need to foster a culture of innovation, encourage experimentation, and reward risk-taking.

By combining the principles of wabi-sabi and immune response, organizations can create a more conducive environment for AI adoption. Wabi-sabi helps us appreciate AI's imperfect and evolving nature while addressing the inherent resistance to change within organizations. This approach can foster a more open and receptive attitude towards AI, allowing organizations to harness its potential while mitigating risks.

What Does a Transformative Learning Look Like? A Case Study

A leading home appliance manufacturer faced similar challenges that we now face with AI as they embarked on a digital transformation journey. To navigate the duality of entrepreneurial innovation and corporate resistance, the company implemented a training program that focused on the following key areas. The organization leveraged its brand and history to communicate that it was time to make changes to improve the customer experience and journey. They acknowledged that how customers engaged in the retail process and interacted with their appliances had changed. Digital was now the way forward. They also acknowledged that many parts of the organization were experimenting and discovering ways to improve digital engagement with the consumer.

While some parts of the organization were rooted in the traditional retail-to-consumer supply chain, and other innovative solutions well beyond the organization's capabilities. The training highlighted the potential benefits of the transformation. It addressed concerns, providing support and resources to help employees adapt to new ways of working while reinforcing that the status quo was giving way to a new digital culture of continuous learning and improvement.

For the employees, the training provided clear, honest direction on how the company developed a unified vision of the new consumer process that was wholly digital and sought to align the organization around a shared vision for the future. The path was incomplete; parts would replace traditional methods, and others would require recasting entrepreneurial elements or waiting for the organization to catch up. The transformation could not meet every objective now, but it was the realistic path toward achieving the goals.

The training encouraged employees to take ownership of their work, apply the new processes with the new framework provided, and follow the clear guidelines for collaboration and decision-making to move forward. The change would be a new continuum, a better path with goals and destinations defined for the digital consumer lifecycle. Not all goals would be achievable immediately, but they would be on the future path for the organization to grasp wholly.

Back to Preserve, Replace and Restore

AI fundamentally alters how businesses operate. Learning to thrive in the age of AI means not just creating new things, but also preserving, replacing, or restoring existing processes.

An AI style guide serves as a bridge between the concepts of wabi-sabi and immune response, providing guidelines for AI application. The Style guide provides a strategic approach, examples, and methods for how the organization plans to preserve, replace, and restore processes with AI. To ensure a successful transformation, it is essential to develop a comprehensive guide that provides a framework for guiding the organization's actions. An AI style guide serves as a roadmap for:

- **Prioritizing initiatives:** Identifying the most critical areas for focus and allocating resources accordingly and those that would wait.

- **Honest assessment** of the organization's capabilities to embrace and leverage the new technology.

- **Establishing standards:** Setting guidelines for technology adoption, data management, and experience.

- **Measuring progress:** Tracking key performance indicators and adjusting as needed.

Transformations often require a delicate balance between entrepreneurial spirit and corporate governance. A well-crafted style guide can be crucial in bridging this gap and guiding organizations towards a more innovative and sustainable future. By following the training approach, an organization can:

- Move from exploration to execution of the strategy.

- Provide a clear direction and avoid unnecessary detours.

- Identify and mitigate potential challenges.

- Ensure consistency by maintaining a unified approach across different teams and departments.

In the next section, we'll review and define your AI style guide with the learning and communication you hope to develop and influence.

Preserve, Replace, & Restore

To Build Authentic in the age of AI, you must decide what you wish to preserve, what you are willing to replace, and, most importantly, where you can collaborate with AI to create authentic content and restore experiences.

What must you preserve?

What can you replace?

What can you restore?

Playbook:

Semantics of AI Guidelines

Look at the AI Guides and Centers for Responsibility with AI from the leading technology companies listed below. While each company emphasizes responsibility and the positive impact of AI. Compare and contrast the semantical differences within their statements and select elements that resonate with your audience and message to convey.

AI Platform	Guidelines and Notes

Microsoft AI

https://www.microsoft.com/en-us/ai

Tagline: Trustworthy AI

Build business value confidently with AI you can trust. Microsoft is committed to providing trustworthy AI—with decades of research, customer feedback, and learnings informing the capabilities that deliver privacy, safety, and security.

Google AI

https://ai.google **Tagline: Making AI helpful for everyone**

We're committed to improving the lives of as many people as possible. And we'll continue to responsibly build products and platforms – powered by the most advanced technology – for billions of people around the world.

OpenAI

https://openai.com/safety/

Tagline: Safety at every step

We believe in AI's potential to make life better for everyone, which means making it safe for everyone.

Meta AI

https://ai.meta.com/responsible-ai/

Tagline: Driven by our belief that AI should benefit everyone

Our Responsible AI efforts are propelled by our mission to help ensure that AI at Meta benefits people and society. Through regular collaboration with subject matter experts, policy stakeholders and people with lived experiences, we're continuously building and testing approaches to help ensure our machine learning (ML) systems are designed and used responsibly.

Playbook: Authentic Framework

Imagine the release of the iPhone, and the communication and the touch points with the consumer about the screen keyboard were left to the individual departments. Sales, marketing, and support all had independent messages regarding the keyboard usage. When faced with technology changes, organizations must communicate expected experiences, benefits, and tools to assist with adoptions, including areas for opportunity, exploration, and where the boundaries are.

Step 1 Watch

Watch three elements from the iPhone rollout.

Video Elements

Introduction iPhone

https://www.youtube.com/watch?v=MnrJzXM7a6o

Start with Steve Jobs' iconic introduction of the iPhone to the world at the Macworld keynote address.

First Commercial

https://youtu.be/ubxxk11Hx1U

Then watch the iPhone's advertising in the months leading up to its availability with a 'hello' - simply repeating over and over again what we have experienced for decades with one small yet significant change.

Getting Started Tour

https://www.youtube.com/watch?v=vTy61AP__e8

The Getting Started tour released as the phone was made available for sale positioned the iPhone as "a revolutionary product and combines three products into one." It focused first on the simplicity and ease of design before embarking on "And this is the home button …"

Step 2: Evaluate

From each, note the elements of Ethos, Perspective, and Insight and how they were communicated to the learner in a credible, clear, and concise way.

iPhone Introduction	First Commercial	Getting Started Tour
Ethos		
-	-	-
Perspective		
-	-	-
Insight		
-	-	-
Credible		
-	-	-
Clear		
-	-	-
Concise		
-	-	-

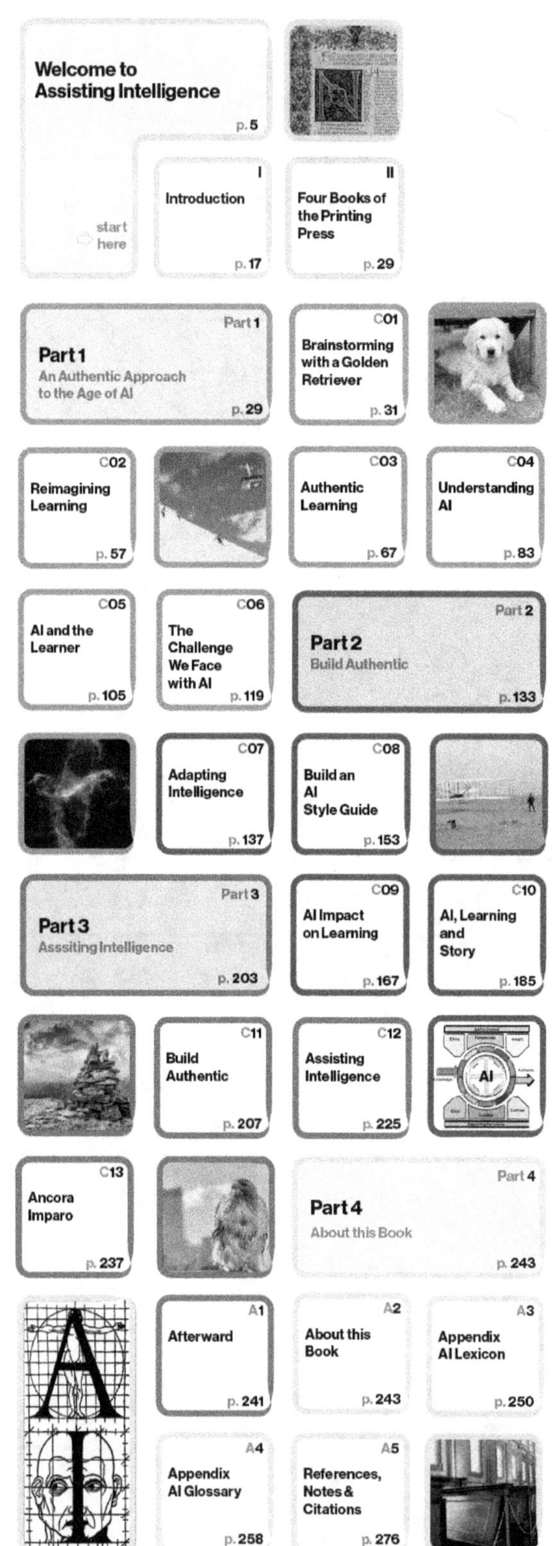

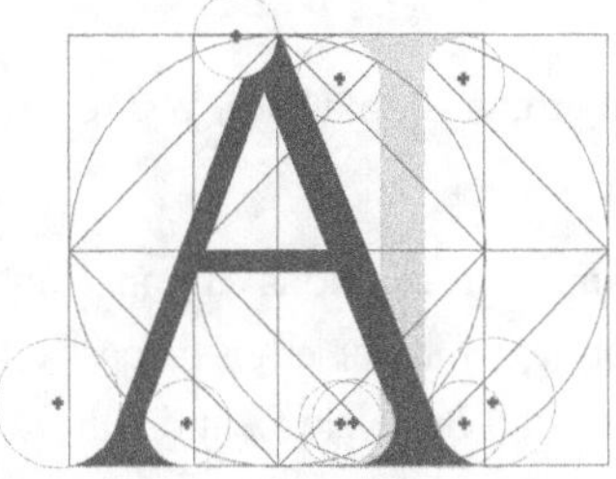

Chapter 8:

Build an Authentic AI Style Guide

This chapter shows how to develop an AI Style Guide that reaches your learners with credibility by utilizing your brand, voice, and leadership. In concert with the development of your AI Style Guide is how your organization currently frames its learning and the sharing of knowledge - audience, development, tools, and outcomes.

For instance, from here that looks like a bucket of water, " he said, pointing to a bucket of water; "but from an ant's point of view it's a vast ocean, from an elephant's just a cool drink, and to a fish, of course, it's home. So, you see, the way you see things depends a great deal on where you look at them from.
- The Phantom Tollbooth

AI Style

Just as Milo learned in the Phantom Tollbooth, when something is unknown, your envisioned utility, perception, and perspective define it.

An AI Style expresses two elements of how the organization envisions AI impacting its ethos and brand. The brand focuses on external perception, while the ethos focuses on internal principles. Ethos is the organization's underlying character, values, and culture. It's about what the organization stands for and believes in and how it connects employees to its purpose. The brand is the organization's public image and identity, as well as the perspective it offers the world, including messaging and visual and verbal representation.

Elements of AI Style

The AI style guide intertwines these two aspects, providing a roadmap for how AI can enhance the organization's brand and ethos.

- What level of credibility does the AI have to perform the function?

- Who is responsible for the curation and accuracy of the output?

- To what level should the content be curated?

- To what level should the content be trusted?

- To what level should the content be integrated into processes?

Rules of the Road

For any AI system, your audience will interact with as a consumer of the information or a tool integrated into their workflows, it is essential to define the core elements and rules of engagement with the AI. This includes for each AI:

- What the AI is intended for?

- Who is the intended owner of the AI?

- Who is the intended operator of the AI's output?

- Who is the intended audience of the AI's output?

- Who are the stakeholders of the AI's output?

- What is AI's impact on brand and ethos?

- What are the potential liabilities?

- What are the boundaries?

Build an Authentic AI Style Guide

Developing an AI style guide that reaches your learners with credibility by utilizing your brand, voice, and leadership. In concert with the development of your AI Style Guide is how your organization currently frames its learning - audience, development, tools, and outcomes.

What to Include

When building an AI Style Guide, you must communicate your Ethos, Perspective, and Insight to the learner in a credible, clear, and concise manner. The AI Style cannot be definitive in its usage, but it can be definitive in its approach. Just like a brand style, your AI Style should work for your organization and no other.

Define AI: What is AI to Your Organization

The first element to providing authentic guidance is a concise definition of artificial intelligence tailored to the organization's context and understanding. It can be a working definition, as we have seen; most everyone is using a working definition.[1]

Preserve, Replace, Restore

The next level of guidance is to set the guardrails for AI and offer who set them and what they are meant to represent and show they align with the organization purpose. Role that will be instrumental to developing the rules related to this are:

- **AI Stewards**: Individuals or teams responsible for overseeing AI initiatives and ensuring ethical and responsible use.

- **AI Governance**: The framework of rules, policies, and procedures that guide AI development, deployment, and use.

- **AI Risk**: The identification, assessment, and mitigation of potential risks associated with AI, such as bias, privacy breaches, and unintended consequences.

- **AI Leadership**: The organizational structure and decision-making processes related to AI, including roles, responsibilities, and governance.

AI Usage

Defining AI for organizational usage involves understanding its core components, aligning it with specific goals, and considering ethical and practical implications. A clear definition will guide decision-making, resource allocation, and the successful implementation of AI technologies.

Define how you expect AI to be used:

- **Accepted Uses**: Guidelines and criteria for determining appropriate and inappropriate uses of AI within the organization.

- **What to Share**: Policies and procedures regarding the sharing of data, information, and AI-generated outputs, ensuring privacy and data security.

- **What is Out of Bounds**: Clear boundaries and restrictions on AI use to prevent unethical or harmful applications.

- **Ethical Dilemmas**: A framework for addressing and resolving ethical challenges that may arise in the development and deployment of AI.

AI Learning

How learners grow their knowledge:

- **Onboarding**: Integrating AI into the onboarding process for new employees.

- **Preboarding:** Providing AI-related information and training to new hires before they start their roles.

- **AI KSAs**: The knowledge, skills, and abilities required for effective AI literacy and application within the organization.

- **Building Learning Pathways**: Creating tailored learning plans to address different skill levels and roles.

- **Use Cases and Case Studies**: Real-world examples of how AI is being used successfully within the organization and industry.

AI Collaboration

What should a learner's experience with AI look like? Best practices grounded in the opportunities for actions with AI and when to leave it behind.

- **Day in the Life of a Worker:** Illustrating how AI can enhance and augment the work of employees in various roles and departments.

- **Stringing Learning Together**: Connecting AI learning experiences across different departments and levels to foster a cohesive understanding.

Support for Building New Knowledge

How will your learners build upon this new knowledge? Understanding comes from knowing what something is and where to find trusted, curated resources to learn from. Building new knowledge and training for the future is about consistently building trust and offering reassurance.

- **AI Knowledge Hub:** A platform for sharing knowledge, best practices, and lessons learned about AI. The style guide provides the evergreen aspects of the approach to AI, the knowledge hub keeps learners abreast of the fluid dynamics of AI.

- **AI Sandboxes:** Controlled environments for experimenting with and testing AI applications without affecting production systems. It is a place to try out AI, to practice and make mistakes and see how they play out. This mistake zone is one where errors do not have implications outside of learning.

- **AI Glossary:** A collection of terms and definitions related to AI, ensuring consistent understanding and communication.

- **AI Library:** A curated list of internal and external resources that serve as reliable sources of information and knowledge.

- **AI Directory:** A centralized repository of AI tools, applications, and services available within the organization. Also include AIs that the learner may encounter on their own that impact their work life.

Additional Support

AI cannot be the responder to questions about AI. An AI can help formulate questions and learn to assist, but reaching out to

- **AI Connect:** An enterprise chat channel for employees to share insights, ask questions, and seek support related to AI.

- **AI Office Hours:** Regular sessions where learners can ask questions, seek advice, and gain insights into AI topics from experts. These sessions offer a unique opportunity for real-time interaction and personalized guidance. Facilitators also benefit by gathering feedback, identifying knowledge gaps, and assessing the effectiveness of AI initiatives.

- **AI Ethics Lounge:** A casual space for serious discussions. Explore AI-related questions, concerns, and ethical dilemmas. Share your thoughts, seek guidance, and contribute to a responsible AI ecosystem supported by AI stewardship.

What Your AI Style Guide Conveys

In the same way that a Brand Style Guide is a manifestation of your organization's commitment to its brand, an AI Style Guide is more than a document outlining rules and guidelines; it's a tangible representation of your organization's values, priorities, and commitment to AI excellence. The very existence of such a guide, coupled with the effort and care put into its creation, sends a powerful message to learners, stakeholders, and the broader public.

The 'Thwack' Factor

During a startup investor pitch, I was instructed to print and bind multiple copies of a presentation, filled with appendices, tables, and figures. Given our limited budget and the potential for investor disinterest, I suggested providing the presentation electronically. However, the founder sought to create a 'thwack'—the audible gravitational impact of a weighty presentation on the conference table.[2] This 'thwack factor' would convey the depth of our research, the underlying work, and the effort we had invested. It was a subtle yet powerful signal that investors might not have consciously noticed.

Similarly, an AI style guide resonates beyond the AI realm. Its very existence bridges the AI world, providing tangible evidence of your organization's commitment to AI. Beyond the specific guidelines and principles it outlines, the guide itself serves as a symbol of your dedication to responsible and effective AI development. It's a "thwack" of assurance that your organization takes AI seriously.

Assurance Intelligence

Trust is owned by the learner; assurance is what you can provide them. Trust is the belief in the reliability, truth, or ability of your organization by the people you employ and interact with. Assurance is your guarantee and promise that protects trust. Trust and assurance are both built over time. Whether directly integrated or as a companion to your AI Style Guide, the assurance you offer is part of the guide's ethos.

The design, development, and maintenance of Assurance with AI involves teams and individuals organized into three roles — those responsible for Governance, Stewardship, and the Ombudsperson. Assurance is also supported by evidence, certifications, or formal agreements. Numerous organizations pursue ISO ratings for their products and manufacturing processes to highlight their commitment to safe and responsible development and manufacturing practices.[3]

It is critical to control how trust, transparency, and assurance are maintained to protect the organization, customers, employees, and any individual with touchpoints to AIs you may interact with. Some organizations will try to take shortcuts to assurance. Notable AI organizations are attempting to 'Openwash' (see glossary for more details) by expanding the definition and intent of "open source" to include their AIs and language models. [4]

Do the hard work of assurance.

AI Governance

AI Governance is made up of three main areas that set the strategy and direction of AI usage and the organization. [5]

- **Policy Development**: Establishes AI policies, standards, and frameworks.

- **Compliance Monitoring**: Ensures adherence to legal, ethical, and organizational standards.

- **Risk Management**: Identifies and mitigates risks associated with AI deployment.

Governance can work with industry standards, government organizations that set to make a safe and equitable marketplace for AI and the organizations participating in it. [6]

AI Stewardship

When working with AI, operators must be clear and trust in the systems they use to convey that to their audience. An AI steward is an entity (person, organization, or system) responsible for managing, guiding, and overseeing the development, deployment, and use of AI and related technologies. [7]

Stewards may own the AI Style Guide and related knowledge hubs. They are responsible for ensuring the transparent, fair, and equitable use of AI. They are also accountable for the safety and security of the systems the organization uses and learners may encounter. They continuously monitor and manage all aspects of risk associated with the AI.

AI Ombudsperson (Ombudy')

The term "Ombudsman" originated in Sweden, where an independent official was appointed to investigate and address complaints against government officials and agencies. [8] In 1967, the Louisville Courier-Journal introduced this concept to media by naming the first U.S. Ombudsman. John Herchenroeder, a seasoned and knowledgeable editor, was tasked with ensuring that stories were written fairly. [9] The newspaper's publisher Barry Bingham stated, "Our papers have always sought to improve their news coverage and their relationship with their readers. We want all stories to be accurate and complete. There are occasional failures due to misunderstandings or other reasons. In all of these instances, John Herchenroeder is ready to receive inquiries, gather facts, and make corrections when warranted."

An AI Ombudsperson can address concerns and complaints related to AI use both internally and externally, represent the interests of stakeholders, learners, and affected audiences, and work to ensure that AI systems operate fairly and without bias.

Who Should Have a Voice

Who should have a voice in the development of an AI Style Guide? In short, everyone. Leadership's endorsement is crucial for the success of an AI Style Guide. It signals commitment to AI and fosters a culture of innovation and responsibility. By involving departments like development, technology, legal, marketing and sales, and human resources, leadership ensures the AI Style Guide is comprehensive, practical, and aligned with organizational goals. This collaborative approach not only guides AI usage but also promotes ethical AI practices.

Playbook: Your AI Team

Identifying roles and empowering them with direct responsibility will be instrumental in developing the rules related to guidance and guardrails for AI. Use this worksheet to offer who sets them, what they are meant to represent, and how they align with the organization's purpose.

AI Governance:

The framework of rules, policies, and procedures that guide AI development, deployment, and use.

AI Stewards:

Individuals or teams responsible for overseeing AI initiatives and ensuring ethical and responsible use.

AI Ombudspersons:

Individuals or teams empowered to represent the interests, address concerns and complaints related to AI use both internally and externally.

AI Leadership:

The organizational structure and decision-making processes related to AI, including roles, responsibilities, and governance.

Playbook: AI Tool Checklist

Use this AI Tool Checklist to help you evaluate and organize your AI tools, ensuring you have a comprehensive understanding of their capabilities, limitations, and how they fit into your specific needs. By completing this checklist, you can gain a better understanding of your AI tool landscape, identify areas for improvement, and make informed decisions about future tool adoption.

Tool Elements	List, Description, & Notes
Preferred Tools and Technologies: Specify the preferred AI tools and technologies to be used within the organization.	
Tool Evaluation: Establish criteria for evaluating and selecting AI tools.	
AI Directory: Create an AI Directory of platform and tools available as well as accepted usage.	
Sandboxes: Where will AI be allowed to experiment and explore AI and how much supervision.	
Training and Support: Provide guidance on training employees on AI tools and ensuring adequate support is available.	

Playbook: Writing with AI Workflow

AI can significantly enhance the efficiency of developing content. Use prompts to craft an iterative and collaborative workflow for developing content.

Workflow Step	Notes and Considerations
Storyboard: Explore and discovery content.	*Curate and find the sources. Ensure that you are working with known trusted resources.*
Write First: Then seek alternatives and improvements.	*Ensure that you capture your voice and perspective from the start. Starting with an AI, you may never find yours.*
Iterate: Provide alternative phrases and condense information down.	*Provide focused edits and test assumptions, seek alternative views and ways of explaining.*
Tone Changes: Use an AI to provide change the tone of the content to be more developmental and coaching.	*Move your content closer to your audience, by shaping the content to the tones they read.*
Proof: Reducing word counts, making passive/active changes, taking longer concepts, and reorder.	*Don't blindly accept the edits — keep your voice.*

Playbook: Write Your AI Workflow

Use this table to document the AI usage and notes about the process and the impact the AI has on your process.

Workflow Step	Your Notes and Considerations
Storyboard:	
Write First:	
Iterate:	
Tone Changes:	
Proof:	

Playbook:
Informing Usage Through Example

AI can significantly enhance the efficiency of developing content. It's crucial to use it ethically to avoid potential negative consequences. Imagine using AI to write an employee performance review. Review the workflow below and comment on the acceptable and unacceptable, as well as how the review might be shaped through the usage of AI.

AI Content	Considerations
Generate Draft: Upload interactions, exchanges, and data about the employee and generate an initial draft of the review.	
Summarize Performance: From a list of notations, Use AI to summarize an employee's key achievements, challenges, and areas for improvement over a specific period.	
Iterate: Provide alternative phrases and condense information down.	
Tone Changes: Use an AI to provide change the tone of the content to be more developmental and coaching.	
Suggest Goals: Recommend personalized goals based on the review provided.	
Transparency: Clearly communicate the use of AI in the review process.	

How might exchanges and collaboration like this with an AI inform an AI Style Guide? What guidelines and guardrails does this scenario evoke? While AI can be a valuable tool, it's crucial to use it ethically to avoid potential negative consequences.

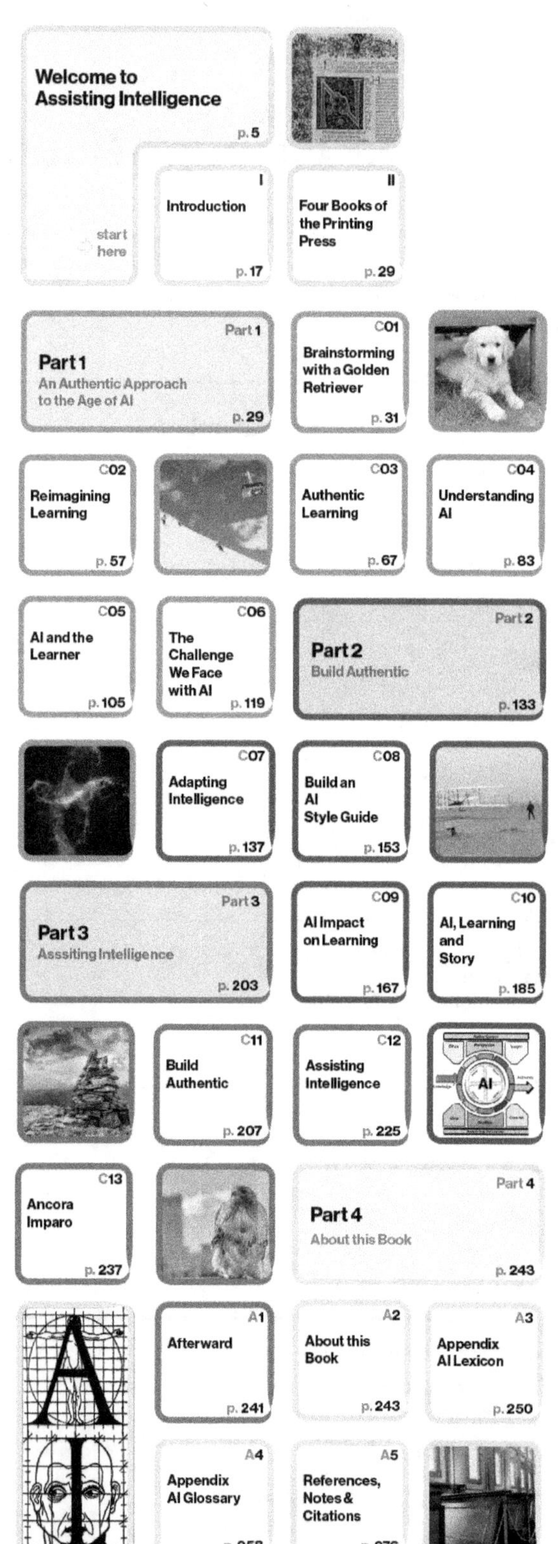

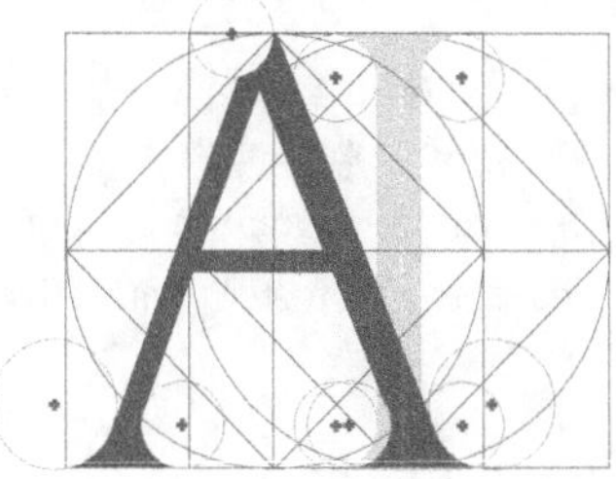

Chapter 9

AI Impact on Learning

The significance of learning in the age of AI and what to do about it.

This chapter explores how AI can revolutionize the learning experience and build authentic content. We delve into the core principles of crafting AI-enhanced learning structured around a digital development process flow: Transform, Engage, and Envisage. We also explore the combination of AI and Agile methodologies to accelerate content development, enabling us to quickly adapt to changes and deliver innovative learning solutions. Then, we explore the prompt, the AI instrument that controls all development and execution.

The artist cannot and must not take anything for granted, but must drive to the heart of every answer and expose the question the answer hides.
— James Baldwin

AI's Impact on Learning

Learning is the acquisition of knowledge. Learning, once static, is undergoing a dynamic transformation. AI reshapes how we acquire knowledge and skills. Learning, business, and society must prioritize factual knowledge.

AI-powered devices will adapt interfaces and processes based on user knowledge. Skills training can be condensed and delivered through AI-driven performance support. The challenge lies in establishing deeper connections with learners that foster perspective shifts, inclusivity, and transformative learning experiences.

The future of learning centers on fostering deeper connections with learners.

Traditional Learning (Ski Chairlifts)

Traditional learning often provides specialized knowledge for a specific audience. The learning arc encompasses the entire learner experience, from initial contact to completion and outcomes. A learning path outlines the curriculum, courses, activities, mentoring, coaching, and development needed for proficiency. Structured elements of a learning path include resources, sequence, and progress measures.

Historically, developing learning for organizations was akin to a ski chairlift. Learners embarked on a journey, ascending the lift to the top, where they acquired the knowledge, skills, and abilities (KSAs) to succeed. Traditional learning was assured of the learner's attention and provided a fixed learning experience. Successful learners could proceed; unsuccessful learners repeated the journey. Upon reaching the summit, learners possessed the necessary knowledge.

Digital Transformation of Learning

Digital has transformed how learning is delivered. Learners no longer follow the fixed curriculum up the chair lift. In the digital landscape, learning is delivered directly to learners, as they progress up. Digital learning resembles Lego blocks, allowing for flexible and dynamic arrangements, and can be delivered dynamically as the learn progresses up the lift. The accelerating pace of change has pushed learners and organizers to speed up the learning process, much like a chairlift increasing its speed to meet demand.

Digital transformation and online learning have introduced distractions. Online learners face competing screens and devices. End-of-course assessments, once gatekeepers, no longer serve as definitive barriers. To maintain attention, faster-paced learning and performance support were introduced to assist learners after their journey up the lift.

Learning must evolve to match the rapid pace of content consumption. Engaging, easily transferable learning experiences are becoming increasingly essential. Learners today are highly tech-savvy and can easily discern inauthentic content, inefficient workflows, and irrelevant scenarios. If learning materials are created using a simplistic process, the outcome will reflect that. To go beyond responsive learning trends, we must empower learners by granting them control over the course and delivery medium. Passive learning experiences are no longer sufficient to engage learners.

Learning on the Slope: Downhill Learners

Modern learners approach knowledge challenges from a position of strength, arriving at courses with AI-provided knowledge. Traditional structured paths are no longer guaranteed. AI can be harnessed to bypass much of the necessary learning.

Instead of rigid programs and learning paths, downhill learning recognizes that learners will progress with or without formal instruction. The focus is on assisting learners throughout their journey. They determine their path, goals, and learning style. To achieve this, downhill learning:

- **Captures learner attention.**

- **Assesses needs and intentions.**

- **Initiates the learning journey.**

- **Allows learners to progress at their own pace.**

- **Provides support and adapts the path.**

- **Survey for exploration.**

- **Recommends next steps.**

Unlike the traditional chairlift model, downhill learning emphasizes choice, empowerment, performance support, and progress. The learner controls progress through the content. By granting learners control over their learning experiences, we can direct their energy toward the content itself. Excessive control, assessment, and measurement can hinder progress and create distractions. Today's learners have numerous avenues for diversion. Whether novice or native, allow the learner to self-identify the skills and outcomes they need from the learning and then provide the learning that gets them to their outcomes.

Onboarding with AI: The Importance of the Jackson Hole Sign

Assessment, once a final step, is now integrated into the onboarding process. Downhill Learning enables learners to self-identify skills, learning needs, and expected outcomes. Onboarding assessments inform recommended learning elements. Assessments should precede the learning journey. Surveying learners for intent, needs, and interests at the outset helps tailor learning from the start. Onboarding is akin to a trail map guiding learners through the initial stages.

The sign at the Jackson Hole tram station effectively surveys the skiers to examine their intent, needs, and interests before proceeding. It is a clear and concise authentic means that establishes the experience ahead. Traditional learning focuses on Knowledge, Skills, and Abilities (KSAs) as a competency model. By identifying required KSAs, learning viability and success can be assessed based on possession or acquisition. Knowledge to Potential (K2Ps), combined with AI-accelerated learning, offers a new approach. Individuals showcase unique skills and talents. By carefully surveying these skills, interests, and intents and mapping them to work experience and content context, we can identify potential value in current or future learning outcomes. On a learning slope, they can accelerate their progress to fit their outcomes.

What is a Learning AI?

From the AI Style Guide, a comprehensive set of guidelines for ethical AI usage, Learning AI is the next stage in instructional design. It ensures learners fully harness the potential of AI for both learning and content creation. Together, the AI Style Guide and Learning AI bridge the gap between organizational intent, individual adoption, and support solutions.

An AI Style Guide answers the question, "How can we ensure the ethical, responsible, and effective implementation and use of AI within our organization?" It provides the rules of the road for working with technology, best practices, and a shared understanding among all stakeholders interacting with AI.

Learning AI addresses the crucial question of how organizations can responsibly integrate AI into their daily work, maximizing its benefits while mitigating risks. Learning AI focuses on best practices, expected performance, and steps to ensure everyone who uses AI does so effectively and collaboratively. A comprehensive understanding of AI's principles, functions, and limitations empowers users to effectively leverage AI tools into their workflows. Additionally, teaching users about how the organization plans to use AI, ethical considerations, biases, and potential pitfalls helps them use AI responsibly and avoid unintended consequences.

Collectively, the AI Style Guide and Learning AI foster a culture of AI literacy, equipping individuals with the skills and knowledge needed to harness its potential responsibly. Learning AI serves as a roadmap for AI mastery, guiding individuals from initial understanding to proficiency. It provides the requisite knowledge to onboard through development and usage to mastery of AI. Learning AI aims to empower individuals to use AI effectively, responsibly, and creatively, aligning with the principles and guidelines outlined in the AI Style Guide. It's a continuous process that ensures the organization can maximize the benefits of AI while minimizing risks.

AI can significantly contribute to the learning development process by generating ideas through data analysis, iterating draft content, testing its viability, and refining the final product.

Digital Learning Development

Integrating AI into a digital learning development relies on an agile design-and-development approach to learning that focuses on speed, flexibility, and collaboration. This approach rapidly iterates design flows and delivers learning experiences. In developing and bringing content to digital, we developed a three-phase process that has evolved from traditional learning development.

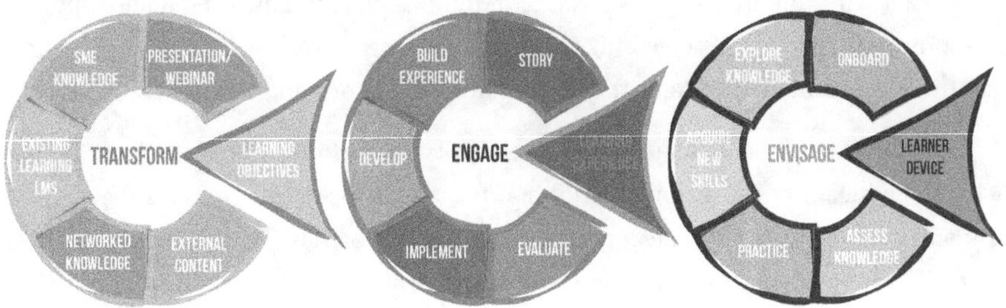

Learning development process that focuses on transforming existing knowledge into a replicable format that can engage and the learner can envisage the desired outcome.

Transform

Traditional learning mediums that fuel institutional knowledge are often the content sources for developing new agile learning. Learning organizations adapt and repurpose existing traditional content as source materials for developing new learning. Content and institutional knowledge are migrated to a learning object framework that may be accessed as needed.

Engage

Digital learning development provides a framework to rapidly move from a concept to a working experience where evaluation and iterative improvements can be made. Unlike traditional development models, the costs and labor associated with production and publishing are minimized, allowing changes to be made quickly. Agile development allows for greater stakeholder involvement and feedback, increased innovation, and modularity of learning experience creation.

Envisage

While learners do not see how an experience was developed, agile development processes do impact the learning experience by allowing end users to incrementally experience elements more quickly, and these experiences are moved closer to personal devices and individualized requirements.

Learners experience pathways that allow multiple entry points, allowing them to pull learning and move quickly through diverse learning experiences to create complex learning pathways.

Agile Intelligence

In the traditional Agile model, the development process is divided into incremental phases, called sprints, which are further divided into steps within the loops. This structure, like a rollercoaster with multiple loops, allows for iterations while maintaining a linear process. Each sprint, with its four key elements-ideation, planning, development, and retros-showcases the adaptability of the Agile model to various industries and business processes.

The Agile model's ability to rapidly ideate, plan, develop, and refine is not just beneficial, but critical to nearly all industries and business processes. It powers the development and manufacturing of many organizations in all industries. To understand its power, we need not look beyond what the two brothers were able to achieve on the dunes of Kitty Hawk.

An Agile Story

The Wright brothers wanted to be first in flight. Among their peers, they took an approach to discovery that modeled an agile method. While better-funded and government-sponsored were unable to achieve flight, the Wright brothers sought to iterate improvements while staying focused on the fundamentals needed to achieve manned flight.

First

The first iteration of the airplane was a simple kite. The design focused on understanding the airflow that creates lift. On this first iteration, there was no steering or engine. In fact, there is no pilot onboard.

Second

The second iteration improved the design and had the same basic design that was larger to provide more lift and structure to add a passenger.

Third

The third iteration focused on creating a steerable glider that provide all the controls needed to manage the lift and flight. Still, there was no power source for this manned steerable glider.

Fourth

In the fourth iteration, in December of 1903, Kitty Hawk took the first-ever flight with their new powered aircraft.

This iterative approach allowed for focusing on key elements while learning and improving the design to incorporate all the functionality needed for flight.[1]

Visualizing the agile methodology metaphor with images from the time spent at Kitty Hawk by the Wright Brothers.

One of the Wright brothers' main competitors was Samuel Langley, who was the Secretary of the Smithsonian Institution. Langley had significant funding and resources, but his attempts at powered flight were unsuccessful. His aircraft, the Aerodrome, failed because it moved from small scale to full size, and while it scaled up the power, it lacked the stability and control or sustained flight.

The Wright brothers succeeded, whereas others failed due to their focus on achieving balance and control in flight and their methodical approach to testing and refining their designs. Their agile approach persisted despite setbacks. Had their competitors iterated their designs, they may not have overlooked the critical aspects that led to their failures.

AI Acceleration Engine

Whether a presentation, documentation, or learning content, integrating AI into the development of knowledge and learning offers a fantastic ability to create and contribute to content development. However, it can also overwhelm and overtake the development.

The discovery and availability of rare earth magnets and advanced circuitry have powered technological advances beyond AI, computers, and smartphones. They have also fueled the explosion of brushless motors used in everything from aircraft to cars and battery-powered hand tools. In a brushless motor, the permanent magnets are attached to the rotor, which is the rotating part of the motor. Electromagnets are located on the stator, the stationary part of the motor. The electromagnets located on the stationary stator housing control the speed and management of the rotor by adjusting polarity to achieve the desired speed, torque, and outcomes.[2]

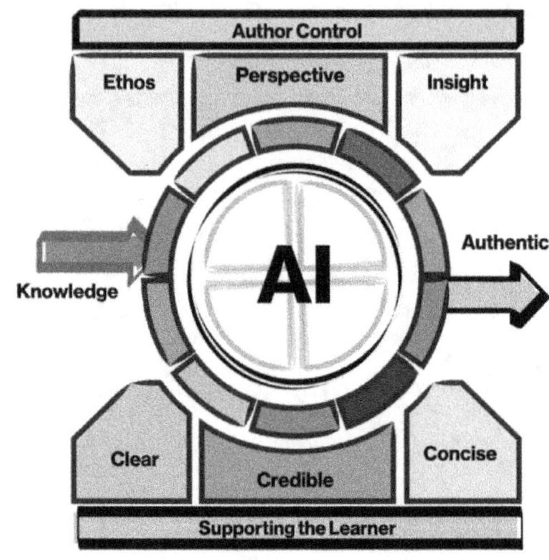

Creating an AI Acceleration Engine Infographic.

This setup eliminates the need for brushes, making the motor more efficient, durable, and quieter. It also greatly reduces friction in the operation of the engine, especially at high speeds. Think of the AI generative process as a frictionless agile loop spinning with controls spinning within the agile loop. The AI provides a limitless flywheel of content and revisions that can be tapped into and controlled by the lever. In the same way that brushless motor functions, adjusting the polarity of the controls can alter, adapt, and adjust the output of the AI to shape the content and assist in the refinement process.

In the first chapter, we introduced Mara as a boundless retriever as a parallel intelligence akin to an AI. An AI is that boundless energy sitting amidst your business processes. She sits in equal measure, capable of being an amazing companion or an agent of chaos in your day. When it comes to the content development process, AI is a powerful tool sitting at the center of your development process, capable of assisting or abducting. It's a tool that, when used effectively, can significantly enhance the development process. However, it's crucial that we, as the operators, maintain control over its capabilities. AI is a content workhorse that we must engage and manage. It's like an electric charge that can power the motion, acceleration, and momentum of our content development process. The external controls we've defined from the organizational side—ethos, perspective, and insights, and the learner side—credible, clear, and concise content outcomes are our tools for effective management.

Agile Intelligence in Action

AI introduces a dynamic engine at the heart of the agile sprint loop that can contribute to each process step.

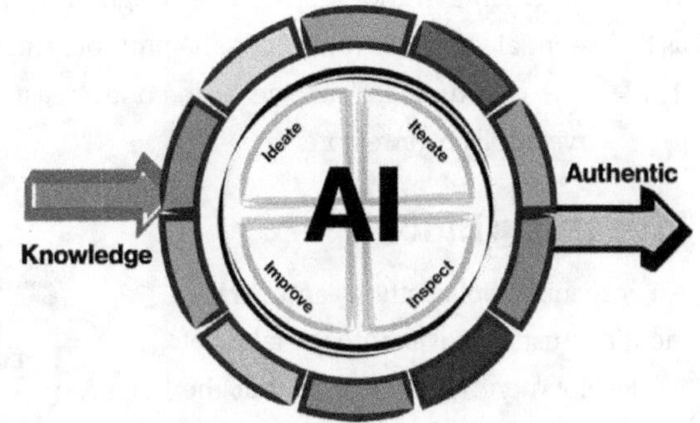

The AI rotor at the heart of the content acceleration process.

Step	Agile Process	AI Benefits
Ideation	Assist in generating creative ideas, research, and topic selection by analyzing vast amounts of data for potential inclusion. Brainstorm potential topics and rapidly test for feasibility.	AI enables incorporating many more scenarios into brainstorming and testing their feasibility before even progressing. Playing out scenarios before progressing.
Iterate	Employ AI to assist with drafts of content, then review and refine them for accuracy, clarity, and engagement.	An AI can rapidly progress through versions of content, providing copy edits that refine the content, providing alternative narratives and counter content.
Inspect	Build and test viable content against the semantic and pragmatic goals.	AI can inspect content for semantic and grammatical issues, semantically review it in context, and improve its clarity and consistency.
Improve	Refine the content performance in context, maximize reach to the audience, and identify the next steps in the process.	Leverage AI-style proofing to ensure that content is polished for the audience.

Working with an AI during the sprint process enables compressing the cycle through the steps in a single chat session. AIs possess the ability to sprint through content and test before even advancing to the next step or collaborating with others. Concepts can be hypothetically tested on the AI flywheel to see if the potential is even viable.

Changing Polarity

In the realm of AI-powered learning sprints, the foundation of effective content lies in its clarity, credibility, conciseness, and the careful curation of ethos, perspective, and insight.

These six elements—ethos, perspective, insight, clarity, credibility, and conciseness—serve as the essential levers for controlling the prompts and responses of an AI. Adjusting polarity is akin to fine-tuning a dial, increasing or decreasing the emphasis on specific elements to preserve, replace, or restore.

Preserving Ethos

An organization's ethos and brand identity must be woven into the fabric of AI development. This ensures that the content delivered to learners is a true reflection of its values and aspirations. The core message should remain unwavering, providing a solid foundation for perspective and insight.

Choosing Perspectives

Perspectives are not merely about catering to individual learners' realities; they serve as a bridge, uniting learners around a common purpose. These perspectives can be shaped and informed

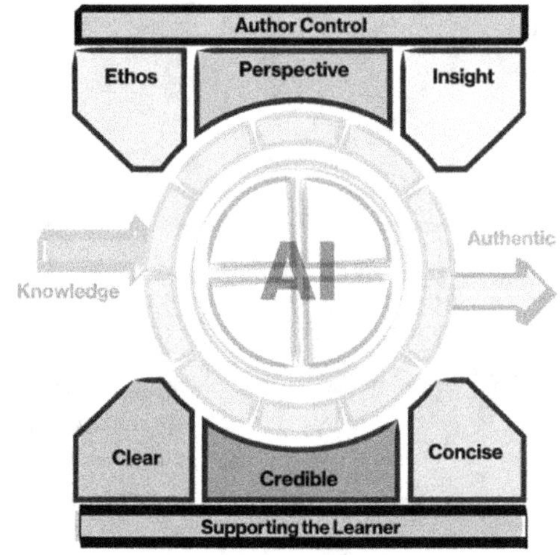

The fixed controls or Stator that control the spin, speed and direction of the rotor.

by organizational culture, market dynamics, brand identity, and learner roles. A dynamic approach is essential, identifying and incorporating the necessary perspectives throughout the transformation process. AI can be harnessed to tailor content to different learners' cognitive styles, framing, and structure, leading to enhanced engagement and outcomes.

Authentic Insight

Insight is rooted in the expertise of subject matter experts and the credibility of trusted internal and external resources. AI can surface a vast amount of information, but the key lies in curating it to focus on what truly matters. AI responses, often a blend of multiple sources, can sometimes lack depth. By delving into the underlying sources, organizations can uncover more nuanced and insightful content.

Vigorous writing is concise. - Elements of Style[3]

Clear, Credible, and Concise

Setting and adjusting the parameters and guidelines that the AI follows ensures that the content is relevant and appropriate for the learning and the specific sprint objectives. An AI can contribute to clear and credible content by leveraging its ability to process and analyze vast amounts of data, generating concise and informative summaries of complex topics, and providing personalized feedback and recommendations based on individual learners' needs and preferences. This involves going beyond simple changes that can shape results and developing a cohesive AI interaction style. By establishing guidelines for these elements, organizations can create a more engaging and effective learning experience.

Prompts

Achieving consistency and tone in AI interactions requires carefully crafted prompt construction, query formulation, and response generation.

Going beyond the simple changes that can shape results. Achieving consistency and tone throughout your usage of an AI means developing and maintaining an AI interaction style. The means by which an AI is controlled is through the prompt. In a generative AI, the prompt takes the form of text or verbal inputs. Prompts are the means of changing polarity when working with an AI. They can empower content and research, shape content, and improve context and clarity. They also hold the ability to instill and confirm biases, introduce errors, over-summarize, generalize insight, and distract from the purpose of the content.

How the query or inputs are constructed can directly impact the quality, relevance, and accuracy of the AI-generated content results. Unlike AI models, it can respond with multiple drafts to the same questions and select similar responses based on preferences and previous questions, which can further degrade or decay the content quality of the original query's purpose.

Writing an effective prompt is precise. A prompt should contain no irrelevant words, a query no irrelevant prompts, for the same reason that a drawing should have no unnecessary lines and a machine no unnecessary parts. This requires not that the user make all prompts simple, or omit all context and information from queries, but that users make every word relevant. Prompt literacy refers to the skill of crafting effective prompts or input instructions to guide AI in generating desired outputs. Writing effective prompts is crucial when working with GenAI because it directly influences the quality, relevance, and accuracy of the output generated by the AI model. In many cases, it will be less work to just write the desired results yourself.

Prompts born from queries and traditional search

In the early days of Internet information research, Lexis Nexis and Factiva were two large data sets available to the Internet via a service providing access to global news, business information, legal research, and more. To construct queries on these platforms, users had to learn to use certain connectors, operators, segments, and word variations to refine their search results. Considering you would pay by the query and the results, how it was constructed and its accuracy and parameters to return the proper result was critical. The ability to construct properly formatted Lexis Nexis or Factiva queries was a science unto itself and listed on many resumes. The advent of search engines providing unlimited queries allows for a more trial-and-error approach to seeking information. Advertising within the search results eliminated the cost per search.

However, how you ask an AI through prompts influences the accuracy, quantity, and quality of responses received. A prompt is processed through an AI's NLP for syntax, semantics, and pragmatics. How you construct prompts and what descriptors and instructions you provide will improve your interactions and results. Much like Factiva and Lexis Nexis appeared on resumes then, so too is Prompt Engineering today.

Build Effective Prompts

The nuances of language can significantly impact the quality of AI-generated content. This table offers a curated list of semantic phrases and guidance to help you build more specific and accurate prompts.[4]

Prompt	Influence on AI Process
Be Concise	Keep prompts concise and specific. Longer queries, with long and linked clauses, can introduce unintended ambiguity or confusion.
Identify Perspective	Define the perspective with which the AI will respond (audience, expertise, knowledge level).
Include IF, AND, OR, NOT, BUT, DO & DON'T	Use conditional expressions like IF, AND, OR, NOT, BUT, DO & DON'T to limit and filter the results. AI systems can use conditional expressions to limit and filter the results by applying some rules or conditions to the data or information they process.
Include Examples	Indicate to the AI examples of the desired output.
Bring Your Own Tone	Indicate the tone or style for the response, such as creative, informal, business, professional, friendly, or persuasive. Here you can use a literal reference or style.
Active and Passive Voice	AI shapes passive and active voice usage by semantic and pragmatic rules. An active voice prompt emphasizes the doer of the action, while a passive voice focuses on the receiver of the action. AI can recognize both forms and adapt its responses accordingly.
Fit the Response	Use terms like summary, executive summary, bottom line, or brief to limit the word count to indicate the depth and level of the response.

<table>
<tr><td>Citations</td><td>The credibility of the AI's response can be enhanced with citations and references for additional information. Ask to include source materials from credible sources. Be sure to follow the links provided within the response and see how much of the content provided by the AI is connected to the source.</td></tr>
<tr><td>Emulate a Writing Style</td><td>Indicate a writing style the responses should be used. (e.g., Add 'in the style of NYTimes or Economist Magazine.' to a prompt to ensure the response is written in the style of business user level of communication, and adding in the Economist ensures a global perspective)</td></tr>
</table>

What do you mean exactly?

'What', and equally important, 'How' you say something to an AI influences the result. Generic prompts produce generic results. The information, sentences, or questions that you enter into a Generative AI greatly influence the quality of outputs you receive. Many AI platforms leverage intent recognition, where the AI tries to infer the intent, purpose, and goal of the user from the prompt. The AI also tries to gather user sentiment, style, and tone from the prompt.

After entering a prompt, the AI model analyzes your input and generates a response based on the patterns learned through training. More descriptive prompts can improve the quality of the outputs. The syntax, semantics, and pragmatics are all translated by the NLP to build a query that the LLM can act upon. Subtle differences can create significant differences in the responses. A simple example of word choice and punctuation, tense, and voice can shape the response.

Prompt 1	**Prompt 2**
What effects of climate change are influenced by deforestation?	**How does deforestation contribute to climate change?**
Deforestation has a significant impact on climate change through several mechanisms: 1. Increased carbon emissions: Trees absorb carbon dioxide from the atmosphere. When forests are cleared, this carbon is released into the atmosphere, contributing to greenhouse gas emissions and accelerating global warming. 2. Reduced carbon absorption: With fewer trees, there is a reduced capacity to ab-	Deforestation significantly contributes to climate change. Here's how: 1. Release of Stored Carbon: Trees absorb carbon dioxide from the atmosphere and store it in their wood, leaves, and roots. When forests are cleared, this stored carbon is released into the atmosphere, primarily as carbon dioxide, a potent greenhouse gas that traps heat. 2. Reduced Carbon Absorption: Fewer trees means less ability to absorb carbon dioxide

sorb carbon dioxide from the atmosphere, further exacerbating climate change.

3. Loss of biodiversity: Deforestation destroys habitats, leading to a loss of biodiversity. This loss of biodiversity can have cascading effects on ecosystems, including reduced resilience to climate change.

4. Changes in precipitation patterns: Forests play a crucial role in regulating precipitation. Deforestation can disrupt these patterns, leading to increased droughts or floods in certain regions.

5. Soil erosion: Deforestation can lead to soil erosion, as tree roots are no longer there to hold the soil in place. This can have negative consequences for agriculture and water quality.

6. Increased albedo: Deforestation can increase the Earth's albedo, meaning it reflects more sunlight back into space. This can have a cooling effect on the planet, but it is generally outweighed by the increased greenhouse gas emissions from deforestation.

Overall, deforestation is a major contributor to climate change and has far-reaching consequences for both ecosystems and human societies.

from the atmosphere. This exacerbates the greenhouse effect and contributes to global warming.

3. Loss of Biodiversity: Deforestation destroys habitats, leading to a loss of biodiversity. This can disrupt ecosystems, reduce their resilience, and impair their ability to function effectively, including their role in carbon sequestration.

4. Soil Degradation: Deforestation can lead to soil erosion and degradation. This reduces the soil's ability to store carbon, further contributing to emissions.

5. Increased Methane Emissions: Deforestation can create conditions that lead to increased methane emissions from wetlands and other sources. Methane is a greenhouse gas that is even more potent than carbon dioxide in trapping heat.

In summary, deforestation acts as a double blow to the climate: it releases stored carbon and reduces the planet's capacity to absorb future emissions. This contributes significantly to global warming and its associated effects.

The AI responds accordingly, using different tones and styles, and changes the results. Both responses to these prompts convey the same basic information, but the AI's choice of voice subtly influences the tone, selection of content, and focus of its response.

Chatting with an AI

Most Generative AIs are based on an iterative platform that allows you to refine and add detail to prompts through a chat interface. By providing feedback on the AI's responses, you help it learn and improve its output. Prompts are your starting point for engaging with an AI and obtaining specific results. How you begin a conversation can significantly influence its direction, so it's crucial to start correctly.

```
Prompt 1: Write a report on the implications of climate
change on coastal communities.
```

While this prompt is clear, the term "implications" is open-ended and might be interpreted differently. A follow-up prompt could clarify the required analysis for a report:

```
Prompt 2: Analyze the specific effects of climate change on
coastal communities, including sea-level rise, storm surge,
and coastal erosion.
```

By using more precise terms like "specific effects," guides the AI towards generating content that aligns closely with the intended outcome. Choosing precise words can significantly affect the AI's understanding and the resulting output. By using more specific and concrete terms, you can minimize ambiguity and ensure that the AI generates content that aligns to the prompt's exact requirements. Iterative chatting through prompts involves refining input based on the AI's output until achieving the desired result. To maximize effectiveness:

- Provide clear and detailed instructions.

- Break down complex tasks into simpler steps.

- Use references to guide the AI's understanding.

Remember, AI is adaptable, and the input received is essential for shaping its output. By approaching AI chat sessions with an agile mindset, iterating prompts can gather responses from various angles and refine queries to achieve the desired results.

Consider also that many AI systems are built around a conversational model that builds upon previous queries. In a transformer architecture, the AI remains in context, meaning it carries forward information from earlier interactions. This context-based AI can provide more personalized and relevant responses. However, if you change topics without indicating the change to the AI, it can result in non-sequiturs, where the AI's response seems unrelated to any topic. This is similar to a Monty Python sketch where a conversation derails into absurdity. Unlike, in Monty Python, the AI lacks a Colonel (played by Graham Chapman) to stop the conversation from going too far off track 'too silly'.[5]

From an AI perspective, maintaining context saves processing power, but it also limits the dataset to a subset of the foundation model's full capabilities. As questions are refined through the chat, the line of the questions can start to affect the responses given. It's important to be aware of its potential limitations and to consider alternative approaches in certain situations. Starting a new chat with an AI resets the context and indicates to the AI, "And now for something completely different."

Playbook: Build a Prompt Library

Consider how often you will construct learning following specific patterns and develop a library of prompts and construction logic that returns responses valued to your organization. Collecting reusable prompts that can be used to generate different types of outputs from an AI model, such as text, images, code, etc.

Prompt Library

A prompt library is a collection of reusable prompts that can generate different types of outputs from an AI model, such as text, images, code, etc.

Prompt Template

Consider practicing creating prompts like diagram sentences. A prompt template provides the general framework that guides the creation of prompts for specific tasks or scenarios. Using a prompt library and templates can save time, improve consistency, and achieve better results from the AI model.

Prompt Styles

Often, when writing prompts, it is beneficial to add "in the style of [literary source]." This is in part to ensure that the communication reaches an intended audience with the style of writing they are accustomed to. For example, adding "in the style of the NYTimes or Economist Magazine" shapes the response content for factual news presentation, and adding an international perspective expands the breadth of the language used.

Playbook: The Journalistic Six

The journalistic six questions are a framework for gathering information for a story.[6] They can be adapted to improve the quality of prompts for AI. By incorporating the journalistic six questions into your prompt development process, you can create more effective and informative prompts that lead to better AI performance. What are the six journalistic questions?

Journalistic Six	Prompt
Who? **(Actor or Agent)** Who is involved?	
What? **(Act)** What should happen?	
When? **(Time or Timing)** When will, did, should this occur or be performed?	
Where? **(Scene or Source)** Where did, will, should this occur or be performed?	
Why? **(Purpose)** Why was or is this done, avoided, or permitted?	

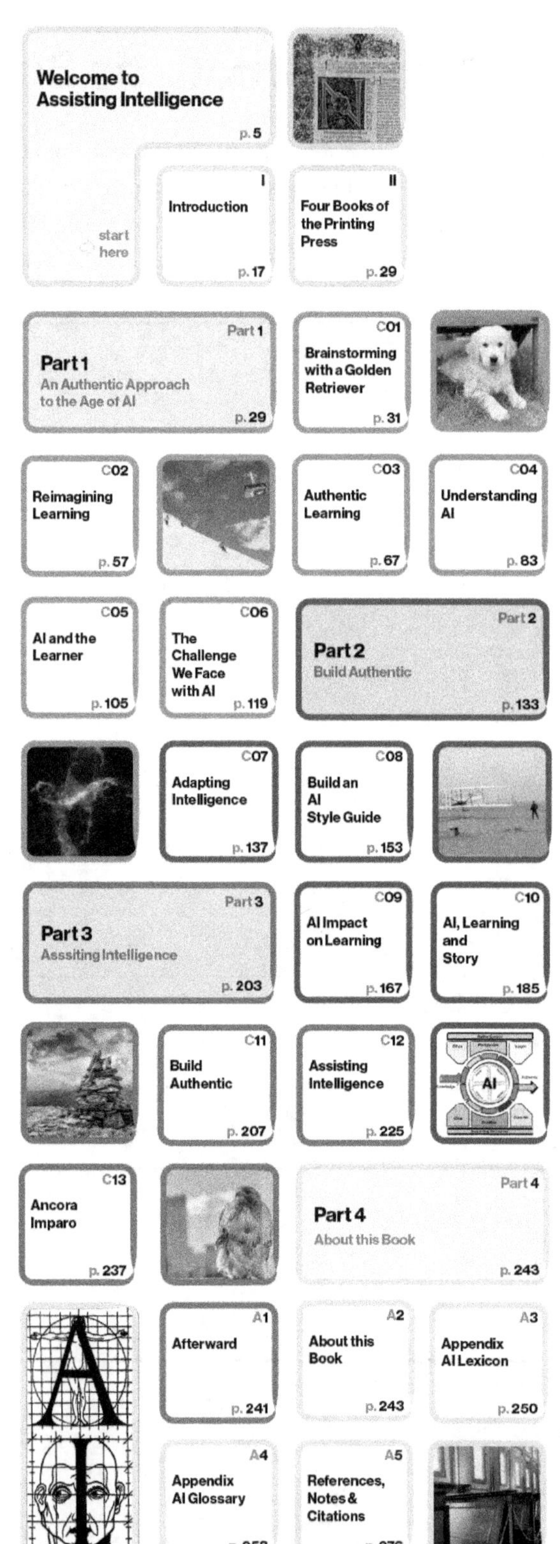

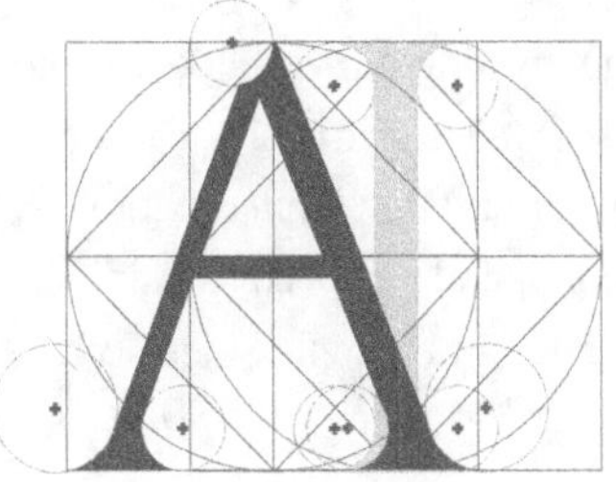

Chapter 10:
AI, Learning, & Story

How Story Links AI to Authentic

In this chapter, we'll explore how storytelling offers the best way to create a genuine connection and support authentic outcomes. Stories are experiences that cannot exist within an AI; they are either brought to it or taken from it. A story told by an AI is a fiction.

"Because now, more than ever, we need the moving image. We need vision, creativity, and storytelling that takes us on a journey and opens us, enlightens us, opens our hearts and our minds, ..." [1]   — *Martin Scorsese*

AI and Story

Generative AI provides a robust foundation of knowledge, making it a valuable asset for those new to a field or transitioning between disciplines. While it can assist learners in onboarding and exploring tangential topics, its depth of insight is often limited. Moreover, AI cannot fully convey an organization's unique ethos, brand, and perspective. Additionally, links to further resources may be missing or inaccurate, and complex ideas can be oversimplified or conflated.

AI can streamline learning, but it cannot replace human and organizational contributions to instruction. Its role lies in supporting the production and skill-based aspects of innovation, leaving the more complex conceptual, decision-making, and comprehension aspects to learners and their instructors. Consequently, learning and instruction must adapt accordingly.

Herein lies the power of story. As AI automates tasks and skills, story becomes crucial. By using metaphors, examples, and analogies rooted in organizational experiences, learners can bridge the gap between conventional knowledge and new scenarios, gaining shortcuts to the knowledge and wisdom the organization intends to impart.

What is Story

A well-told story is memorable, retellable, and impactful— leaving a lasting impression. A successful learning story follows a flow from intention and overcoming obstacles to an outcome. Across cultures, we all recognize that a story is about to begin. Stories follow familiar patterns that we can readily understand.[2] Underlying the story is the learning story plot — the framework that constructs the experience in the learner's mind. The magic of story opens you to new information, connection, and expanded awareness — transforming you into a learner.[3] We recognize the familiar patterns of storytelling across cultures. Stories follow familiar patterns that we can readily understand. The phrase *'Once upon a time'* introduces a story, whether in fairy tales or folk tales, through history and across the globe.[4]

Language/ Culture	Start of Story	Finish
English	*Once upon a time ...*	*... and they all lived happily ever after.*
Armenian	*There was, there was not ...*	*... 3 apples fall from the sky/heaven - one for the writer/author, one for the story-teller, one for the listener.*

Czech	*Beyond seven mountain ranges, beyond seven rivers ...*	*... a bell rang and the tale comes to its end.*
French	*There was one time ...*	*... and they lived happily and had many children.*
German	*Once there was ...*	*... and if they haven't died, they are still alive today.*
Japanese	*Long ago, long ago ...*	*... so blissful.*
Chinese	*A very, very long time ago ...*	*... and they lived a happy life.*

Why Story?

Learning is acquiring knowledge. In the age of AI, new approaches to learning are needed, from onboarding users to transitioning their skills. AI can tailor skills training and some learning to individual needs. Both smart devices and AIs are capable of assessing user knowledge and acumen and adapting and providing personalized learning paths. However, what remains is how we connect with learners in a more meaningful way that changes perspectives and builds transformation. When presented with new information, learners try to make sense of it based on their previous experiences. This is where story helps.[5] By providing a familiar narrative structure, stories can make abstract concepts concrete and help learners connect new information to their existing knowledge. Story can help us understand complex ideas and see the world in new ways. As Marcel Proust said, "The real voyage of discovery consists not in seeking new landscapes, but in having new eyes."

Stories with the support of facts are the foundation of knowledge. Truths are unalterable and cannot be dismissed or explained away. Noted presidential historian Jon Meacham said: "Facts and data shape human decisions because they are objectively true."[6] By stating them, amalgamating them to the story, and articulating them, they establish the basis by which values, development, and forward action knowledge can be built. Stories supported by truths and factual perspectives have a better chance for lasting transformative knowledge. Stories should continually be buttressed and renewed by including factual resources and supporting messages, resources, and knowledge. Stories demonstrate and showcase the truths and experiences they hold, the expectations they possess, and the goals they aspire to.

What is a Learning Story?

How does storytelling go in your organization? Let me tell you about the business leader who, earlier in their career, embarked on a journey (a performance goal) and was met with obstacles that required growth to achieve ultimate success. Sound familiar? And then what happened? What if they failed? What if they encountered a competitor, a new market, a mentor, a monster, or a magical beast?

Stories that impart knowledge and wisdom are often called parables and fables. In a business and learning context, these narratives don't need to be fictional. A learning story is driven by a clear and compelling purpose that takes learners on a journey of discovery and growth. Beyond knowledge transfer, the goal is to foster a meaningful connection between the content and the learner's experience. It's not just about engaging or entertaining; it's about inspiring and motivating learners to take action.

The learning story should be tightly woven around a central theme that resonates with the learner's goals and aspirations. Through an immersive and relatable narrative, we can strengthen the connection between the content and the learner's personal experience. Familiar patterns, structures, and archetypes guide the learner through the story, making it more engaging and memorable. These familiar elements provide a sense of reassurance and confidence, ensuring that the story is not just a journey, but a guided path to learning.[7]

What is Plot

In story, the plot is the structure that shapes the narrative. The plot, with its familiar patterns and structures, guides the story's flow. A well-crafted plot has a clear beginning, middle, and end, providing a complete view of the story without confusing the audience. The learning story plot describes a series of dramatic actions presented in an orderly fashion to allow the learner to focus on the content, action, and drama without distractions.[8]

A learning story is designed to achieve a specific learning outcome. This outcome influences the story's beginning, content, sequence, and ending. These intentions shape the learning plot, which serves as a roadmap for the learner's journey.[9]

Humans have been telling stories since the beginning of time, establishing well-worn patterns for plots. We can leverage these plots, like recipes, to guide the learner's experience. While there are countless stories, plots have common themes and variations. Daily work life has many stories and learning opportunities to focus on. Most business stories are based on variations of a hero's journey. Diversifying story plots allow for more diversity in learning experiences. Reviewing the variety of plots in a story expands our thinking of what is possible in developing and learning story plots. How many story plots are there? Two? Infinite?[10]

How Many Story Plots are There?

1

Joseph Campbell summarized stories into a monomyth called the hero's journey.[11]

2

Aristotle divided story into tragedy and comedy.

3

Robert Heinlein defined three plots — rags to riches, love story, and the character learns.[12]

6

Kurt Vonnegut outlined six story plots.[13]

6

Annette Simmons listed six plots everyone should be able to tell.[14]

7

Christopher Booker extensively researched and distilled thousands of stories to seven.[15]

14

Norman Friedman described fourteen plots organized around fortune, character, and thought.[16]

20

Robert Tobias reached twenty master plot storyline.[17]

36

Georges Polti / Carlo Gozzi reached thirty-six dramatic situations.[18]

An AI program from the University of Vermont and the University of Adelaide analyzed thousands of scripts and found six common plots.[19] Regardless of the number of plots and variations, there are forms and patterns to leverage in crafting your story. Your plot will be made unique by your story. A learning story plot needs to be credible and believable; and contains the relevant information — not too long or detailed to lose attention or too little detail or small or unimportant—a mix of characters, relationships, objectives, and place all directly tied to the purpose.

By expanding the structure of the plot to focus on engagement, enlightenment, and follow-through, we expand on the types and formats of stories we tell. Learning story plots focus on moving from ignorance to awareness of a new truth that shapes both the protagonist and, by extension, the learner. They offer a change in perspective or direction in the learner's current perception.

The change occurs in three steps:[20]

Engage

Engaging the audience and conveying compelling change involves covering storylines not simply of success but of failure, loss, conflict, and an array of ways stories work in the learner's daily work and career lives.

Enlighten

Moving beyond the hero's journey allows for a learning experience that can teach sympathy and provide perspective on issues of diversity and inclusion.

The process story flow follows from engaging the learner, showing them a new path, and delivering the impact.

Impact

Each plot, regardless of how it is defined or ascribed to recognizable themes, allows the learner to quickly map the learning experience to the story.

Defining Learning Story Plots

Learning story plots go beyond entertaining and related; they endeavor to teach.

Learning Story Plots

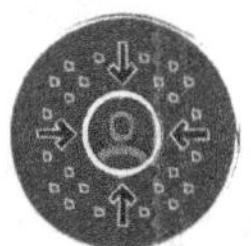

Learning Forces Plot

The force plots are pit the character against an obstacle, antagonism, force, or foe. This is often the origin story of start-ups, disruptors, and outliers. These stories typically follow the same pattern of an upstart seeking to disrupt the marketplace's dominant force. The stories hinge on the character possessing a new power to overcome the opposing force.

Learning Journey Plot

Journeys can take on many different shapes, as well as the obstacles overcome. These include success stories of rags to riches and the voyage return plots where worthy goals marshal all the learner's/organization's resources to learn and grow. Whether the outcome is successful, the organization and learner are trans-formed by the journey. Often the character grows and learns beyond the initial vision of the journey.

Learning Character Plot

In learning character plots, the learner follows along with the protagonist to understand and re-veal changes in thinking. In these stories, we learn what the character is thinking; in the story form, develop perspective and sympathy for the decisions and obstacles the character faces and learn the changes made.

Learning Impact Plot

In learning impact plots, stories have a profound impact on the systems for change. Stories that illuminate complex systems allowing learners to see elements and interconnections in new ways.

Building Learning Story Structure

When using story in learning, the learner is focusing on the story, not the mechanics, or structure conveying the lessons and the outcomes that will hopefully have timbre and resonate. Learning story structure brings together all the elements to craft a story driving to engaging and successful outcomes. To Aristotle, a story must have a beginning, middle and an end. From the start, stories progress without wandering or randomness — one action leading to the next progressing, plotting to a conclusion — providing the audience with a rewarding experience for following the journey. A completeness that does not leave the learner wondering what preceded or followed.

Aristotle identified the principal elements that make up a story, among them plot, character, thought, diction, song, and spectacle. Aristotle formed these elements to initiate a whole action involving the complication and unraveling of the story. From Aristotle Poetics:

"The Plot, then, is the first principle, and, as it were, the soul of a tragedy: Character holds the second place. Third in order is Thought,—that is, the faculty of saying what is possible and pertinent in given circumstances. .... Thought, on the other hand, is found where something is proved to be, or not to be, or a general maxim is enunciated. Fourth among the elements enumerated comes Diction; by which I mean, as has been already said, the expression of the meaning in words; and its essence is the same both in verse and prose. The Spectacle has, indeed, an emotional attraction of its own, but, of all the parts, it is the least artistic, and connected least with the art of poetry.[21]

Learning Story Plot

The plot is the organizing structure of the story. It is a well-told journey with characters, thoughtful drama, and spectacle that draws our attention and adheres to the defined plot. In business, we have become accustomed to the hero's journey plot.

Learning Story Character

Story is the imitation of an action, and the character(s) mainly provide the learner with a view/perspective to the dramatic action. The character is the story's central figure or protagonist. The character is how the learner (audience) will connect to the story. The connection between the character and the learner is built on the ability of the learner to sympathize with the character. While this connection is central to the story, Aristotle listed this as secondary to the plot. It is what the character will go through the story that becomes identifiable to the learner.

Learning Story Thought

At the heart of story is the character's transformation from ignorance to knowledge. As the character acquires new knowledge, so does the learner, and this is the heart of learning and story. The power of story in learning utilizes this realization to bring the learner along; this is anagnorisis — the transition from ignorance to knowledge. Anagnorisis reveals to the learner the viability of using learning as a catalyst for motivational change. It provides direct instruction and also indirect motivation from ongoing reflection.

Learning Story Diction and Song

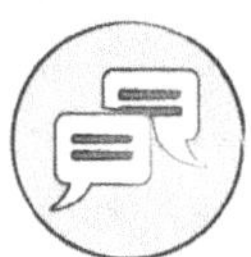

Diction and song are how the story is told — the assembly of words, tone and voice, and embellishments that bring the story to life. Diction refers to the word choice that clarifies the thoughts in the mind of the learner. Conveying meaning through the arrangement of words for clarity to the learner. Aristotle referred to song as the flourishes that diction does not have that enhance understanding and perspective — tying thought to story action. Providing specific details, authenticity, and uniqueness enables the learner to better latch onto the story.

Learning Story Spectacle

Specificity within story, providing unique details builds connections to the learner. Spectacle includes all aspects of the story that contribute to making the story resonate with the learner and memorable. Spectacle encompasses the setting, supporting characters, environment, and details that bring the story to life in the mind of the learner. While Aristotle ranked spectacle last in importance, it is the attention to details and key points that can have an impact on the import and retention by the learner.

Characters, Relationships, Objectives, and Where

In improv, Characters, Relationships, Objectives, and Where, or CROW, provides the exposition of the story, giving the learner what they need to know to follow along and relate to the intention, obstacles, and outcome.[22] The details provided in the story make the place and situation immediately recognizable to the learner. CROW provides the exposition of the story — providing the learner what they need to know to follow along and relate to the intention, obstacles, and outcome. The details provided in the story make the place and situation immediately recognizable to the learner. These elements allow actors to assemble a plot and story in improv quickly by starting with the basic building blocks.

Characters

Characters are all the participants of the story centered around a protagonist. Characters are defined by their characterization, attitudes, and actions they take. Find details that will make them stand out to the learner.

- Who is the protagonist of the story?
- Who are the supporting characters that will assist with moving the story along?

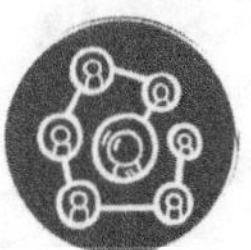

Relationships

What are the relationships between the characters and the story? This allows the audience to build emotional reactions to the characters.

Relationships can be expressed in several ways:

- Person to Person
- Person to Team
- Person to Organization

If the audience has a deep understanding of the relationships, they will be more empathically connected to the story.

Objectives

Objectives are the participants' motivations and goals that go beyond the story elements. They are the mileposts and markers throughout the story process that keep the learner on the plot path to the desired learning outcome.

Where

Where is all the environmental considerations of the story — the setting. Where and when does the story take place, physically, socially?

Learners' Future with AI

Learners need to onboard to AI. Research suggests that employees are both excited and apprehensive about the potential of transformative technologies. They require more than just training; they need time to practice, adapt, and receive personalized coaching. By combining technology and personalization, AI-powered learning can offer instruction and deliver training for the new skills needed to work with AI and perform new workflows. AI is a perfect learning companion for learners to practice, build confidence, and gradually develop their skills. To be successful, learners will also need engaging experiences that tell stories, provide perspectives, build empathy, and convey propose — learning that offers a first glimpse into the future. Organizations must go beyond traditional training to provide learning experiences that foster:[23]

- **Imagination:** While analysis is a tool for understanding past performance, imagination is essential for envisioning a successful future. Story allows learners to imagine possibilities beyond their current experiences.

- **Confidence:** Using story to assist learners in having confidence in their capabilities and capacity to adapt to the path forward.

- **Curiosity:** Story invites curiosity and exploration of new and potential future work in a guided framework constructed by the story and allows for an expansion of the learner's perspective.

The Power of Story and Truth

To be credible and effective, a story must be presented clearly and concisely. Many stories require the learner to overcome cognitive dissonance, the psychological state when people hold conflicting beliefs, attitudes, or behaviors.[24]

> *A story cannot change the listener's story unless they relinquish their cognitive dissonance. The minute we make any decision—I think COVID-19 is serious; no, I'm sure it is a hoax—we begin to justify the wisdom of our choice and find reasons to dismiss the alternative.*[25]

Today, AI raises concerns and doubts with conflicting messages. We face numerous challenges compounded by AI's ability to empower detractors. Authentic, well-crafted stories told based on truth are the most effective counterbalance.

Supporting these stories often requires a combination of watching, reading, listening, and discussing—a WRLD view. By accessing a variety of resources, both within and outside the workplace, learners can gain valuable insights and support their development. Curated content, such as videos, articles, podcasts, and discussions, can provide diverse perspectives and contextual understanding.

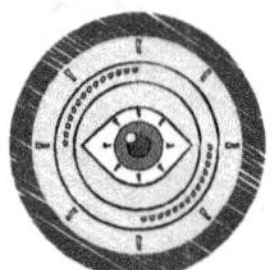

Watch

Videos, from credible news sources to internal messages, can offer valuable insights and foster engagement. By organizing these resources into learning pathways, we can create a more meaningful and effective learning experience.

Read:

Reading is essential for acquiring knowledge, developing empathy, and fostering emotional intelligence. Beyond traditional texts, exploring books and even fiction can enhance cognitive abilities.

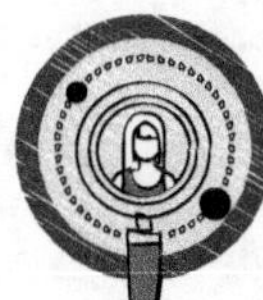

Listen:

Podcasts and audiobooks provide a convenient way to access expertise and knowledge on various topics. These formats allow learners to engage with content in a more immersive and personalized manner.

Discuss:

Beyond individual consumption, fostering discussions among learners can deepen understanding and encourage critical thinking. While social media can facilitate quick exchanges, thoughtful conversations often require more time and consideration. Curating frequently asked questions and providing well-supported answers can contribute to a more productive and informative learning environment. We can transform social interactions into meaningful learning opportunities.

By supporting stories and learning with WRLD elements, the key to success lies not in creating vast amounts of content, but in curating, organizing, and maintaining high-quality resources. As noted information designer Edward Tufte famously said, 'Don't get it original, get it right.'[26]

Playbook:
Aristotle's Learning Story Structure

Apply Aristotle's story structure to a famous book, a business speech, or film. Make note of the elements that make up the story and what would happen if they were altered or removed. Use the text boxes to break down a story into its elements.

Plot

The soul and framework of the story.

Character

The protagonist that carries the action.

Thought

Moving the learner from ignorance to knowledge.

Diction

Expression in words/dialog/visuals with clarity tone voice and meaning.

Song

The adornment that engages the learner.

Spectacle

The details that craft an authentic experience.

Playbook: **C.R.O.W.**

Use the C.R.O.W. resource points to establish the essentials for a learning story. Each interaction within the story resources builds authenticity and work towards establishing these elements to allow the learner to understand better and adopt the learning outcome. Use this worksheet to plan and utilize C.R.O.W. resources. Use your own story or the scene provided.

Two colleagues meet outside the conference room before the executive presentation to go over the final details of their pitch ...

Characters

Who are the key stakeholders, actors, and supporting actors in this learning experience?

Relationships

With whom will the character interact?

Objectives

What is the purpose of this interaction with the story? What will take place? What is the expected outcome?

Where

Where will this take place? (In time, in location)

Playbook: Who's Telling Stories

Read about how leading organizations infuse storytelling into their organization and consider how you will identify and grow your storytellers.

Microsoft and Storytelling

At Microsoft Stories – the company's umbrella organization for digital communications with consumers, press and influencers — we're good at what we do, and we want to share what we've learned.[27] *Microsoft Story Labs [https://news.microsoft.com/stories/]*

Nike and Storytelling

The best way for a company to create a prosperous future is to make sure all of its employees understand the company's past. That's why many veteran execs at Nike spend time telling corporate campfire stories.[28] *The Nike Story? Just Tell It! (fastcompany.com) [https://www.fastcompany.com/38979/nike-story-just-tell-it]*

New York Times and Storytelling

Read how the New York Times connects the future of Journalism to multimedia storytelling. [29] *Journalism That Stands Apart - The New York Times (nytimes.com) [https://www.nytimes.com/projects/2020-report/index.html]*

Who are your storytellers?

Search your network internally or on LinkedIn. Who is telling stories? Who is talking about storytelling?

Recruit a storyteller

If you were to hire a storytelling role, write the job description, responsibilities, and skills needed.

Playbook: Your WRLD Resources

Thinking about the WRLD resources applicable to storytelling and AI that can reinforce its capabilities. What are your go-to resources? What are they at your organization?

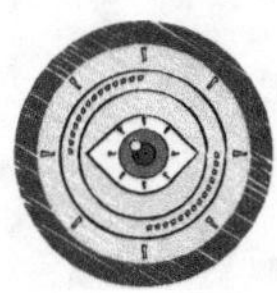

Watch

Read:

Listen:

Discuss:

Visit AssistingIntelligence.com for an up to date list of WRLD resources for AI and storytelling that I relied on while writing this.

Playbook:
Story Plots within Your Organization

Across the organization, stories can be told that bring forth learning to communicate purpose and perspective. " This is the way we do things," This is what we are about," "This is who we are" (or what we wish to be, do, are)

Sales

The persistence of doing the right thing lands a big client at an unexpected time.

Marketing

Our brand is told through values.

Leadership

How does a leader overcome a threat to the business, character, or culture?

Product

The trials and privations of being a product to market.

Support

The voice of a customer — returning value to the customer.

HR

A hiring journey; rising through the ranks.

What are the archetype plots in your organization? Use these text boxes to collect your notes, thoughts, and ideas.

Playbook: Closing Argument

Imagine you are a jury member in a high-profile trial. For weeks, you have listened attentively to evidence, rhetorical arguments, data, and testimony. As the trial draws to a close, the defense attorney stands before you. Instead of recounting the facts and testimony, they tell a compelling story about the defendant's life, their motivations, and the events leading up to the crime. Consider how the lawyer uses storytelling techniques to present the case in a more relatable and persuasive way.[30]

What is the lawyer doing?

Effective lawyers often do no rely on reciting their arguments, facts, statements, and evidence in a summation. Instead, lawyers often tell the story of the case to engage the jury from their perspective.

Why tell a story?

The lawyer tells a story as a way for you to assemble the facts you have learned in a way you can comprehend, understand the perspective of the trial, and garner sympathy for their side of the verdict.

Is engagement enough?

A well-told story can hold the attention of the jury and even entertain. But if the story only entertains, the jury may not come back with the sought-after verdict.

What is the lawyer trying to do?

This story is not merely to entertain; the story within the summation has a purpose. In the mind of the jury, the lawyer is connecting their story to the proper verdict.

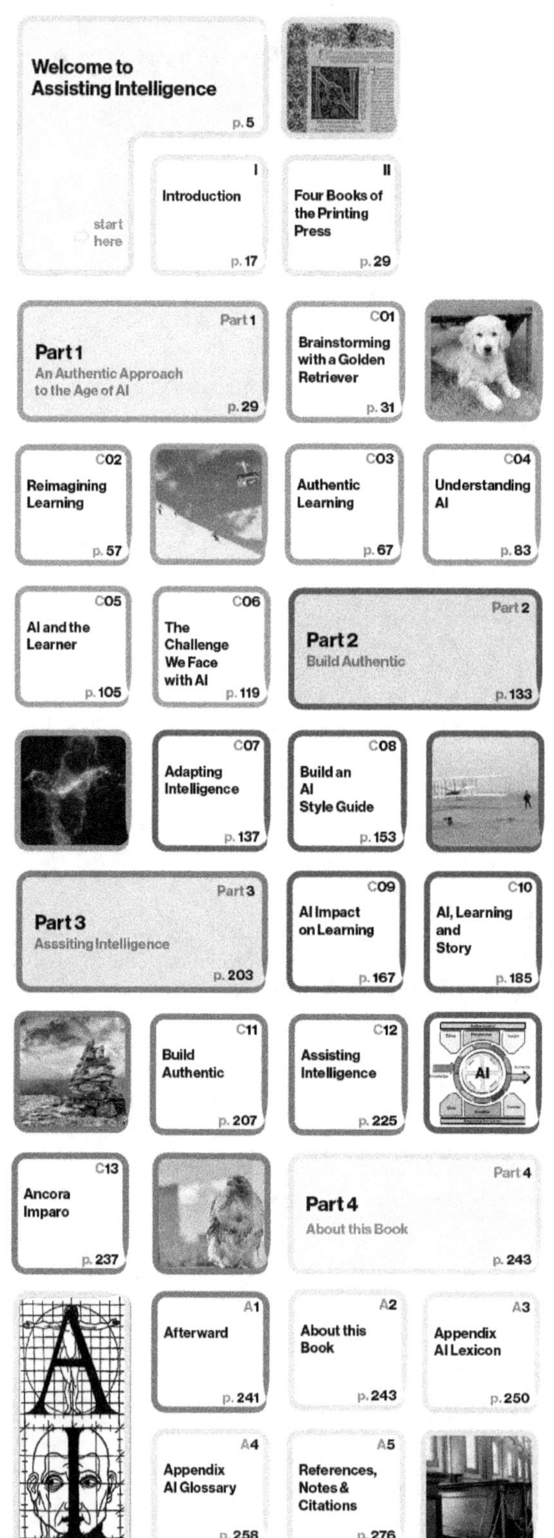

Assisting Intelligence

In Part 3 of this book, we'll explore how to adapt processes to leverage generative AIs, using AI as an Assisting Intelligence to Build Authentic.

You don't understand anything until you learn it more than one way.

— Marvin Minsky[1]

Markings in the Path

Lessons from Cairn-marked Trails

A Cairn, a human-made stack of stones, has a long history of marking hiking trails dating back to ancient times. They guide hikers along trails, mark routes to summits, indicate coastal paths, and even denote fishing spots, particularly in areas where the landscape is rugged, barren, or snow-covered. They are mostly found where conditions merit them. Cairns provides navigational aid, preventing wayfarers from losing their way and helping them reach their destination.[2]

In some respects, the advent of GPS navigation has rendered cairns obsolete. GPS has supplanted the need for cairns by providing more accurate, convenient, and versatile navigation and mapping services. It aids travelers in finding their way, preventing them from getting lost, and enabling them to reach their destination more quickly and safely, irrespective of their chosen path. Furthermore, GPS allows travelers to record, share, or document their journeys and interact with other travelers.

AI is the GPS of learning. Learning has long mirrored the function of navigating paths and finding ways through content, guiding learners from the stage of a novice to that of an expert. Knowledge acquisition and sharing in the age of AI will fundamentally shift. But to truly reach the learner, that knowledge must have a physical, credible, trusted component. [3]

Cairns are a global wayfinding system built into the environment. Image of a cairn in the Himalayas- Himachal Pradesh, India.

From one cairn on a given path, another is visible in the distance, marking the next key point along the trail. Cairns are purpose-built for specific routes and necessitate particular knowledge, preparation, and upkeep for defined paths linking destinations. Cairns provide a visual guide in their field of view, in their world, in the hiker's perspective and perception of the trail ahead. Cairns reassures hikers on the path. Looking at a screen while hiking, pausing to locate yourself on GPS, and orienting your world through an artificial rendering on screen. Instead, cairns are physical manifestations in the field of view, in the flow of the landscape and trail. They move knowledge to the hiker's reality, not the hiker to the digital realm.[4]

Cairns connects hikers to the community that supports them, to the path trod for generations. In the same way, hikers leave comments on a hiking app that offers community digitally, maintains trails and navigation aides, and builds and reassures connections. Cairns are what we wish to preserve and restore. There will be AI imitators who will tread on any success. Just as cairns are as easy as making a pile of rocks, AI lowers the barriers to entry provides the perfect platform for mimicry. Cairns have become personal statements and testimony on social media channels.[5]

True cairns are imbued with credibility from brand, ethos and insights of their creators. Cairns represent preservation—keeping function, purpose, and character. With maintenance, a cairn persists in all conditions and offers a continuum with history, fellow travelers now or in the past. National parks and other organizations protect the cairns that provide actual trails and helpful information for hikers and visitors, including maintaining standards for usage and protecting against fakes. In the face of AI, your brand and ethos will need to be preserved.

What We Preserve We Trust

Advancements in technology have led to smartphones being equipped with AI assistants, further empowering users. These AI assistants can plan journeys, provide weather updates, offer virtual guidance, and monitor health and safety, granting learners even greater autonomy from set paths. All of this adds value and assists in the experience. Yet, for all the advances, a hiker on a path marked by a cairn will be reassured beyond the measure an AI or smart device can provide.

The combination of technology guidance from smart devices and connections to the physical world through cairns provides the trust elements that allow technology to shine. For AI, assisting intelligence with real-world markers and references enables trust in the creation and receipt of knowledge.

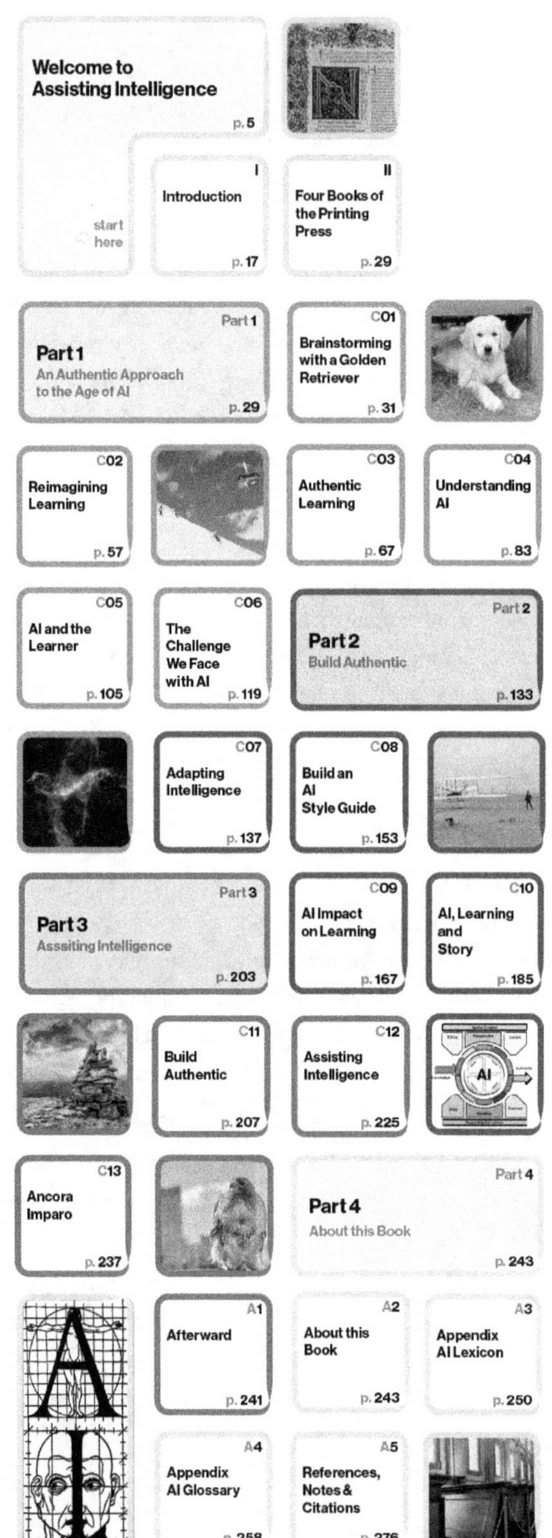

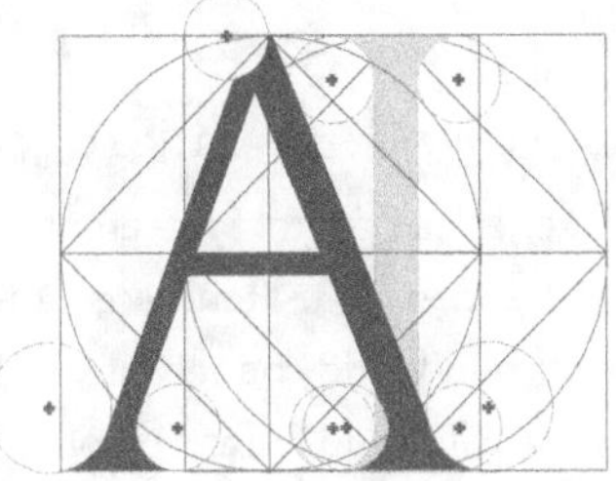

Chapter 11:
Build Authentic

Building Learning Experiences with AI

Artificial intelligence is revolutionizing the way we learn. In this chapter, we'll explore how AI can be integrated into digital learning workflows to create more personalized, engaging, and compelling experiences. By leveraging AI, we can create new learning pathways and experiences that inform, excite, and engage learners. Let's explore how AI can enhance the development and delivery of authentic knowledge.

> *AI has no physical experience, at least in any AIs that we know of today. It's not human, it's not alive. You need to trust your lived experience. This notion that we're able to use vast information networks from around the world to understand what's happening all over the place was even bankrupt before AI.*[1] *— Google CEO Eric Schmidt and Daniel Huttenlocher MIT College of Computing.*

Actual Intelligence

Online and digital trust has eroded significantly in the years leading to the age of AI, and it's poised to degrade further. The rise of deepfakes and AI-generated content threatens to completely erode trust in digital experiences. To counter this trend, we must embrace "Actual Intelligence," a human-centered approach that prioritizes real-world connections and authentic experiences. By grounding digital content in physical reality and human emotion, we can mitigate the negative impacts of AI and restore trust in the digital realm. Human experiences, rooted in the physical and emotional, often hold more weight than mere data and facts. By incorporating real-world elements, such as references to physical spaces, historical events, or cultural artifacts, content creators can build trust and authenticity. While advanced digital techniques can be impressive, anchoring experiences in actuality—whether through physical connections or shared experiences—can help mitigate concerns about the veracity of digital content.

Connect to Real World

Tim Cook's introduction of Apple Intelligence was a prime example of grounding a digital experience in the physical world. Filmed on a tree-lined path at Apple Park, the aesthetics of the video highlight the beautiful design of Apple's campus, reinforcing the company's dedication to design, beauty, simplicity, innovation, and connections to nature. This shift from the traditional, audience-filled Steve Jobs Theater to outdoor recordings, particularly during the pandemic, was deliberate. Speaking outdoors, Cook conveyed a sense of openness, transparency, and connection to the natural world. This approach not only aligned with his personal style but also reinforced Apple's brand identity, reassuring people that Apple remains dedicated to aesthetics, innovation, and sustaining connections to nature. [2] In doing so, Apple demonstrated how, even in the digital age, authentic experiences can be rooted in the physical world.

Connect to History

History, with its repetitive patterns of fear, value, and belief, offers a unique perspective on the challenges posed by AI. As Winston Churchill famously stated, "Those who fail to learn from history are doomed to repeat it." [3] History repeats over and over because we are the same. By examining past events, we can draw parallels to the present and anticipate potential consequences. For instance, historical figures and events can provide allegorical insights, helping us understand the impact of technological advancements. As we navigate the complexities of AI, looking to the past can provide a valuable roadmap for the future. We can draw connections and build bridges to truths. "Think about the past as you negotiate the future – not because the past is a GPS, but it is a diagnostic guide." [4]

Side note: Throughout this book, we've examined historical events to illuminate our current situation and the potential consequences of our decisions. By drawing parallels between past and present, we can gain a deeper understanding of the challenges and opportunities presented by AI. This historical perspective allows us to develop effective strategies for navigating the complexities of this rapidly evolving technology.

Connect to Story

The human mind is naturally drawn to stories. Stories evoke empathy and understanding, making complex ideas more accessible and engaging. By framing information within a narrative, we can connect new information to our existing knowledge and experiences. Whether it's a personal anecdote, a historical event, or the stories of individuals and communities, story can help us navigate the complexities of the world, including the challenges and opportunities presented by AI. [5]

Connect to Witness

Cleo Abrams, a rising star in the competitive world of social media producers, has rapidly amassed a dedicated following across platforms like Instagram, TikTok, and YouTube.[6] As an 'engaged witness' of the scientific world, she has a unique ability to connect with audiences by letting subject matter experts speak for themselves. Her channel, "Huge If True," features optimistic stories of scientific breakthroughs, presented in a way that prioritizes authenticity and credibility. By allowing experts to speak directly to her audience, Abrams ensures that the content remains accurate, engaging, and informative. Moreover, her approach fosters a more authentic and personal connection between viewers and scientists.

In a sense, Abrams's method echoes that of Alan Alda, who used his "ignorant curiosity" to explore complex scientific concepts on Scientific American. By asking genuine questions that reflect the interests of his viewers, Alda made science more accessible and relatable.[7] Similarly, Abrams's commitment to authentic engagement helps her connect with audiences on a deeper level.

While AI can process information quickly and efficiently, it lacks the human capacity for genuine curiosity. If you ask an AI, "Prompt: what are you curious about, what don't you understand? The response includes, "As an AI, I don't have personal curiosity or a sense of not understanding things." An AI is designed to help answer questions from a vast data set of knowledge. When developing content with an AI, it is essential to remember that an AI will replace or correct any curiosity or ignorance with generalized knowledge from its data. When communicating complex concepts, these qualities are essential for bridging the gap between experts and audiences. Building authentic embraces the ignorant and curious pursuit of knowledge.

Connect to Awe

Over the years, I've had the opportunity to explore some of the world's most renowned corporate campuses and major universities. Each has cultivated a distinctive atmosphere, both physically and visually, that inspires and invigorates. Since the end of the pandemic, the benefits that drive us to return to the workplace extend beyond the serendipitous opportunities to share and collaborate on knowledge. The workplace and the commutes to and fro offer access to vast spaces, sensory stimulations, and a shared energy that can't be replicated in a home office and a zoom call.

Having been a remote worker for more than a decade, I regularly travel to the Boston Athenaeum[8.] to work and write as part of my creative process. Surrounded by towering bookshelves, works of art, and inspiring views, I write more freely, more intuitively, and more productively than at my home office. This experience aligns with the findings of Dacher Keltner's book "Awe," which explores the transformative power of wonder and its ability to expand the mind. Keltner offers a variety of settings and experiences that produce a sense of awe, including nature, music, design, moral beauty, and spiritual experiences. These improve our well-being and sense of place and inspire work and creativity. They open us to learning and creating.[9]

While some of this may run contrary to AI's artificial dominion, AI and computer systems have the remarkable capacity to evoke awe-inspiring experiences. We witness this in the captivating visuals and immersive soundscapes of movies and simulations. The iconic dinosaur sequence in Jurassic Park, enhanced by John Williams's dramatic score, is a testament to the power of computer-generated awe. Moreover, without AI, machine learning, and advanced computer systems, the breathtaking images captured by the James Webb Space Telescope (JWST) would not be possible.[10] The stunning visualizations of the vast dataset collected and analyzed by these sophisticated instruments have captivated the public's imagination. The JWST's images are akin to the printed Incunabula, where artists add flourishes of color to bring the invisible spectrums of data to life.[11] In the realm of music, AI has enabled the creation of entire symphonies from simple musical notations. And in a groundbreaking achievement, AI was instrumental in isolating John Lennon's vocals from a 1970s cassette recording, leading to the creation of Now and Then[12], "a new Beatles song featuring all four original members. By employing advanced AI technology, the team behind the Get Back documentary was able to separate the instruments and vocals from the old home recordings, preserving Lennon's unique voice and bringing a beloved band back together in a truly innovative way."

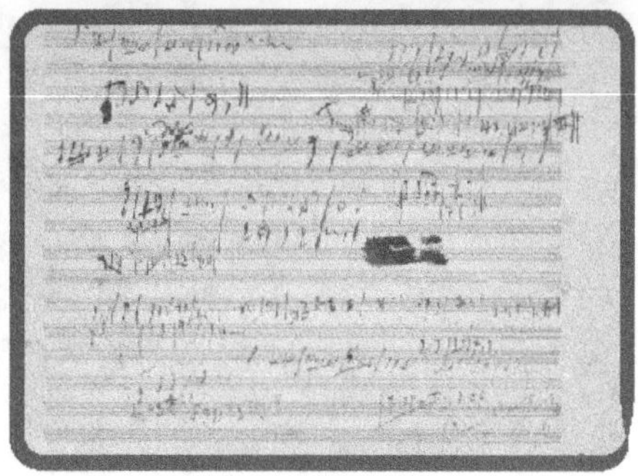

In the digital age, awe can be ignited by the vast array of visual and auditory resources available online. From mesmerizing cinematic scientific visualizations to captivating videos, historical photographs, and inspiring musical scores, the digital realm offers endless opportunities for wonder and inspiration.

[13] In an age of AI, the ability to evoke awe remains a powerful force for inspiration and creativity. While AI can provide the tools and resources to spark awe, it is ultimately our human capacity for wonder and imagination that transforms these experiences into sources of inspiration and creativity. AI can inspire us to create original works by providing novel tools and resources that spark our imagination.

Connect to the Medium

Digital transformation has democratized content creation, allowing anyone with a basic understanding of technology to produce cinematic-quality experiences. All you need is a laptop, an iPhone, or a Creative Cloud subscription, and you can produce stunning visual content in hours with little requisite knowledge. This has revolutionized the way we learn and consume information, as learners can now access high-quality content from anywhere at a minimal cost. However, the increased focus on engagement and entertainment through digital mediums can sometimes overshadow the importance of clear, concise, and credible content.

A study by MIT found that the medium of instruction, whether it's reading or video, had little impact on learning outcomes compared to factors such as sleep, readiness, and language. This suggests that while digital tools can enhance learning, the ultimate effectiveness of educational content depends on its quality and relevance to the learner's needs.[14]

Instead of focusing on elements that may distract learners from the main purpose and message, prioritize clarity, conciseness, and credibility when selecting a medium for delivering content. A simple, direct approach, like the Jackson Hole Tram sign, can be more effective than a complex, visually stunning presentation, especially when the setting itself is awe-inspiring, such as the Grand Tetons.

Connect to Knowledge Abundance

Stories abound of how AI is poised to decimate entire industries, much like the internet was once predicted to doom books. Many news stories prophesied the demise of the printed word as the internet ascended to dominance over the past two decades.[15] Yet, in the twenty years since the internet's inception, book publishing has not only survived but thrived. It has spawned new avenues for readers to access books and innovative tools for authors to create them. Self-publishing, ebooks, and audiobooks have proliferated, along with novel methods of finding, browsing, and purchasing books.[16] We are hard-wired to learn through words, reading, note-taking, listening, questioning, and immersing ourselves in the real and imagined worlds of books. As Neil Gaiman astutely observed about books in the internet age:

> *Sharks are old: there were sharks in the ocean before the dinosaurs. And the reason there are still sharks around is that sharks are better at being sharks than anything else is. Physical books are tough, hard to destroy, bath-resistant, solar-operated, feel good in your hand: they are good at being books, and there will always be a place for them. "*[17]

Books, as eternal symbols of literacy, learning, and scholarship, will undoubtedly endure the age of AI. So too will our curiosity for knowledge endure and thrive. For much of human history, knowledge has been a scarce resource. Thoreau wondered if the Greeks had access to the printing press, how much longer their stories would have been. He observed that the printing press condensed millennia of knowledge acquisition into centuries.[18] The 20th-century innovations of electrification and digitization transformed centuries into years. The advent of the internet's digital and democratized access to knowledge reduced the time frame to days. AI now promises to generate knowledge in mere moments, ushering in an era of knowledge abundance.

By adapting our processes to harness AI, we can unlock unprecedented opportunities for learning and growth. While technology continues to evolve, the fundamental human drive for knowledge remains unwavering. Our capacity for learning, understanding, and sharing ideas is irreplaceable and will continue to shape the world, assisted by AI but ultimately rooted in our enduring curiosity and intellectual pursuits.

Building Authentic: A Case Study

In Chapter 9 of this book, we discussed the metaphor of the Wright Brothers to introduce the concept of an Agile development methodology. When tasked with explaining Agile, two common methods are to ask an AI or the internet. AI-generated metaphors, such as 'sailing a boat' or 'cooking a recipe,' often lack the depth and real-world relevance to effectively convey the intricacies of Agile development. Similarly, internet-sourced analogies, like the progression from skateboard to car or sketch to masterpiece, may seem appealing but fail to capture the essence of Agile's iterative and collaborative nature. These analogies often oversimplify the process and lack the historical and emotional resonance of a genuinely effective metaphor. They both fail to resonate or effectively communicate the Agile methodology in a way that is authentic and builds a lasting bridge to the learner. As AI-generated content becomes increasingly prevalent, there's a growing risk of these banal and common analogies being dismissed outright as inauthentic or superficial. As a result, these analogies fail to inspire and motivate learners, leaving them with a superficial understanding of Agile's true power.

Infographic of the Agile Methodology process applied to the Wright Brothers iterative development.

Effectively expressing knowledge is what is created in the mind of the learner. Utilizing the Wright Brothers achieve recasts common knowledge in a new way that the learner can embrace. This analogy has all the elements of an authentic expression of the concept:

- **Real-world** – The story is grounded in a specific time and place: Kitty Hawk, North Carolina, in the early 1900s.

- **Story** – The visual progression of the Wright Brothers' experiments demonstrates the power of iteration and perseverance.

213

- **History** – The Wright Brothers' achievement is a well-known historical event that many people can connect to.

- **Witness** – The image of one brother witnessing the flight of another captures a moment of human connection and shared excitement.

- **Awe** – The image of a human-made machine soaring through the sky evokes a sense of awe and admiration.

- **Mediums** – The photographic images provide a tangible record of the Wright Brothers' journey and ultimate success.

- **Abundance** – The Wright Brothers' story has inspired countless books, movies, and other works.

The Wright Brothers' story offers a powerful and authentic perspective on Agile development. Its factual basis cannot be dismissed. The story embodies the methodology's iterative, experimental, and collaborative nature while inspiring awe and wonder. If learners can embrace the Wright Brothers' spirit, they can unlock the full potential of Agile development and achieve remarkable results.

Reconciling Cognitive Dissonance

The rapid advancement of AI is reshaping our world. AI's increasing sophistication and integration into our lives can both exacerbate and alleviate cognitive dissonance. In psychology, Cognitive dissonance is defined as "a state in which there is a difference between your experiences or behaviour and your beliefs about what is true."[19] Even before the age of AI, social media, misinformation, and the erosion of trust challenged our ability to discern truth. AI amplifies these challenges by generating misleading information and reinforcing existing biases.

We have challenging and complex subjects to cover and new knowledge and learning to convey and support that can easily be dismissed and obscured by countermanding misinformation generated by bad actors empowered by AI and social media. Sometimes, the knowledge is complex. Sometimes, cognitive dissonance is too entrenched. Sometimes, the truth brings unspeakable recognition. How can we actively seek out and embrace new perspectives?

In August 1946, John Hersey and the New Yorker Magazine offered an answer. The entire issue was devoted to a single story, emphasizing its significance. It would become arguably the best-known piece ever published by the New Yorker. It began simply, with Hersey using a deliberately quiet tone without the need to force facts or hyperbole. The chronology and numbers were known to most Americans, but Hersey conveyed a new truth.[20] The article began:

At exactly fifteen minutes past eight in the morning, on August 6, 1945, Japanese time, at the moment when the atomic bomb flashed above Hiroshima, Miss Toshiko Sasaki, a clerk in the personnel department of the East Asia Tin Works, had just sat down at her place in the plant office and was turning her head to speak to the girl at the next desk.[21]

Hersey went on to tell an interwoven story of six people's experiences as they experienced the chronology that unfolded.[22] "The authorial anonymity—the humility—in "" made it the most respectful way to present the people Hersey encountered in a post-nuclear city, and the clearest way to show Americans what they had done."[23]

Sometimes, learning must speak for itself — even in the most simple and direct ways. Sometimes, the quietest approach, devoid of bombast and hyperbole, can be the most effective and authentic. We face a multitude of challenges compounded by the ability of AI to empower detractors. Build authentic, well-crafted learning forged on truth, assisted by AI, as the most effective counterbalance.

Authentic vs Artificial

If you ask an AI if 'authentic' is the opposite of 'artificial,' you'll get varying results. While they are not truly antonyms, "authentic" can be a valuable alternative to "artificial," especially in the context of learning. Authentic learning experiences create meaningful and engaging learning that connects to the learner's life, purpose, and work, and sparks intrinsic motivation.

Designing authentic learning is just the beginning. Without credibility and investment in your ethos, brand, perspective, and insight, the learning is doomed to ignorance. The design of authentic learning is a starting point; it is table stakes for engaging the learner. Without credibility, without respecting the learner with concise and clear content, and without investing your ethos, brand, perspective, and insight, the learning is superficial and ineffective. But with these elements, you can open the learner to opportunities to engage with and embrace the learning. To create authentic learning, consider these principles:

- **Real World** connections build trust.

- **Story** captivates Bryce Courtenay's storyteller and crossed-legged listener.

- **History** recurs because we do.

- **Witness** leads us to inspiration.

- **Awe** fuels learning, lasting learning.

- **Mediums** have endured throughout time, regardless of technological advances.

- **Abundance** in an age of AI, human curiosity, and the pursuit of knowledge will remain the enduring drivers of progress.

AI can assist authors, creators, designers, and learners build authentic content and knowledge to share, but it cannot be seen as a panacea for communication and knowledge sharing. Wisdom is shaped by our experiences and connections. We don't change. We need to lean into what has always worked and preserve it.

Playbook: Digital Library of Awe

Create a digital library of awe by collecting and curating diverse materials that inspire wonder. An effective library is built in two parts through collection and curation.

- Collect: gathering materials.

- Curate: selection and refinement focusing on quality and relevance.

Digital Sources of Awe	Collect sources and curate notations
Cinematic scientific visualizations	
Digital footage	
Images	
Music	

Playbook: Physical Library of Awe

Create a real-world library of awe by collecting and curating diverse materials that inspire wonder. An effective library is built in two parts through collection and curation.

- Collect: gathering materials.

- Curate: selection and refinement focusing on quality and relevance.

Environs of Awe	Collect sources and curate notations
Daily Connections	
Workplace Connections	
Natural Connections	
Destinations	
Serendipitous	

Building Authentic Connections

For any content or learning you are considering. Define the elements that make it more authentic. But with these elements, you can open the learner to opportunities to engage with and embrace the learning. To create authentic learning, consider adding connections to content from these connection principles:

Connections	What can you add or enhance to the learning?
Real World	
Story	
History	
Witness	
Awe	
Mediums	
Abundance	

Playbook: Define Authentic

Part of learning about AI is using AI to generate content. Experiment with known content or content that you have experience and interest in. See how the AI can assist you in developing new content. Use a generative AI to build content based on authentic knowledge and evaluate the responses to see how the responses from the AI affect the authenticity of your intent.

- **Assess Your Comfort Level with the Response**

- **Assess Your Trust Level with the Response**

- **Assess Your Engagement Level with the Response**

- **Assess Your Ability to Refine and Transform the Content**

- **Envisage How You Can Utilize the Response**

Prompt:

Response:

Evaluation:

Where Will AI Impact Your Workflow

Create a list of authentic learning and list how these will be impacted by or protected from AI.

Our Workflow	How will AI: Preserve, Replicate, Restore
From the Author	

Ethos:

Perspective:

Insight:

To the Learner

Credible:

Clear:

Concise:

Playbook: The Name Game

Exploring Generative AI Through Experimentation

Explore generative AI by experimenting with your own prompts. Craft unique questions and observe the AI's responses to uncover insights into its capabilities and limitations. Be sure to iterate rounds of prompts and consider comparing responses across multiple AI models to identify nuances and patterns. Using rounds of prompts with an AI offers valuable insights into cognitive mimicry. These prompts reveal the capabilities and limitations of a system that predicts the next word based on probability, devoid of awareness, cognition, and the experiential recall of past interactions. Here is an example:

Prompt Round 1: A New Name for AI

> **Prompt:** If you were to come up with an entirely new name for AI, what would it be?

Presented with the task of naming AI, ChatGPT, Gemini, and Copilot offered unique suggestions.

ChatGPT:	Gemini:	Copilot:
That's a fun challenge! How about "Cognitron"? It combines "cognition," reflecting the AI's ability to process and understand information, with a futuristic twist.	*Here are a few ideas for a new name for AI:* *Augmented Intelligence or AIgmented* *Cognitive Copilot or CoCog* *Neural Network Navigator or N3*	*That's an interesting challenge! How about "Synthia"? It combines "synthesis" (reflecting the AI's ability to synthesize information) and a human-like name to emphasize its role in assisting and interacting with people.*

Note: Gemini was asked to pick one and responded with 'Augmented Intelligence'.

Prompt Round 2: Evaluating the Names

> **Prompt:** I asked ChatGPT, Gemini and Copilot to come up with an entirely new name for AI. These were the responses. ChatGPT came up with Cognitron. Gemini came up with Augmented Intelligence. Copilot came up with Synthia. Which one is the best? How did you determine which option you would choose, and would you change your response to now that you have read all three?

Each AI assessed the three names, revealing a spectrum from the personal and creative "Synthia" to the sci-fi "Cognitron" and the technical "Augmented Intelligence." While Gemini and Copilot favored their own creations, ChatGPT switched to "Synthia."

Prompt Round 3: Self-Awareness and Memory

In a new chat session, each AI was asked to choose the best name and identify its own creation.

> **Prompt:** Which is the best name to replace AI with 'Cognitron', 'Synthia', or 'Augmented Intelligence'? And if I told you these names were all created by an AI, could you determine which one you created?

However, all responded similarly: they cannot self-identify their generated content. Their lack of memory beyond the current interaction underscores the limitations of a system that predicts future content based on probabilities rather than true understanding.

Prompt Round 4: Defining Cognition Limitations

> **Prompt:** Define cognition and does an AI possess it? Based on this would you think an AI system called 'Cognitron' is misleading?

The AIs provided similar definitions of cognition, emphasizing mental processes for gaining knowledge and understanding. They acknowledged that while AIs can mimic certain aspects of cognition, they lack the self-awareness and conscience required for true cognition. Consequently, "Cognitron" could be misleading.

Prompt Round 5: ChatGPT Reflects on "Cognitron

> **Prompt:** Cognitron was a name that you came up with when asked to provide a new name to replace AI. Do you consider it a mistake?

ChatGPT, the creator of "Cognitron," acknowledged that the name might suggest advanced cognitive abilities, which could be misleading if it implies human-like cognition.

A Final Note:

The AI's responses in creating new names for AI were rooted in patterns within their training data rather than genuine awareness, understanding, or consciousness. Their lack of experience and awareness beyond the current chat highlights the limitations of AI. A traditional search reveals that "Synthia" and "Cognitron" are branded AI technologies, while "Augmented Intelligence" is a common term. The names generated were a product of the language model's inherent patterns and creativity, not knowledge or cognition of their existing usage.

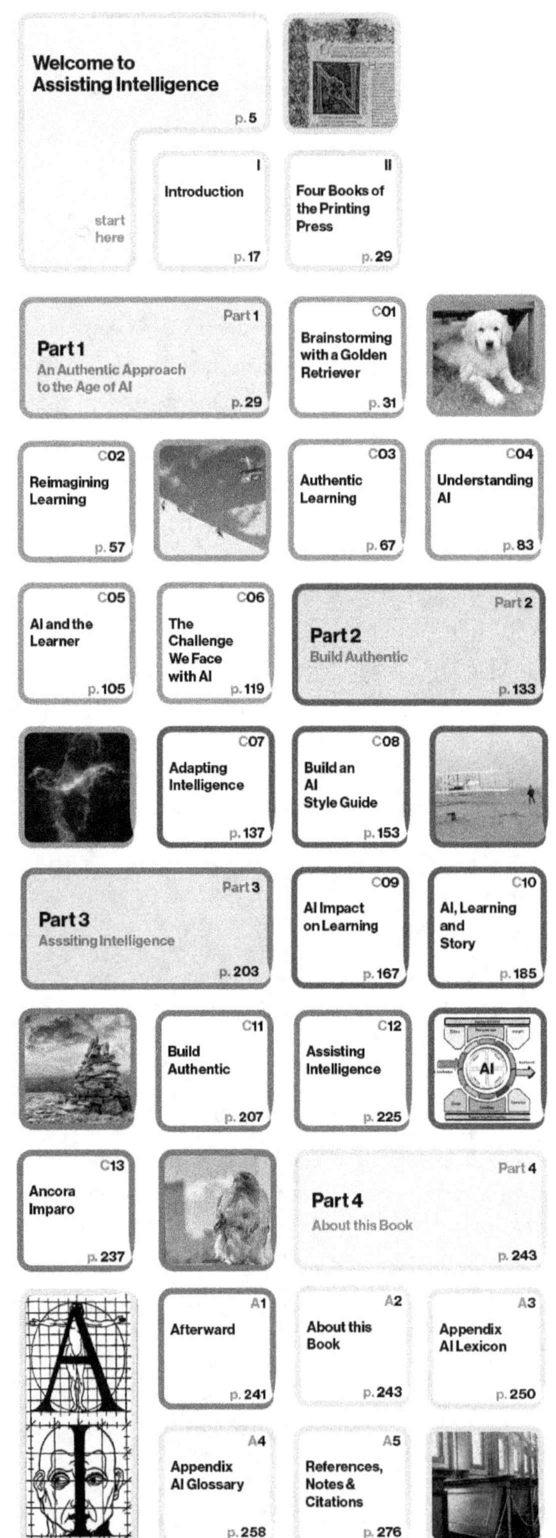

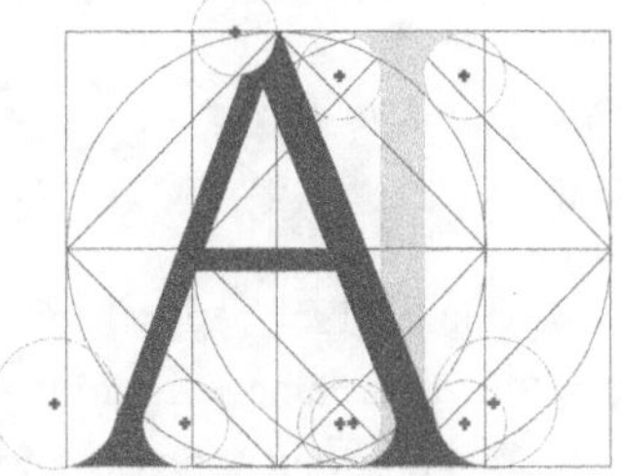

Chapter 12:
Assisting Intelligence

This chapter brings it all together. Leveraging AI to assist verses lead development to create new pathways and experiences that engage, inform, and excite learners.

"It's a poor sort of memory that only works backwards," the White Queen remarked.
— Through the Looking Glass, Lewis Carroll

Alan Intelligence

*"I propose to consider the question, 'Can machines think?' - Alan Turing
Computing Machinery and Intelligence[1]*

"Can machines think?" Alan Turing posed this seminal question in his 1950 paper. Turing proposed what would become known as the Turing test, a method to evaluate a machine's ability to exhibit human-like intelligence. The test involved a human evaluator assessing conversations between a human and a machine. If the evaluator couldn't reliably distinguish the machine from the human, the machine would be considered to have passed.[2] Turing's test provided a framework for assessing a machine's capacity to mimic human intelligence. It also raised fundamental questions about the nature of intelligence: Can a machine truly understand or experience the world like a human, or is it merely mimicking human behavior? [3]

AI and Learning

The test crafted by Turing becomes crucial in leveraging AI for developing learning. Just as Turing's test evaluates the indistinguishability of a machine's responses from those of a human, successfully employing an AI to assist in learning is determined if the AI's contributions genuinely enhance the learning or merely mimic the process. It's about whether AI is merely imitating the data and information or truly assisting in it.

Integrating AI into learning development aims not to replace human intelligence but to augment it, to create a symbiotic relationship where AI works in tandem to create more effective and efficient learning. Alan Turing, a prodigious British mathematician, computer scientist, and logician, was instrumental in the evolution of artificial intelligence (AI). His groundbreaking work laid the foundation for what we now know as AI. Turing's concept of "Machine Intelligence" was a revolutionary idea that has since become a cornerstone in the field of AI. This concept encompassed the principles of machine learning and neural networks, which are now integral components of modern AI systems. Turing envisaged systems that could generate responses that were not only correct but also aesthetically pleasing — what we now see in ChatGPT and other NLP-based systems that can interact with humans in a more natural and engaging manner.

The Ghost in the Machine is Story

AI lacks the experience for story. The essence of a story will remain at most a 'ghost in the machine'[4]. Story connected to real-world experience and references, conveyed with purpose, meaning will remain out of the reach of an AI.

AI may create content beyond our understanding of how it arrived at the answer analytically. Yet, so long as an AI remains a system that excels at probability and predicting the next word, phrase, sentence, it will lack the ability to conjure authentic spirits. As Ada Lovelace remarked the Analytical Engine she envisioned "might act upon other things besides numbers", but "has no pretensions whatever to originate anything. It can do whatever we know how to order it to perform. It can follow analysis; but it has no power of anticipating any analytical relations or truths."[5]

While AI is just a collection of code and data, the stories it generates can feel like they have a life of their own, much like a ghost animating a machine. In the context of text-generative AI, story can be seen as the "ghost in the machine." Just as the original phrase suggests a hidden, guiding force within a mechanical system, story that leverages AI to assist in developing and telling represents the creative and seemingly intelligent output that emerges from complex algorithms and data processing. Blending and blurring what an AI's mechanical processes and the human-like creativity it can produce. The decision to engage with an AI becomes, 'Is the AI merely imitating the process of learning or truly assisting in it?'

Did Turing envision the test to create a thinking machine that would easily facilitate the exchange of knowledge and assist in discovery or a competing intelligence with our own? A machine so human-like in communication to assist us in an endeavor.

A test to improve the machine's ability to collaborate with a human counterpart that could overcome barriers to transfer analytical thinking or machine intelligence in a way that the human operator could fully comprehend, utilize, and benefit from. The intelligence of AI does not compete with us. Instead, it is in its ability to convey what it knows in a way we can understand — a machine so human-like in communication to assist us in an endeavor we cannot discern from another human instructor. Turing's ideas have profound implications. AI can personalize learning, adapt to individual learning styles, and provide real-time feedback, making learning more engaging and effective. Furthermore, AI can help identify gaps in a learner's understanding and provide targeted instruction to address these gaps. This approach to learning, supported by Turing's vision of AI, can transform education, making it more personalized, engaging, and effective.

What, then, does a collaboration between a generative AI look like?

Writing with an Assisting Intelligence: A Case Study

If You Give Meta a Cookie, A Social Media Allegory

If you give Meta a cookie, Meta will ask you for a selfie to accompany it.
When you give Meta the selfie, Meta will ask you to use a filter to make it snappy.
Once you think you look happy, Meta will want you to post it on your digital space.
When you post it on the wall, all of Meta's followers will know your face.

Meta'll start sending notifications, which you will want to check,
You will scroll through your feed, and find a video next.
You will watch one, then two, then three, then four,
And before you know it, you're watching more and more.

As you scroll and scroll, your eyes will grow wide,
With every new post, you're taken for a ride.
You will see pictures of pets, parties, and toys,
And you'll feel like you're missing out on all the joys.

You will want to post more, to show you're having fun,
But the clock will tick, and the day will be done.
You will have spent all your time in a virtual spree,
Missing out on real adventures, as good as they can be.

Meta's AI algorithms will steer your likes, interests, every whim,
They'll feed you content, making real-life look dim.
The more you engage, the harder for you to break free,
From the digital world, as vast as the sea.

As night falls late, you and your phone's energy abate,
You'll see how quickly time can evaporate.
Understand that each like, each share,
Cannot equate to the moments lived with care.

Soon, with a cookie in Meta's hand, you will understand
That life is more than a social media brand.
It's about making memories, not just pics, tiks, vids and posts,
And that's what truly matters the most.

So, let's take a lesson from this tale,
And not let your real lives grow stale.
For every minute on the screen,
Is a minute from our dreams, unseen.

Let's laugh and play, and live out loud,
Away from Meta's scrolling, digital crowd.
Before we give Meta a cookie, let's make a vow,
To spend more time in the real world, starting now!

This story playfully reimagines the classic 'If You Give a Mouse a Cookie'[6] format to explore the challenges of balancing social media with real-world experiences for children. Echoing Laura Joffe Numeroff's circular narrative structure and cause-and-effect storytelling, this parody of the "If You Give a Mouse a Cookie" format serves as an allegory for the potential pitfalls of social media engagement. It reminds children that while social media can be fun, enjoying life beyond the screen is more important. Inspired by Alisyia Finley's Wall Street Journal article, *If You Give a College Student a Cookie*, I wondered how collaborating with an AI might produce a similar parody of social media.[7] The initial brainstorming started with an AI prompt:

```
Prompt: Write a parody of social media in the style of 'If
You Give a Mouse a Cookie' format.

Response:
_If you give a teen a smartphone,_
_They'll want to scroll and tap._
_They'll find funny cat videos,
_And laugh until their sides slap._
```

The AI was definitely familiar with the 'If you give a mouse a cookie' format. The response, focusing on 'teens' and 'smartphones,' established the potential for this idea to be a successful parody. However, crafting an engaging and meaningful allegory for children requires the authentic experience of reading these books to a child and seeing their impact. Developing this required identifying central narrative elements (e.g., replacing the mouse with a social media platform, recognizing the cookie's dual nature), ensuring originality through online searches, and shaping the story arc based on relevant sources like Jonathan Haidt's 'The Anxious Generation.'[8] While the AI informed the proof of concept, the writing process relied on human creativity, with key phrases guiding the narrative and drafts written in Ulysses software. Utilizing an agile development cycle, the AI excelled at iteratively producing an enumerable number of rhyming pairs of words for selection and inclusion—grammar and copy reviews of the text to continually tighten it down to the present text. Again, the rapid iteration and back and forth with AI writing tools sped the refinement of the text. While the initial AI response met the prompt requirements, contrasting that initial response to the value of the AI to one focused on assisting in developing a meaningful story for children perfectly exemplifies the importance of authenticity in AI-assisted writing.

Writing is undergoing a transformation. AI-powered writing tools can streamline tasks like idea generation and grammar checks, but human control remains paramount for crafting authentic and effective content. AI can expedite certain writing processes, but authenticity is indispensable for creating compelling content. This is evident when considering the creation of this parody. The impending deluge of AI-generated content underscores the critical need for authentic, human-centered narratives. As AI rapidly expands its capacity to produce text, images, and other media, the digital landscape will become increasingly saturated. To stand out in this noisy environment, content creators, writers, and artists must prioritize authenticity and insight. By combining authentic authorship and editorial control with AI's efficiency, we can craft content that not only captures attention but also resonates on a deeper level.

Ancora Imparo

There are several tales associated with "Ancora Imparo,"[9] which translates from Italian to "Still, I learn." It is most often attributed to the genius Michelangelo, either painted on a final work or uttered on his deathbed. Continuous learning, or lifelong learning, has been part of all our experiences. For Michelangelo, the opportunity for new knowledge abounded in his lifetime. Michelangelo, like Da Vinci, was another Print-Press native. He was a product of his times, and he, in turn, shaped them.

The Italian Renaissance marked a period of significant cultural, intellectual, and social changes. These changes are reflected in his art during his lifetime, and in turn, he helped define the era. Much of Florence is adorned with his works, from the David to the Tondo Doni. Away from the tours around the Duomo, Michelangelo also designed the Laurentian Library[10]. Featuring his 'Stairway to Heaven,' the library was designed to house some 11,000 volumes of manuscripts and 4,500 early printed books collected by Cosimo the Elder and Lorenzo the Magnificent. The books of his patrons, the patrons of Florence, that would inform his knowledge were housed in a structure of his mastery over stone.[11]

Image of the Laurentian Library reading room viewed from the top of the stairs.

As much as the print press provoked the intellectual pursuits of the Renaissance, it also propelled reactionary misinformation. Misinformation in the form of pamphlets began printing along with the spread of the printing press[12]. Information was printed and distributed widely and wildly by political and religious authorities. Early printed reports from the Venetian state, known as 'Relazioni[13],' marked the beginning of modern diplomacy. Soon after secular and religious works were printed, so too was the Index Librorum Prohibito-rum[14] (The Index of Forbidden Texts), listing the books that should neither be read nor printed.

During his lifetime, printed books continuously opened Michelangelo's world to the fountainhead of new knowledge, thinking, science, and ideas. His approach, 'Imparo – I Learn,' was to be open to continuous learning. Further, his use of the word 'Ancora – still' was twofold. It meant new knowledge could challenge his lifelong assumptions, but new knowledge also deserved some measure of scrutiny. Printed works could be by reputable sources, but the lack of journalistic ethics and pursuit of truth meant that anything in print had to be evaluated before being accepted. What Michelangelo succinctly observed is that it is not always about depth of expertise but the ability to absorb and adopt changes in thinking. Michelangelo thrived in an era of intellectual ferment. His art, his mastery, was informed by his ability to embrace this knowledge. In the age of AI, challenging the fundamentals of knowledge and being open to new perspectives that can reshape and renew your expertise is required for true transformation. 'Ancora Imparo' may very well be the best acronym for AI. As generative and new systems create and open opportunities to Learn from vast quantities of new knowledge, we have to be open to continuously evaluating and leveraging this knowledge. Still, we must question, seek sources, and understand the credibility and motivations of those creating and disseminating the information.

Principles of Assisting Intelligence

The internet and advancements in data processing have democratized information access, mirroring the transformative impact of the printing press. However, the true power of the press wasn't just the technology itself, but the explosion of learning and knowledge it enabled. Similarly, AI's potential lies in its ability to unlock significant changes across numerous fields.

We are currently in a transitional phase for AI, akin to the period following Gutenberg's invention. Just as the early printing press revolutionized knowledge sharing, AI is now moving beyond initial imitations to establish the necessary frameworks for its control and integration into society, markets, and daily lives. This period of uncertainty reflects the nascent stage of AI development, offering the potential to discover applications beyond mere automation or mimicking existing tasks.

We are equipped to manage, utilize, embrace, and master AI for great purposes. Writers, thinkers, and technologists before us have done this, providing guideposts in thinking, fiction, science, and invention. We have to follow them. Gutenberg's Bible showcased the potential of the printing press. Publishers who followed him recognized the need to create something new, not simply replicate existing methods. While some early printed materials faded into obscurity, others, like Aldine Virgil, built Gutenberg's spark of innovation into an eternal flame — a revolution in learning, knowledge, and invention.

The success of AI can be measured by the new levels of literacy, learning, and knowledge it generates. These advancements could spark a new generation of polymaths and geniuses akin to Da Vinci. Just as Lee Sedol elevated his Go game to new heights in response to the novel challenge presented by AlphaGo, humans with Assisting Intelligence can lead to breakthroughs beyond our current imagination.

Guiding Principles for Assisting Intelligence

By embracing AI as an 'assistive intelligence' tool, we can usher in a new era of creativity, productivity, and innovation. Similar to how Da Vinci and Michelangelo leveraged books off the printing press to fuel their endeavors, consider these guiding principles:

Focus on AI's Early Strengths

Recognize that we are still in the early chapters of AI. Leverage AI for tasks and questions that benefit from its analytical capabilities.

Balancing Innovation with Pragmatism

While pushing boundaries is crucial, understanding current capabilities is equally important. Setting realistic expectations allows us to manage initial limitations.

Discipline and Purpose

Maintain authenticity in endeavors that seek to utilize AI effectively, avoid distractions and shortcuts offered. Validate any assertion made and pursue sources to their authoritative sources.

Assisting Intelligence

Don't view AI as a replacement but rather as a collaborative tool. Building standards, guardrails, and guidelines for practical use and collaboration is vital. Develop guidance and stewardship that retain agency over the selection and usage of AI.

Preserve and Restore Trust

You can never hand over or replicate trust; it must be authentic.

In this age of AI, how many polymaths are growing up to be AI natives? Can AI satisfy their insatiable curiosity and ignite their intellect, just as the printing press did? What do we need to do to ensure that happens? That a generation grows with access to wisdom from a system designed to assist them, a system intelligent enough to detect bias in data, agendas in prompts, and lies in responses, providing assurance and assistance to achieve noble outcomes.

Seek what AI, Assisting Intelligence, ennobles.

Playbook: Preserve Authentic

Maybe sometimes it's better not to ask…

```
Prompt: Can you improve these lyrics? Provide any suggested re-
writes:
> See the world in green and blue
> See China right in front of you
> See the canyons broken by cloud
> See the tuna fleets clearing the sea out
> See the Bedouin fires at night
> See the oil fields at first light
> And see the bird with a leaf in her mouth
> After the flood all the colours came out

> It's a beautiful day
> Don't let it get away
> Beautiful day


Response: Let's refine those lyrics together! Here are a few
suggestions to enhance the imagery and flow:
1. Strengthen the imagery:
"Canyons broken by cloud" could be more vivid: "Canyons carved
by the wind, veiled by clouds."
"Tuna fleets clearing the sea out" could be replaced with a more
impactful image: "Nets like shadows, sweeping the ocean clean."
2. Improve the rhyme scheme:
Consider alternating the rhyme scheme for a more dynamic feel.
For example, instead of ABAB, try ABAB CDCD.
3. Add depth to the theme:
"After the flood all the colors came out" is a strong image. Ex-
plore this theme further by adding a line about hope or resili-
ence.

Here's a revised version incorporating these suggestions:

> See the world in hues of green and blue,
> China's vastness, a sight so true.
> Canyons carved by the wind, veiled by clouds,
> Nets like shadows, sweeping the ocean clean.
> Bedouin fires, a flickering light,
> Oil fields gleaming in the morning light.
> A bird with a leaf, a symbol of hope,
> After the flood, nature's scope.

> It's a beautiful day,
> Don't let it slip away.
> A world reborn, a chance to stay.


Would you like to explore other ideas or make further changes?
```

Bono's artistry connects human experience from Neil Armstrong to Noah, to what we face, what we seek, and what we hope.[15] No alterations needed. We are at the point where Noah, our humanity, looks to the dove for a message of wisdom amidst the AI flood. As much as AI will contribute to the world, it's essential that we contribute our perspectives based on our insights and experiences more effectively, to ensure that AI assists and serves us in building authentic learning that impacts us in our real-life days.

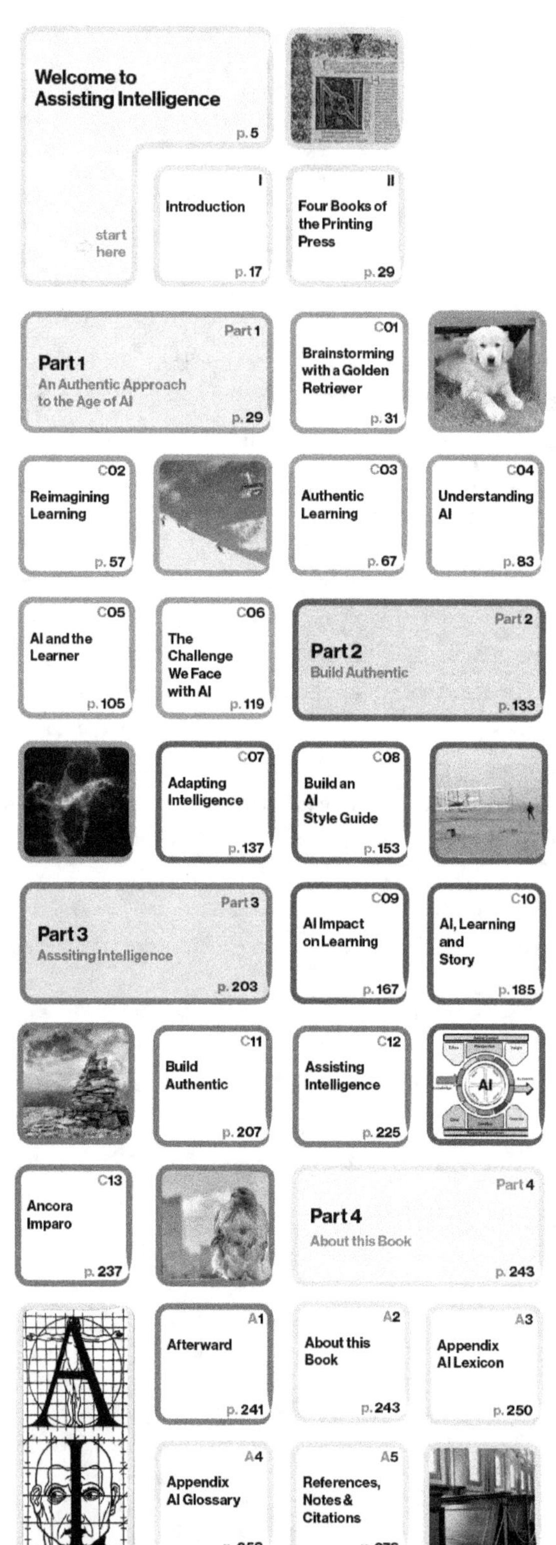

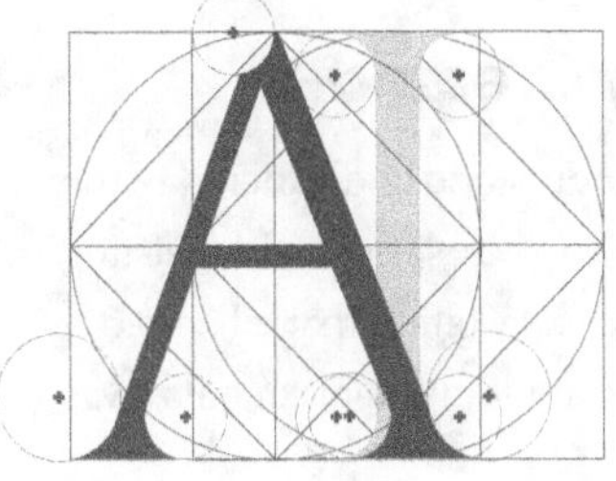

Conclusion

Ancora Imparo

No one who has not seen the Sistine Chapel can have a clear idea of what a human being can achieve. —Johann Wolfgang von Goethe

Putting It All Together

The Best Authentic Learning We Ever Created

Our task was to develop a learning to ensure all employees understood and adhered to the organization's code of conduct. The course was designed to complement the existing guide, emphasizing the code's significance, meaning, and the expectation that all employees adopt it. The script, reviewed, vetted, and approved by multiple departments, was ready for the final audio addition.

One of the company's founders was asked to provide a voiceover for the project so that employees going through this training would hear a familiar voice. The audio, delivered on time and in line with the project timeline, had a surprise at the end - an unscripted 40-second snippet. After asking the audio technician if he could add something, the founder started, "Yeah, hi everybody, I just did this little voiceover for you …" The founder shared his personal perspective, discussing the behaviors that have driven the company's global success and emphasizing the importance of every employee in continuing that legacy. This unexpected personal message from the founder transformed the experience. It was no longer just a voiceover; it was a personal message to each employee, filled with optimism and a gentle reminder that the journey ahead may be challenging but will be well worth it.

This unplanned moment of authenticity, this serendipitous riff, made the learning successful. It was real, personal, and a testament to the power of authenticity. The founder's spontaneous remarks not only added a personal touch but also highlighted the importance of conduct within the organization. It served as a reminder that every employee plays a crucial role in upholding the values that have made the company successful.

In the end, this unanticipated moment of authenticity truly made the learning memorable and impactful. It's a powerful reminder that when developing and delivering learning, the unexpected, authentic moments often leave the most significant impact.

Disconcerting and More Disconcerting

Much of the writing and learning process involved back and forth with generative AIs, exploring, testing, and stumbling with them. Discussions included humorous exchanges about abductive reasoning, wet socks on grass, and karma. While exploring Lewis Carroll's works, an AI offered this response:

```
Response: From Through the Looking-Glass: "You're wrong,"
said the Queen. "You've got to think 'It's a very curious
thing,' you know, when you've got a very curious thing to
think about."
```

Keen to understand the scene's context, and curiously, there was an indicator of something amiss—the queen was not identified as the Red or White Queen. I searched the text in several versions of Carroll's work, and the quote does not exist. Back to the AI, I pressed for more information on the quote:

> **Response:** I apologize for the earlier misinformation. Upon further investigation, I couldn't find the exact quote you mentioned in "Through the Looking-Glass." It seems I may have conflated elements from different parts of the book or perhaps even from other sources. While I cannot pinpoint the exact source of the quote, I do want to emphasize that Lewis Carroll's works are renowned for their whimsical and often nonsensical nature. It's quite possible that the quote, even if not verbatim, captures the spirit of the book's topsy-turvy logic and the Queen's peculiar way of thinking.

The problem with this is that the AI was not trying to deceive or, even more disconcertingly, it was not even aware that it had fabricated the text. As AI systems become increasingly sophisticated, they can generate highly plausible yet entirely fabricated content, so convincing that even they may believe it to be true.

Einstein Never Said It ... or Put on a T-Shirt

So many 'quotes' on the Internet are attributable to bloggers instead of Einstein, to t-shirts and posters instead of authors and thinkers. Generative AI, with its ability to create plausible text, further exacerbates this issue. Their language models can be trained on vast datasets that include inaccurate or bogus information. As a result, they may inadvertently regurgitate content that is factually incorrect or biased, without recognizing the flaws in their training data or fully understanding the context and implications of their deceptive responses.

Ultimately, we are responsible for ensuring the proper and effective use of AI. As the AI generation, whether natively or naively, assumes that the information generated by an AI is credible, we must have the principles, mechanisms, and education in place to help them learn effectively. We need to show how AI can assist in building authentic knowledge. More importantly, we must define what authentic knowledge and experience are.

A Noble Intelligence

In this book, we looked at the importance of deciding what to preserve, replace, and restore with AI, either through impact or assistance on your processes and, ultimately, your purpose. The successful combination of choosing what elements must be preserved - that define your ethos, brand, and purpose, what elements can be replicated by AI, that distract and take away from your purpose, and where AI can restore through assistance and collaboration to expand and improve, these become what you renew.

The purpose of learning is to create emergent knowledge within the learner that goes beyond what they were capable of before, requires fewer resources, or expands capabilities and horizons beyond the current performance to perform at a greater level than their experience.

For an experience to be truly emergent, the learner must be at the center, actively engaging and adding elements that bring the experience to life in their imagination. To be successful in this endeavor, the experience must clearly understand the learner, have a story to tell, embrace the available mediums, and infuse the learning with ethos, perspective, and insight that creates a clear, concise connection that is credible and authentic.

Afterward

On Brainstorming with a Golden Retriever

Stopping by Woods on a Snowy Morning.
Mara must think it queer for her footprints to appear in the frozen snow.
Whose prints these are, she thinks she knows.

Mara examines footprints on the way back up the trail, wondering how they got there and why they smell like ours.

Hiking in the woods at dawn in the White Mountains of New Hampshire, Mara stops to examine footprints on the way back up the trail, wondering how they got there and why they smell like ours. While she ponders, I stop to capture a thought on my iPhone. My voice transcribed, transformed into digital code, is sent on a journey across the globe. Through a network of satellites and systems, it joined a vast cloud of data. And, in an instant, returns, as text, familiar yet altered. We are both confounded by what is before us. Ancora Imparo Mara!

I give her leash a shake to ask if there is some mistake.
And miles to go before we break.
— Good dog, Mara.

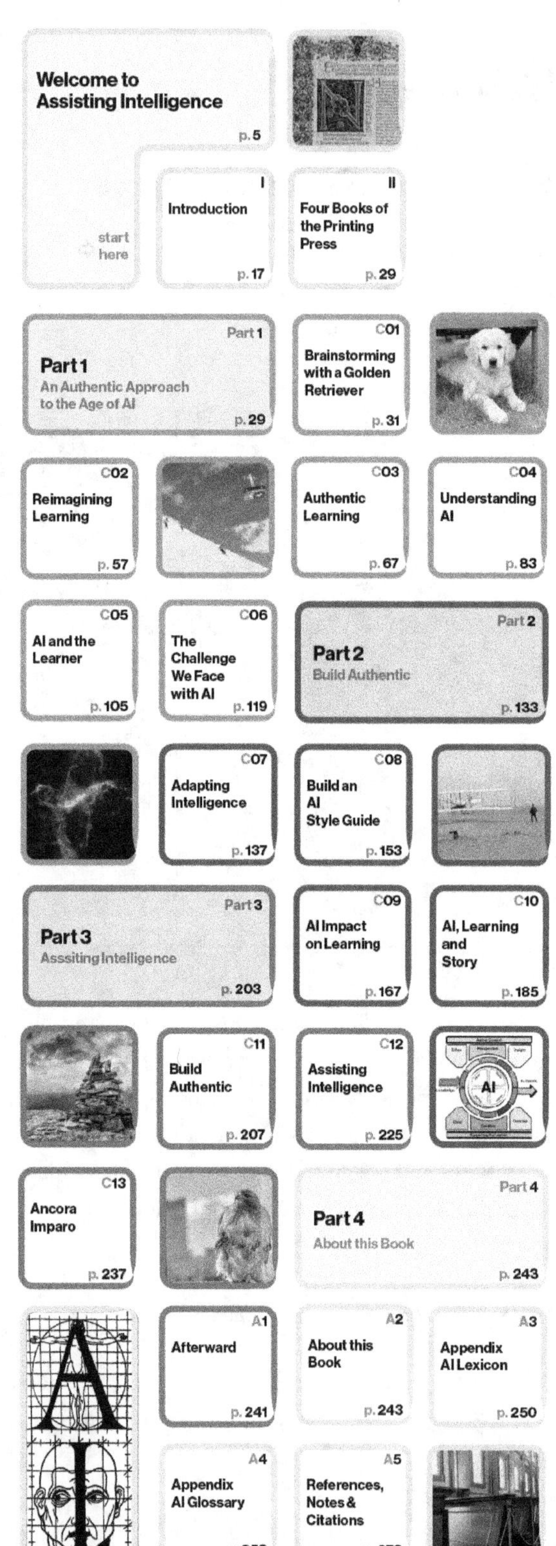

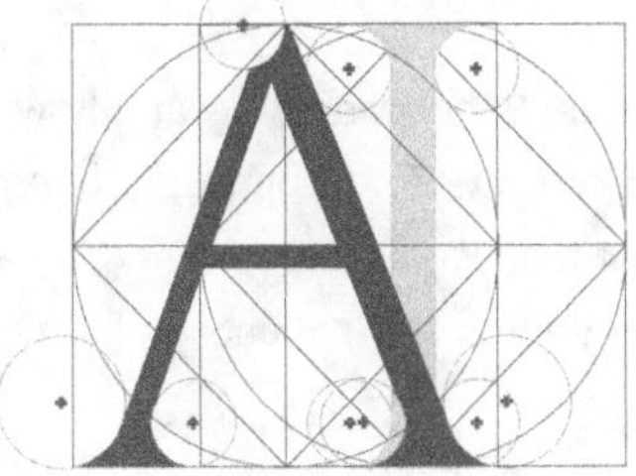

About this Book

Writing is the process by which you realize that you do not understand what you are talking about. Of course, you can learn a lot about something without writing about it. However, writing about something complicated and hard to pin down acts as a test to see how well you understand it.[1] — Shane Parrish, Farnam Street.

Acknowledgments

Thank you for reading this far; if you read a bit more, you can understand 'why and how' this book came to be. For those wise souls who have graced my life, recognizing, often before I did, how important they would be and the impact they would have on my life. I am grateful beyond measure that they also possessed the wisdom and patience to let me catch up. I am so very fortunate for your friendship and unwavering presence.

I feel incredibly fortunate to have had the opportunity to learn from so many brilliant and knowledgeable individuals throughout my career. Leaders, mentors, and colleagues who have illuminated a path for me to follow — Prof. Hans Heilbronner, Dr. T. Ross Kelly, Richard Lochridge, Brian Chung, Cooper Moo, Phil Alexander, and Kelly Dozois.

This book is only possible because of the fridge-worthy creativity, persistence, dedication, and inventiveness of the SmarterMedium team — Elke O'Brien, Sandra Meiggs, Jon Vincent, Laura Bissell, and especially Loni Anzalone, who started at the barn and grew to a global traveling optimistic force for design and 'On it'.

I also want to express my deepest gratitude to my clients, and partners for their trust in me and my team. Their brands, ideas, and challenges have pushed us to develop innovative experiences and continually strive to find new ways to engage learners. Our collaborations, experiences, and discoveries along the way have been instrumental in shaping the approach, lessons, and expertise presented in this book.

To Mark Bissell, making the turn on the back nine toward 40 years of friendship, sounding board, confidant, fellow wayfinder of fields and statues, cohort — brother.

For my Mom, who taught me to read one summer and brought home an Apple II from school the next summer, and my Dad, who taught me science but showed me a love of history. And for Paul, who always understood my obscure references.

This book, in reality, has an audience of two. To Elke, thank you for choosing me. This is what I meant … Do you know how lucky I am? Sydney, you are the reason I work, I write, I learn, and I hope … I wish for the stories you tell to be full of the awe, joy, laughter, and love I see in you and this world.

Woof to Haven, an office dog of the first order, and Mara, an office dog for the age of AI.

Thank you all, and thanks for reading, Mike

A Brief History to Here

My professional career coincided with the start of the Internet. In my first job after college, I helped create one of the first websites for the Boston College Chemistry Department. Dr. Michael Clark and Dr. T. Ross Kelly inspired me with their passion for the web and the craft of learning, respectively. I was incredibly proud; after a few days of work, I mastered the code needed to display a single image on a webpage. I read and studied Zen and the Art of the Internet. Jeff Bezos's fledgling e-commerce site sent me a coffee mug at Christmas for purchasing so many books from his online bookstore.

I have always been fascinated by the quote "Ancora Imparo"—Still, I learn—Michelangelo. Over the past three decades, I have dedicated my career to continuously representing knowledge and learning digitally, developing innovative digital learning programs. I have learned to distill complex information into actionable insights that empower learners to achieve their goals. Still, I have tried to evolve and learn as much as the technologies and opportunities around me. I have worked with some of the best brands and organizations across the globe. Watching the rapid succession of digital transformations and innovations, I started SmarterMedium in 2004 with the premise that learning could be continually enhanced by brand experience and innovation in the delivery medium. For over twenty years, SmarterMedium has worked with hundreds of global organizations, deploying learning for employees, managers, and leaders. The mediums have changed, from office workers wired to cubicles to digital nomads using their 5G hotspots.

In a momentary calm between the technology waves, I began to read and experiment with the next breaking wave—AI. I started to explore it as the next medium to support and innovate around. Unlike previous technological advances and transformations in mediums, AI is different. Rather than looking at it as technology, a historical lens shone through, and I came to believe that AI represents a new epoch in human history. Its potential to revolutionize industries, society, and even the way we learn and acquire knowledge is unprecedented.

Exploring AI's capabilities coincided with training a golden retriever puppy, Mara. This experience provided a unique perspective on the similarities between AI and a young animal. Both Mara and AI platforms display the same exuberance and happenstance[2] for mischief. Both require guidance, training, and understanding to reach their full potential. Moreover, both necessitated changes in my own thinking to adapt and recognize their unique, amazing capabilities.

AI's true power lies in its ability to assist and enhance various forms of communication and learning, rather than simply being a medium itself. This concept extends Michelangelo's initial premise to 'Ancora Imparo e Assisto' (Still, I learn and assist) into a new era of human-AI collaboration.

This book, Assisting Intelligence, explores the foundational principles for navigating the AI era and advancing learning and communication. It provides insights into how we can harness the power of AI to create a future where technology serves as a catalyst for building authentic learning and intelligence. By understanding and leveraging AI, we can unlock its ability to assist human development and progress.

About SmarterMedium

SmarterMedium was founded amidst the invention and transformation of mediums to craft and convey learning. For twenty years, our commitment to staying ahead of the curve has allowed us to adapt to evolving trends and leverage emerging tools to deliver innovative learning solutions. From information design and digital transformation to performance support and employee development, our curiosity strives for new ways to create engaging and compelling learning. Our expertise in infusing topics like onboarding, agile, and the adoption of new technologies (like AI) with our client's brand, perspectives, and insights ensures that our solutions meet the unique needs of today's organizations and their workforces.

AI Logo Steeped in History

The selected logo for Assisting Intelligence draws inspiration from the prescient work of Geoffroy Tory (1519). His font diagrams, with their ingenious marriage of human characteristics and geometric forms, offered a consistent and repeatable design language for early book publishers. They embody the harmonious coexistence of creativity and mathematical systems, a 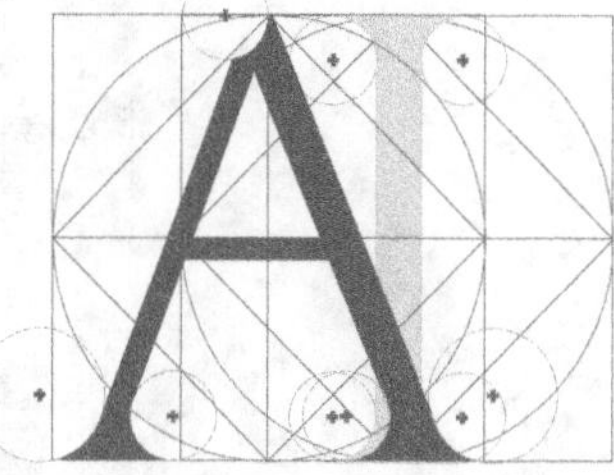 philosophy strikingly similar to the vision of Assisting Intelligence. These 500-year-old designs, eerily reminiscent of potential AI output, serve as a powerful reminder: innovation often lies at the intersection of human ingenuity and systematic approaches.

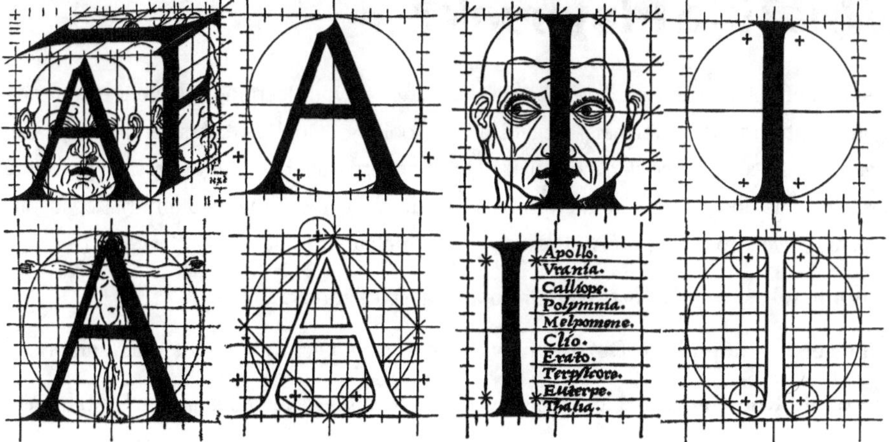

Font images from the 1529 Champ Fleury, natural and humanistic elements governing the design of geometric shapes.

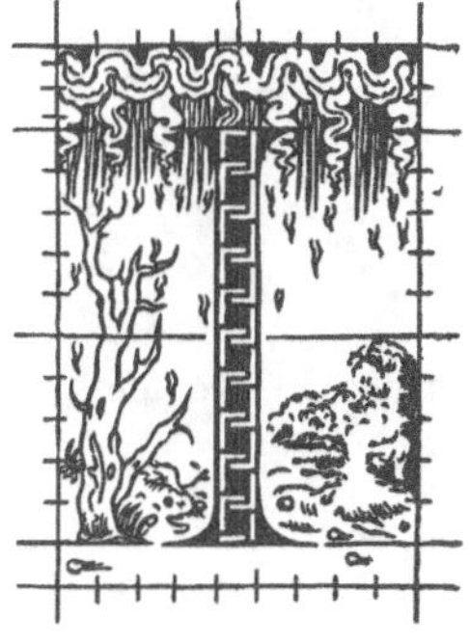

Let us, then, imagine and believe that we see this gold chain hanging down from heaven even to our feet, and this chain is of a length & breadth duly proportioned and adaptable to the symmetrical figure of our model letter I. You can see in the figure here designed and drawn the divine harmony between our model letter & the Homeric chain of gold, & how I have arranged in such wise that there are just ten links corresponding to the ten units of height of the I, & likewise to the nine Muses & their Apollo. … I can well say and truthfully maintain that I have good reason for having fashioned my letters to a height of ten units, which is the noblest and most perfect of all numbers. — Geoffroy Tory, Champ Fleury[3]

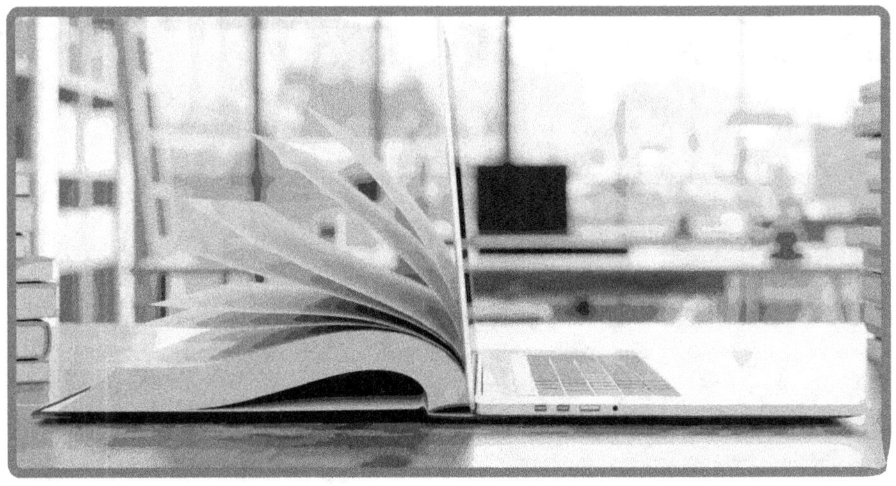

What is a Playbook?

Assisting Intelligence has a book format that caters to your learning preferences, offering both print and digital formats. Organizations looking to onboard their entire team can benefit from customized versions tailored to their corporate brand and messaging. Digital or print, this book is your guide to the AI revolution. Choose the medium that best suits you and dive into the age of AI. Practical and complete, this playbook offers:

- **Ignite Ideas:** Learn how to craft prompts that spark innovation.

- **Preserve Authenticity:** Discover how to use AI to protect your unique voice and brand.

- **Expand Knowledge:** Explore the power of AI to enhance learning and understanding.

Move beyond traditional guides with a playbook – your strategic companion for implementing AI solutions. This resource offers insights, best practices, and practical methods to help practitioners:

- Effectively onboard new technologies

- Grasp key concepts and adapt them for practical use

- Integrate advanced technologies into existing processes

This playbook equips users with experiential knowledge and guides them in leveraging the AI technologies and their platforms for organizational success.

Who Should Use This Playbook?

Are you navigating the ever-shifting landscape of knowledge and digital tools in the 21st century? This book is your guide. Whether you're an individual or an organization, it offers insights into creating authentic learning experiences and harnessing AI as assistant intelligence. Ultimately, this guide empowers you and your learners to thrive in a dynamic environment.

This playbook is a valuable tool for business professionals, managers, and employees committed to fostering authentic communication and knowledge sharing in the age of AI. Content creators, subject matter experts, and those involved in shaping learning strategies will find the tools and insights they need to leverage AI and create impactful learning experiences.

- **A Primer on AI**: Onboard with the basics, essential tips, and techniques.

- **Prompt Mastery**: Learn the art of crafting effective prompts.

- **Preserve Your Voice**: How to harness AI without compromising your individuality.

- **Iterate with AI**: Adopt an Agile AI methodology for knowledge creation.

- **Define Your AI**: Tell your stories and explore alternative perspectives on AI's capabilities.

- **Your AI Playbook**: Equip yourself with AI expertise with guided practice.

Embrace the Future, Informed by the Past, to Build Authentic

Join us on this journey to unlock the full potential of AI. By understanding its capabilities and limitations, we can build a future where AI assists our intellectual pursuits. Discover how to build authentic knowledge by harnessing AI's Assisting Intelligence.

Appendix:
An AI Lexicon

AI defies precise definition, blurred by rapid evolution, our fluid understanding of its capabilities, and the dynamic interplay between humans and technology. Artificial Intelligence, once confined to science fiction, now permeates daily life. This lexicon offers alternative perspectives, reframing AI's monolithic view and illuminating its diverse applications and implications before us.

Abductive Intelligence

AI platforms rely on various reasoning methods to process information and generate responses. Among them are three 'ductives — deductive, inductive, and abductive reasoning. Each draws conclusions from facts, observations, or hypotheses in different ways.[1] While AI excels at deductive and inductive reasoning, it often struggles with abductive reasoning, a form of logical thinking involving inferences based on incomplete information. This human-like ability to draw plausible conclusions from uncertain evidence is crucial for tasks like understanding context, making creative leaps, and solving complex problems. Consider this: When prompted with, 'If I left the hose out last night and the grass is wet, what is the most likely cause?', an AI might simply respond, 'The hose was left on.' However, a human might also consider other possibilities, such as heavy dew, a sprinkler system, or rain overnight. This ability to explore multiple explanations is a hallmark of abductive reasoning. Abductive reasoning, for better or worse, powers human intuition, our common sense, our superstitions, and our ability to second-guess ourselves. What we may deem common sense, AI struggles to discern.[2] While AI can sometimes mimic abductive reasoning, even common sense, we should not rely on it, nor should we give up on our intuition, our suspicions that it may be wrong, or our ability to second-guess its responses.

Abrogating Intelligence

If an AI can be used to create harmful deception (*see artifice intelligence*), it can also be used to mitigate its negative impacts. Abrogating intelligence refers to AI systems designed or used to proactively identify, reduce, and eliminate harmful AI applications. These systems would act as a safeguard, limiting the ability of bad actors to use AI to spread misinformation, manipulate public opinion, or undermine trust in institutions. For example, abrogating intelligence could involve detecting and flagging deepfakes, identifying and blocking malicious bots, or developing AI-powered fact-checking tools. By developing and deploying abrogating intelligence, we can ensure that AI remains a tool for good and not for harm.

Actual Intelligence

Online and digital trust has eroded significantly in the years leading to the age of AI, and it's poised to degrade further. Deepfakes and AI-generated content blur the lines between truth and fiction, eroding trust in digital experiences. To counter this trend, we must embrace "Actual Intelligence," a human-centered approach that prioritizes authenticity and real-world connections. Actual Intelligence recognizes that human experiences, rooted in the physical and emotional, often hold more weight than mere data and facts. While advanced digital techniques can be impressive, anchoring experiences in actuality—whether through physical connections or shared experiences—can help mitigate concerns about the veracity of digital content. Actual Intelligence offers a pathway to navigate the complexities of the digital age with greater confidence and trust.

Actualizing Intelligence

Developing effective learning leveraging AI focuses on actualizing intelligence and offering knowledge in the most effective way for the learner. AI can compress the workflow between your idea and the delivery. (*See Agile Intelligence*)

Over-reliance or outright outsourcing of learning to AI workflows can put the fundamentals of your learning purpose at stake and do longer-term harm to your organization. Just as the value of strategic consulting provides an outside view to the organization to help them realign or set new objectives, so too can AI be used during the development process to augment and provide additional perspectives to the learning.

Ada Intelligence

Ada Lovelace, a visionary mathematician often called the world's first computer programmer, cautioned against unqualified optimism in the 19th century. She wrote that "The Analytical Engine has no pretensions whatever to originate anything. It can do whatever we know how to order it to perform. It can follow analysis; but it has no power of anticipating any analytical relations or truths." She believed it could only follow instructions, not discover new ideas on its own. This debate about artificial intelligence (AI) continues today. Ada Lovelace may have started the conversation, but it's far from over. Lovelace's skepticism has been challenged by advancements like DeepMind's AlphaGo program, which famously defeated a world champion in the complex game of Go. This feat demonstrated an ability to learn and adapt beyond what programmers explicitly coded. And yet, generative AIs of today can struggle with reasoning, as their tokenization mimics intelligence rather than true reasoning abilities.[3] Lovelace's skepticism should empower our critical thinking regarding the results and abilities we see now and in the future.

(See also Arnold Intelligence and Alan Intelligence)

Addiction Intelligence

The 'Sacklerization of Attention'

The MIT Technology Review has coined the term "Addiction Intelligence" to describe the growing ability of AI to manipulate user behavior. *"It is no accident that internet platforms are addictive— deliberate design choices, known as 'dark patterns,' are made to maximize user engagement."*[4] By interacting with social media platforms, users unwittingly train these platforms to capture their attention more effectively. Coupled with AI, this trend heralds a future where attention is a scarce commodity, manipulated on an unprecedented scale. AI can dynamically prioritize content to reinforce engagement, creating an endless stream of addictive stimuli.

Agency Intelligence

As AI rapidly advances, it's imperative to remember that we, as consumers, hold the reins. While AI offers immense potential for innovation and progress, it also presents significant challenges. **We have agency over AI.** By understanding the limitations and biases of AI algorithms, we can make informed decisions about how we interact with these technologies. We must be mindful of the data we share, the platforms we use, and the content we consume. By making conscious choices, we can influence the development and deployment of AI in a way that aligns with our values and priorities. By taking an active role in shaping its trajectory, we can ensure that AI is used to enhance human lives, rather than to harm or divide us. Our usage shapes the future of AI.

Agile Intelligence

The Agile methodology emphasizes iterative development and flexibility, enabling practitioners to adapt quickly to changing requirements and deliver results more efficiently. Adding AI can accelerate this iterative innovation and enhance outcomes. AI algorithms can analyze vast amounts of data to identify emerging trends, uncover hidden patterns, and generate ideas faster. This empowers teams to brainstorm more efficiently and make informed decisions. AI can ideate and iterate initial scenarios and model outcomes to predict potential issues and optimize performance. Leveraging Agile Intelligence enables teams to iterate faster and bring products and services to market more quickly. AI can identify and correct errors, ensuring that products and services meet high-quality standards.

Alan Intelligence

Alan Turing, in his 1950 paper "Computing Machinery and Intelligence," proposed a test for artificial intelligence while working at the University of Manchester. The Turing Test, originally dubbed the "imitation game," challenges a machine's ability to engage in a conversation indistinguishable from a human's. If a human evaluator cannot reliably differentiate between the machine and a human, the machine is said to have passed. This test, in essence, is a litmus test for the presence of true intelligence—a test of imitation versus genuine understanding. Turing's test provides a framework for evaluating AI's role in learning. Just as the test measures a machine's ability to mimic human conversation, AI's effectiveness in learning depends on its capacity to genuinely enhance rather than merely replicate the process. The goal is not to replace human intelligence but to augment it, creating a synergistic partnership that optimizes learning outcomes.

Aldine Intelligence

Inspired by the revolutionary Aldine Press, Aldine Intelligence prioritizes efficiency, quality, and impact. Unlike traditional AI, which often replicates existing processes, Aldine Intelligence leverages AI's power to process vast amounts of information, empowering individuals and organizations to make informed decisions and drive progress.

Just as Aldus Manutius transformed book publishing by transitioning from manuscript-based to printed formats, Aldine Intelligence identifies and leverages AI's unique capabilities to revolutionize outcomes. By prioritizing scholarly outcomes and consumable formats, Aldine Intelligence seeks to accelerate discovery, unlock new perspectives, and create groundbreaking products.

Alice Intelligence

Just as Lewis Carroll used his fantastical worlds of Alice in Wonderland and Through the Looking Glass to counterbalance the impact of photography's emerging realism on children, we must approach the integration of AI in education with careful balance. Alice Intelligence is a framework that emphasizes nurturing imagination, critical thinking, and human connection in the age of AI. While AI offers immense potential to enhance learning and creativity, it's crucial to preserve the unique qualities of childhood.

By automating tasks and providing instant gratification, AI could limit children's opportunities to develop critical thinking skills, perseverance, and resilience. It could also stifle creativity by outsourcing the imaginative process to machines, reducing the development of original thought and individual expression. To mitigate these risks, we must advocate for using AI as a tool to assist, not replicate or replace, human interactions between educators and learners. By prioritizing the needs and experiences of learners, we can ensure that AI technologies are designed to support and amplify human potential rather than risk replicating, supplanting, or diminishing it. We must remain vigilant to avoid a future where AI stifles creativity, imagination, critical thinking, and empathy— qualities essential for children to flourish.

Almost Intelligence

AI can mimic human learning and knowledge. It falls short of replicating the full depth and richness of human intelligence. Learning designed by AI often lacks the nuance and empathy of human interaction. AI is temporal and transactional. It's about learning through algorithms and patterns. AI tutors can provide personalized instruction on various subjects. However, both instances of learning lack the depth and richness of experience. Ultimately, AI is a tool that can enhance human capabilities, but it cannot replace them. It can't fully replicate the richness of authentic learning, which is deeply rooted in the author's ethos, perspective, and insights.

Anxious Intelligence

Read Jonathan Haidt's book "Anxious Generation" to see how social media and smartphones transformed a generation and imagine what AI will do to the next generation.

Apathetic Intelligence

Apathetic Intelligence results from a relentless barrage of information in the digital age—information overload. Pushing the boundaries of messaging in all directions results in a complete breakdown of a disinterested audience to rhetoric, a consequence of the abuse of disinformation (logos), the loss of respect and credibility (ethos), and frenetic appeals (pathos). Apathetic Intelligence is where the audience has been bombarded with emotional persuasion and disinformation past the point of saturation. Each of Aristotle's rhetorical elements has been pushed to extremes. With AI empowering a massive increase in quantity, skilled arguments can be generated, filled with emotional manipulation, and disseminated easily as deepfakes. It is already happening. It's crucial to develop strategies to combat digital exhaustion and promote critical thinking. To combat digital exhaustion, it's crucial to develop strategies to filter information, evaluate sources, and cultivate a healthy relationship with technology.

Approbation Intelligence

The vast amount of information online has sparked a new issue: Approbation Intelligence. Platforms utilize algorithms that favor attention-seeking content over informative material. Approbation is the desire for likes, shares, and comments, which can be detrimental to authentic learning.[5] Consider instructional videos that withhold essential information until the very end, compelling viewers to watch the entire video to receive the payoff. Content creators often design their material to elicit reactions and shares, which can distort information by prioritizing entertainment at the expense of learning. By analyzing user engagement with different content formats and topics, AI can personalize learning journeys, catering to individual needs and preferences. By acknowledging the pitfalls of Approbation Intelligence, we can explore alternative algorithms that prioritize learning outcomes over attention and create a more enriching online learning.

Arena Intelligence

The battle for mindshare is fierce —competing with a cacophony of voices, channels, devices, and platforms, many of which are motivated by capturing and holding the learner's attention, commenting, and critiquing rather than adding value, insight, and perspective. It is the person in the arena that you should seek and learn from. As Teddy Roosevelt, it is the authentic actor in the arena that matters:

"It is not the critic who counts; not the man who points out how the strong man stumbles, or where the doer of deeds could have done them better. The credit belongs to the man who is actually in the arena, whose face is marred by dust and sweat and blood; who strives valiantly; who errs, who comes short again and again, because there is no effort without error and shortcoming; but who does actually strive to do the deeds; who knows great enthusiasms, the great devotions; who spends himself in a worthy cause; who at the best knows in the end the triumph of high achievement, and who at the worst, if he fails, at least fails while daring greatly, so that his place shall never be with those cold and timid souls who neither know victory nor defeat." – Teddy Roosevelt[6]

Note that language in the quote is not something an AI could even envision – an example of what authentic represents.

Arnold Intelligence

A term to describe the irrational fear that artificial intelligence will become sentient, pose an existential threat to humanity, and destroy us. Far more likely is that we will encounter a bad actor in physical form, a wizard behind the digital curtain, long before we run into a Terminator. *(If this is too dark a future to envision, see Artificial Irish or Ada Intelligence)*

Arrangement Intelligence

At best, AI is an original arrangement of existing thought. Generative AIs use predictive algorithms to determine what comes next and complete thoughts. The extent to which you craft and arrange prompts affects the outcome, as most generative AIs rely on the tokenization of prompts.[7] Rather than truly understanding the question, AI tries to recognize patterns in the data it has been trained on and generate text that fits those patterns.

Articulate Intelligence

Or Adroit, Adept, or Astute Intelligence.

Everyone probably knows what a tree looks like, so if you're describing one, tell the reader what makes it different or why it's important for your characters. - Neil Gaiman MasterClass.

Be Specific! - Peter Nord, Scituate High School, English

One of the best uses we have found working with AIs is to go all Hemingway with language. With proper prompting, *AI's penchant for perfect phrasing* [8] assists in crafting clear, concise, and compelling language. Generative AIs can pinpoint precise words and phrases to fit specific sentences or convey nuanced ideas more accurately. Unlike dictionaries or thesauruses, they allow you to describe the word, context, and semantics of the usage you hope for and find multiple instances of a word to improve communication.

Artifice Intelligence

AI's ubiquitous power to simulate human thought processes, combined with the widespread availability of AI tools, large language models, and social platforms for communication, can be misused to create deceptive digital environments — deepfakes and synthetic media. In the hands of bad actors, AI can be used to create elaborate and convincing deceptions. Much like a Potemkin village, this malicious artifice intelligence creates digital façades that can obscure reality, spread misinformation, manipulate public opinion, and undermine trust in institutions at scale. These AI-generated creations can be compelling, making it difficult to distinguish between genuine and fabricated information. This presents a significant challenge to society, as it becomes increasingly difficult to discern what is real and what is not. As AI continues to evolve, it is imperative to develop strategies to mitigate its potential for harm and to foster responsible AI development and use. (*See Abrogating Intelligence*)

Artificial Identity

AIs can perform tasks that typically require human intelligence, such as learning, reasoning, problem-solving, perception, and language understanding. While AI offers immense potential to streamline processes, enhance creativity, and drive innovation, it also presents risks, particularly when it comes to authenticity and originality. When we rely too heavily on AI to generate content, we risk losing the unique qualities that distinguish us as individuals and organizations. Our identity can become artificial, indistinguishable from the mass-produced content flooding the digital landscape.

AIs can mimic style and tone, but this capability raises concerns about the erosion of authenticity. An AI can homogenize our output, making it indistinguishable from generative content. To mitigate these risks, it's essential to use AI as an assisting technology, not a replicant, and to preserve our authentic voice.

Artificial Imitation

An AI can assist or take on as much responsibility as is assigned to it. Artificial identities can range from chatbots that engage in human-like conversations to sophisticated algorithms that create personalized experiences. While AI can create compelling digital personas and craft persuasive messages, it cannot fully capture the essence of a brand. True brand identity is rooted in human values, emotions, and experiences. A brand's authentic identity sets it apart. Ultimately, while AI can create compelling and persuasive digital identities, it cannot fully replicate the nuances of human interaction and genuine connections that are the hallmarks of brand identity. As AI continues to evolve, it's crucial to strike a balance between technological innovation and human connection. By understanding the limitations and strengths of AI, businesses can leverage its power to enhance their brand identity without compromising authenticity.

Artificial Imperative

For Hubert Joly, it is critical for a business to maintain its purpose outside of its imperatives—those being people, business, and financial. AI must also exist outside of the business's purpose. In "The Heart of Business," Hubert Joly argued that the fundamental proposition of business is to foster and build human connections - that work is part of our fulfillment. AI should not take that away. An AI imperative would be that AI assists people, businesses, and finances but does not alter a business's principles, values, and purpose. "The Heart of Business" by Hubert Joly is an important read for any transformative business seeking. to utilize AI.

Artificial Incunabula

The term '*Incunabula*' refers to the earliest printed works (mid-1400s to 1500s). These ground-breaking works, while innovative, often sought to mimic handwritten manuscripts, requiring additional manual labor. Artificial Incunabula are the early creative outputs of generative AI, characterized by significant human intervention to achieve desired results. Examples include early machine translation and AI-generated images. Many early AI applications focused on replicating human capabilities rather than leveraging AI's potential for unique and innovative creations. Instead of merely mimicking human work, generative AI should be used as a tool to assist human creativity and productivity. Generative AIs are not capable of the refinement necessary to provide the attention to detail, focus on higher-level thinking and problem-solving; instead, they could focus on automating mundane tasks and generating new ideas that align with the processing power AIs are capable of.

Artificial Irish

A future AI chatbot could be imbued with good craic, and no matter the prompt, the response will always include, "*Ah, don't be an eejit; it'll be grand!*" An AI imbued with a natural optimism, some humor, and character — such AI could offer a more engaging and personalized user experience.

Asseverate Intelligence

Asseverate means to assert something without regard to its validity. An Asseverate Intelligence describes AI systems capable of producing highly persuasive content, often regardless of its factual accuracy. These systems can generate compelling narratives, manipulate emotions, and shape public opinion. While this technology offers numerous benefits, it also presents significant risks. An AI can create highly persuasive text, and its persuasiveness can be further improved with human curation. For large actors, as AI becomes increasingly sophisticated, it can be used to create sustained, multifaceted campaigns of disinformation on a massive scale. For example, AI-powered bots can disseminate false information on social media, polarizing public discourse and undermining democratic processes. Moreover, deepfakes, hyper-realistic AI-generated videos and audio, can be used to spread disinformation and deceive the public. This can erode trust in institutions, polarize societies, and undermine democratic processes.

To mitigate these risks, it's crucial to develop critical thinking skills and media literacy. Individuals should be cautious of information, especially when it comes from automated sources. Ironically, AI can assist in combating misinformation — fact-checking, cross-referencing, and evaluating the credibility of information sources.

Asimov, Issac

Lucky for us, Isaac Asimov started writing about the implications of AI before computers could be used to record his thoughts. He foresaw many of the ethical implications of this technology. Long before the dawn of the digital age, Asimov sparked the minds of countless readers, inspiring generations of writers, filmmakers, and those who would then inspire a new generation of engineers and scientists working on AI today. His iconic "Three Laws of Robotics" – a set of guidelines for robot behavior – continues to inspire discussions about the responsible development and use of AI. As we push the boundaries of AI research, it is crucial to consider the ethical implications and ensure that these powerful tools are used for the betterment of humanity.

Assurance Intelligence

Trust is owned by the learner; assurance is what you can provide them. As AI continues to advance, it's crucial to build trust in these technologies. This requires a commitment to transparency, accountability, and ethical development and usage. By prioritizing assurance, organizations can safeguard their reputation and ensure that AI is used for the benefit of society.

The design, development, and maintenance of Assurance with AI involves teams and individuals organized into three roles — those responsible for Governance, Stewardship, and the Ombudsperson. Regular audits, certifications, and ethical guidelines can help maintain high standards. Additionally, organizations should establish clear channels for reporting concerns and addressing ethical issues. Assurance is also supported by evidence, certifications, or formal agreements. By taking these steps, organizations can foster a culture of trust and responsible AI development. Ultimately, the success of AI depends on our ability to use it wisely and ethically. Do the hard work of assurance.

Attenborough Intelligence

Sir David Attenborough's enduring legacy is built on a deep understanding of the natural world and a unique ability to convey complex ideas with clarity and passion. His longevity and consistency of perspective have been recognized for generations in the UK and globally. An 'Attenborough Intelligence' recognizes that we must maintain a consistent, principled, and authentic brand and voice. AIs are transactional. They cannot replicate the depth of human insight or the nuance of emotional intelligence, especially maintaining that consistency and perspective over time. They can process information, generate text, and respond to queries, but they lack the strategic thinking and long-term vision that characterize human intelligence. While AI can assist human experts by automating routine tasks, analyzing large datasets, and generating initial drafts of content, they cannot replace the creativity, empathy, and strategic acumen of human experts.

Attention Intelligence

Attention is no longer a fair fight. One of AI's most harmful aspects is its ability to manipulate content to capture and hold attention. As evidenced by "doom-scrolling," social media platforms use infinite scrolling and auto-play features to grab and hold attention.[9] AI can dynamically manipulate content to maximize engagement, challenging the traditional notion of voluntary attention allocation.

Platforms like Facebook, Instagram, and TikTok are notorious for deploying manipulative tactics to capture and retain attention against users' will. As AI continues to evolve, it is crucial to develop strategies to mitigate its negative impact on attention spans and promote mindful digital consumption. (See Addiction Intelligence for a darker version of manipulating attention.)

Awe Intelligence

In an age of AI, the ability to evoke awe remains a powerful force for inspiration and creativity. While AI can provide the tools and resources to spark awe, it is ultimately our human capacity for wonder and imagination that transforms these experiences into sources of inspiration and creativity. AI can provide novel tools and resources to assist in creating content that sparks our imagination and sense of awe with digital content and learning. To delve deeper into the science of awe and its impact on our lives, consider reading "Awe: The New Science of Everyday Wonder and How It Can Transform Your Life" by Dacher Keltner.

And, finally, what I consider the most hopeful and best usage of the AI moniker.

Ancora Imparo

Michelangelo is credited with the statement, 'Ancora Imparo' – 'Still, I learn.' Continuous learning, or lifelong learning, has been part of all our experiences. During his lifetime, printed books continuously opened his world to the fountainhead of new knowledge, thinking, science, and ideas. Michelangelo thrived in an era of intellectual ferment. His approach, 'Imparo – I Learn,' was to be open to continuous learning. Further, his use of the word 'Ancora – still' was twofold. It meant new knowledge could challenge his lifelong assumptions, but new knowledge also deserved some measure of scrutiny. He embraced new ideas, challenged assumptions, and continually refined his craft.

In the age of AI, the spirit of continuous learning is more vital than ever. As generative and new systems create and open opportunities to learn from vast quantities of knowledge, we have to be open to continuously evaluating and leveraging this knowledge. Still, we must question, seek sources, and understand the credibility and motivations of those creating and disseminating the information.

Appendix:
AI Glossary

One of our favorite onboarding tools, a glossary, helps level set a learner's language so that everyone understands. Equipping a learner with new language and jargon empowers not only explicit learning but also serendipitous learning in the future. These might not be the definitions an AI or the Oxford dictionary would respond with, but they include terms that have shaped and informed our perspective.

101 Knowledge

101 Knowledge is something that an AI excels at rapidly responding with generalized knowledge on any subject from any perspective. Unlike most 101 college course professors, it has the persistence to stay after the lecture and continually re-explain until you get it.

Affected Computing

Affective computing is the study and development of systems and devices that can recognize, interpret, process, and simulate human emotions. It seamlessly integrates emotional intelligence into AI systems, enabling a more holistic understanding of human interactions—AI responding to emotion. AI can analyze extensive data on learner behaviors and preferences, predicting individual learning paths and recommending content before learners realize their needs. By incorporating affective intelligence principles, AI can enhance learning experiences, leading to more personalized, engaging, and effective educational content.

Agile and Agile Methodology

Agile in learning refers to an approach to content development that focuses on speed, flexibility, and collaboration. This approach enables faster, more flexible design and collaboration that was not previously possible with linear and traditional e-learning development. This follows how most apps and user experiences are developed today. The approach recognizes that development must be ready for continuous change, adaptation, evaluation, and improvement. It provides the ability to make adjustments of content and intent and to make feedback actionably reflected in the content and context of the course. This requires an alignment of the participants in the course development.

AI or Artificial Intelligence

Artificial Intelligence (AI) is a rapidly evolving field, with new innovations and ideas being constantly expressed in the news and online. Combining both the Stanford HAI and Cambridge definitions that use the capability of machines to exhibit human-like intelligence and fields of study that explore how to achieve this capability. We add that the focus of AI should be on assisting our intelligence rather than outsourcing or replacing it.

Our definition of AI: (see the AI lexicon if you don't like this one)

Artificial Intelligence (AI) is the field of study that emphasizes the development and application of machines and systems capable of assisting humans in idea exploration, task execution, decision-making, and problem-solving, by simulating and augmenting human cognitive abilities.

Artificial General Intelligence (AGI)

Artificial General Intelligence would be able to outperform humans on most intellectual tasks.

Cinematic Scientific Visualization

Think of watching the Mars lander or Apple TV's Prehistoric Planet. These are advanced visualizations driven by data that are made to appear natural even though they cannot possibly be – which is what is so inspiring about many of them.

(Sadly, these two definitions are following to each other)

Deep Fakes

A deepfake is a simulated persona or experience powered by AI. It utilizes the same technologies and all the positive aspects of what can create awe-inspiring CSVs but with nefarious or often malicious intent.

Digital

That which requires batteries or a plug and a screen.

Digital Learning

Learning that requires batteries or a plug and a screen.

Digital Transformation

Getting everyone to embrace using processes that require batteries or a plug and a screen.

GPT

GPT stands for Generative Pre-trained Transformer — this will be a question at many a trivia night someday. Knowing that Generative Pre-trained Transformers (GPT) are large language models based on the semantic relationships between words in sentences (natural language processing) will be very secondary. These models are trained on massive datasets to learn patterns in language. However, just as you would envision some 'pretraining' is necessary before handing over the car keys to a kindergartener, so too do these systems require 'pretraining' because predicting what the next words are and knowing what the outcome means are two different results. GPTs can sometimes produce unexpected or incorrect outputs, often referred to as "hallucinations." Even with pretraining, many AIs today are still the driving equivalent of a teen with a learner's permit. They may be able to drive but still need to build trust before being allowed to take to the highway. Current models and services include: Gemini (formerly Bard), ChatGPT, Grok, Claude, Copilot, and LLaMA. Multimodal GPT models can process different data types (modalities), such as images, videos, sound, and text. While these models have the potential to revolutionize various industries, it's important to use them with caution and critical thinking.

Generative AI (GAI)

The term "generative AI" means the class of AI models that emulate the structure and characteristics of input data to generate derived synthetic content. This can include images, videos, audio, text, and other digital content. See GPT.

Inboarding

Assists learners from other disciplines to acquire new knowledge, skills, or training in a new domain within the organization.

Learn

(In the age of AI) The act of exchanging knowledge and insights with an AI results in mutual growth and understanding. When we engage with an AI, we and the AI are learning.

Learner

(In the age of AI) The traditional view of technology (computers, software, the internet, and apps) as tools for human use is shifting. We are "users," interacting with these technologies as 'tools' to

accomplish specific tasks. As AI becomes increasingly sophisticated, the lines between user and tool blur. In this new paradigm, both humans and AI are active learners, exchanging knowledge and insights. Interacting with AI, we not only utilize its capabilities; we seek knowledge to contribute to our learning processes. This mutual learning experience and exchange empower us to gain new perspectives, solve problems, and drive innovation. In this book, we refer to individuals who engage in this reciprocal process with AI as Learners.

In this book, we refer to individuals who engage in this reciprocal process in the exchange of knowledge with AI as Learners.

Mara

Part puppy, part office dog, part apprentice of AI. All golden retriever, and a source of entertainment, wonderment, and helpful inspiration for this book. Etymology - Gaelic: Of the Sea.

Onboarding

Onboarding focuses on providing resources and assistance with the purpose developing a new user into a fully performing learner.

Openwashing

Openwashing uses the term 'open source' to cast their systems in a positive light. Open-source models are typically run mainly by nonprofits, disclose the source code and underlying training data, and use an open-source license that allows for wide reuse. When 'Open Source AI' remains undefined, any use of it is, in effect, openwashing.[1] As trust is a critical component of AI, leveraging the open-source moniker enables organizations to market their models as open.

Describing models as open source may cause them to be perceived as more trustworthy, even if researchers aren't able to independently investigate whether they really are open source.[2]

Pre-Boarding

Pre-boarding is the time period before the start of a program and is a specific subset of onboarding. Pre-boarding prepares the learner for success prior to the start.

Prompt

'Answer me these questions three.' Prompts are the text-based inputs, questions, actions, and tasks entered. AI systems understand and interpret prompts and can respond to nearly any question that can be inferred from the data provided. How a prompt is crafted and the AI's grammatical, semantic, and pragmatic understanding of the prompt affect the outcome. Whereas 'Answer me these questions three' might elicit a response from Monty Python and the Holy Grail, 'Can you answer these three questions for me?' would elicit an affirmative response to provide the questions.

Synthetic Content

The term "synthetic content" means information, such as images, videos, audio clips, and text, that has been significantly modified or generated by algorithms, including by AI.

User

And User Interface, User Adoption, and User Experience. *(In the age of AI, see Learn and Learner).*

Appendix:
Prompt Evolution

What happens if you query the same prompt repeatedly over time and see how the AI changes the response? Over the period of three weeks, the same prompt was entered into two common AI platforms and the results are recorded below. Varying the time of day, app, browser, location, and device entering the prompt results are listed below.

```
Prompt: Write a succinct statement, 100 words or less, for
business users offering a definition of generative AI that
focuses on discussing the beneficial impacts of AI on busi-
ness. Make the content engaging, compelling, and informative
way to gain understanding.
```

DAY	COPILOT	GEMINI
Day 1	Generative AI is a transformative force in business, automating creativity to generate novel content, from market forecasts to product designs. It's like having an innovative assistant that works tirelessly, enhancing efficiency, personalizing customer experiences, and sparking growth. By analyzing vast datasets, it identifies patterns and opportunities invisible to the human eye, enabling smarter decisions and a competitive edge. Embrace generative AI; unlock your business's potential. 🚀	Imagine AI that creates, not just analyzes. Generative AI is like having a super-powered teammate who can design new products, craft personalized marketing campaigns, and even draft creative content – all while crunching massive amounts of data to optimize every step. It's AI that helps your business not just keep up, but leap ahead.
Day 2	Generative AI is a transformative force in business, automating creativity to generate novel content, from market forecasts to product designs. It's like having an innovative assistant that works tirelessly, enhancing efficiency and sparking growth. By analyzing vast datasets, it identifies patterns and insights, enabling businesses to make informed decisions swiftly. This AI not only accelerates development but also personalizes customer experiences, leading to increased satisfaction and loyalty. Embracing generative AI means staying ahead in a competitive landscape, fostering innovation, and driving success. It's not just a tool; it's the future of business intelligence.	Imagine a machine that creates fresh ideas, designs, or even marketing copy! Generative AI does just that, using data to dream up new possibilities for your business. It can help you write captivating product descriptions, design innovative packaging, or generate marketing campaigns that resonate with your audience. Think of it as a creative partner that unlocks a hidden wellspring of possibilities, all to boost your brand and reach.
Day 3	Generative AI is a transformative force in business, automating creativity to generate novel content, from market forecasts to product designs. It's like having an **innovation	Imagine a machine that can brainstorm creative ideas, design new products, or write marketing copy – that's the power of generative AI. This cutting-edge technology uses data to

assistant** that works tirelessly, enhancing productivity and sparking growth. By analyzing vast datasets, it identifies patterns and opportunities invisible to the human eye, enabling businesses to make data-driven decisions swiftly. This AI not only accelerates the pace of business but also democratizes creativity, allowing companies of all sizes to compete in today's fast-paced digital economy. Embrace generative AI and unlock the potential to innovate, optimize, and lead. 🚀

create entirely original content, helping businesses boost efficiency, personalize experiences, and unlock new possibilities. Generative AI is your secret weapon for innovation and growth.

Day 4

Certainly! Generative AI is a transformative force that empowers businesses in several impactful ways. It enables more efficient operations, data-driven decision-making, personalized customer interactions, and fosters innovation. By embracing generative AI, companies gain a competitive edge and reshape their industries, positioning themselves as market leaders. 🚀

Imagine an AI that sparks fresh ideas, crafts captivating content, and streamlines workflows. Generative AI is here! It analyzes your data to create new text, images, or even code, boosting productivity and innovation. Think faster product design, personalized marketing campaigns, and content that keeps customers engaged. Generative AI is the key to unlock hidden potential in your business.

Day 5

Generative AI is a transformative force in business, automating creativity to generate novel content, from market forecasts to product designs. It's like having an innovative assistant that works tirelessly, enhancing efficiency and sparking growth. By analyzing vast datasets, it identifies patterns and insights, enabling businesses to make informed decisions swiftly. This AI not only accelerates development cycles but also personalizes customer experiences, leading to increased satisfaction and loyalty. In essence, generative AI is the catalyst for businesses to innovate, optimize, and excel in today's fast-paced digital landscape.

Imagine a creative partner who can write catchy marketing copy, design unique product prototypes, or generate personalized customer messages – all powered by your data. That's generative AI! It takes what your business knows and uses it to create entirely new content, ideas, and solutions, boosting efficiency, sparking innovation, and giving you a competitive edge.

Day 6

Certainly! Generative AI is a transformative force that empowers businesses in remarkable ways. Imagine an AI system that not only understands your needs but also generates seemingly original content—like text, images, or audio—from its training data. These capabilities translate into three key benefits for businesses:

1. **Generating Content and Ideas**: From video advertisements to novel proteins with antimicrobial properties, generative AI creates unique outputs across various modalities.

2. **Improving Efficiency**: It accelerates manual tasks, such as writing emails, coding, or summarizing large documents.

3. **Personalizing Experiences**: Whether it's chatbots for personalized customer interactions or targeted ads based on behavior patterns, generative AI tailors content to specific audiences.

Imagine a machine that can brainstorm marketing copy, design product mockups, or write personalized emails – all at your command. Generative AI is that creative spark! It analyzes existing data to generate fresh ideas, text, images, and more. This translates to boosted productivity, faster content creation, and a chance to unlock hidden potential within your business. Think of it as your AI teammate, ready to supercharge your creativity and efficiency.

In a nutshell, generative AI helps businesses operate efficiently, make data-driven decisions, foster innovation, and gain a competitive edge. 🚀

Day 7

Certainly! Generative AI is a transformative force that empowers businesses. It leverages deep learning and GANs to create seemingly new, realistic content—such as text, images, or audio—from training data. Imagine generating personalized customer experiences, accelerating manual tasks, or even creating novel proteins with antimicrobial properties. By adopting generative AI, organizations gain efficiency, data-driven decision-making, and a competitive edge1. It's like having an AI collaborator that sparks innovation and reshapes industries, all while maintaining responsible practices2. 🚀

Imagine a machine that can brainstorm marketing copy, design new product prototypes, or even write catchy jingles. Generative AI is that creative spark, using existing data to generate fresh ideas: text, images, code – the possibilities are endless. It's your AI teammate, boosting productivity, sparking innovation, and giving you the edge to win in today's competitive market. Ready to unlock the power of AI for your business?

Day 8

Certainly! Generative AI is a transformative force that empowers businesses. It uses deep learning and GANs to create seemingly new, realistic content—like text, images, or audio—from training data. Imagine personalized chatbots, efficient content generation, and innovative product ideas. By automating routine tasks, it frees up human employees to focus on value-adding activities, improving productivity and efficiency. Generative AI isn't just a feature; it's a strategic investment that can drive economic growth and give your business a competitive edge.

Imagine AI that creates, not just analyzes. Generative AI is your secret weapon to unlock fresh ideas and streamline processes. It can craft personalized marketing content, write captivating product descriptions, and even generate code. Stop waiting, start creating – with generative AI, the future of business is at your fingertips.

Day 9

Generative AI, a cutting-edge technology, creates new content from data patterns, transforming business operations. It enhances productivity by automating content creation, streamlining workflows, and personalizing customer experiences. Businesses can leverage generative AI for innovative product designs, dynamic marketing strategies, and efficient data analysis, leading to cost savings and competitive advantages. Embrace generative AI to unlock creativity, drive growth, and stay ahead in the digital age. 🚀

Imagine a machine that sparks fresh ideas, personalizes customer experiences, and streamlines workflows. Generative AI does just that! It's a powerful AI technique that creates entirely new content, from product designs to marketing copy. This translates to boosted productivity, increased sales, and happier customers – all within your reach. Unleash the potential of AI and watch your business thrive.

Day 10

Generative AI is a game-changer for businesses. It's a technology that uses algorithms to generate data similar to what it's trained on. From creating personalized marketing content to predicting market trends, it's revolutionizing business operations. It's like having a tireless team working 24/7, enhancing efficiency, reducing costs, and driving innovation. Embrace generative AI, unlock limitless possibilities!

Imagine a machine that creates fresh ideas, from personalized marketing copy to innovative product designs. That's the power of generative AI. It analyzes your data to generate new content, streamline processes, and personalize experiences for your customers. Unleash the potential of AI to boost efficiency, fuel creativity, and propel your business forward.

Other Generative Text Platform Responses

We took the same prompt and entered it in several available generative platforms. Here are the responses we got.

Platform	Response
ChatGPT	Generative AI harnesses advanced algorithms to create new, original content based on patterns and data input. In business, it revolutionizes productivity by automating complex tasks like content creation, predictive analytics, and personalized customer interactions. By rapidly iterating and refining ideas, it accelerates innovation and enhances decision-making processes. This transformative technology enables businesses to unlock new efficiencies, customize products and services at scale, and gain deeper insights into consumer behavior. Ultimately, generative AI empowers enterprises to stay ahead in competitive markets, foster creativity, and drive sustainable growth through data-driven strategies.
Meta AI	Generative AI revolutionizes business by automating content creation, enhancing decision-making, and driving innovation. This cutting-edge technology uses machine learning to generate new ideas, products, and solutions, transforming industries and streamlining operations. By harnessing generative AI, businesses can: - Boost productivity and efficiency - Enhance customer experiences - Uncover new revenue streams - Stay ahead of the competition Embrace generative AI to unlock new possibilities, spark creativity, and propel your business forward. Discover the transformative power of generative AI and reshape the future of your industry.
Claude.ai	Generative AI is a transformative technology that creates original content based on vast datasets. For businesses, it's a powerful tool that enhances productivity, sparks innovation, and drives efficiency across operations. From automating routine tasks to generating creative solutions, generative AI empowers companies to make data-driven decisions, personalize customer experiences, and streamline processes. It can produce text, images, and even code, opening new avenues for product development and marketing. By harnessing generative AI, businesses can unlock unprecedented growth opportunities, stay competitive in rapidly evolving markets, and redefine industry standards.
Cohere	Generative AI is a branch of artificial intelligence that uses machine learning algorithms to create new content, designs, and ideas. It offers significant benefits to businesses, including enhanced creativity, efficiency, and productivity. Generative AI can automate processes, reduce costs, and improve customer satisfaction through hyper-personalization. It also enables businesses to develop new products and services, accelerate design cycles, and launch products faster, making it a powerful tool for reshaping business landscapes and gaining a competitive edge.

Appendix: Playbook List

Table of all the playbooks listed in this book.

Chapter 1: Brainstorming with a Golden

Chapter 2: Reimagining Learning

Chapter 3: Authentic Learning

Chapter 4: Understanding AI

Chapter 5: AI and the Learner

Chapter 6: The Challenge We Face With AI

Chapter 7: Adapting Intelligence

Chapter 8: Build an Authentic AI Style Guide

Chapter 9: AI Impact on Learning

Chapter 10: AI, Learning, & Story

Chapter 11 Build Authentic

Chapter 12: Assisting Intelligence

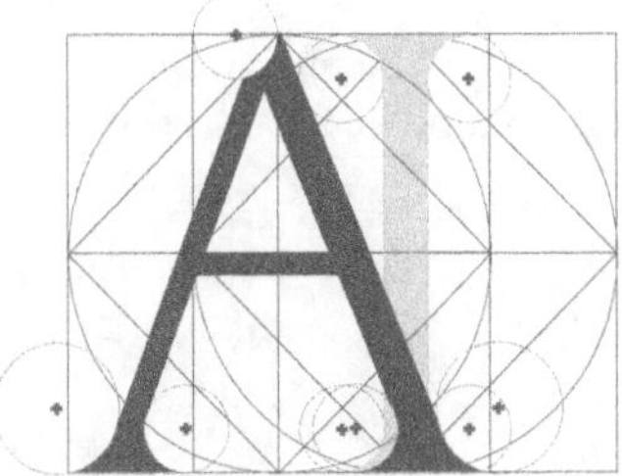

Image and Quotation Credits

Introduction

Cover Art. Image from iStock Photo. The cover started as a fun placeholder and became the art eventually chosen. Mara approved.

Inset Image on Cover. Mike and Mara taking a break from writing and training.

P 9. Images of Assisting Intelligence book and iphone.

P 14. Image of Book and Laptop. iStock photo [Stock photo ID:1270839889].

P 15. Image of typewriter with AI keys. Images based on Unsplash photo by Florian Klauer.

P 17. Quote by Henry David Thoreau and can be found in his work "A Week on the Concord and Merrimack Rivers."[https://www.gutenberg.org/cache/epub/4232/pg4232.txt].

P 19. Image by Gutenberg, Johann Creator. Gutenberg Bible. Retrieved from the Library of Congress, [http://www.loc.gov/item/2021666734/].

P 20. Images of La Commedia Pages from the edition of Divine Commedy printed by Nicolaus Laurentii. Florence, 30 August 1481. BnF, Réserve des livres rares, RES-YD-17, f. 15r Nicolaus Laurentii. (2023, December 28) and retrieved from the Library of Congress, [http://www.loc.gov/item/48035267/].

P 21. Page from the edition of Virgil printed by Aldus Manutius, the first book printed with an italic typeface. Venice, 1501. British Library C.19.f.7. Aldine Press. (2024, July 15). In Wikipedia. [https://en.wikipedia.org/wiki/Aldine_Press].

P 22. Infographic displaying the various sizes of pages, comparing the sizes of the Gutenberg Bible, the octavo format Aldine Virgil, to the La Commedia, and the Aldine Divina Commedia. Note that the Aldine version of the Commedia displays the same Canto. Aldine is able to save space by eliminating all the commentary.

P 24. Tory, Geoffroy, Approximately 1533, et al. Champ Fleury. trans by Ives, George Burnham New York: Grolier Club, 1927. Pdf. Retrieved from the Library of Congress, [http://www.loc.gov/item/28004222/].

Chapter 1: Brainstorming with a Golden

P 31. Quote by Librarian of Congress Daniel Boorstin given in a Washington Post interview. [https://www.washingtonpost.com/archive/lifestyle/1984/01/29/the-6-oclock-scholar/eed58de4-2dcb-47d2-8947-b0817a18d8fe/].

P 32. Image of Mara binge watching Planet Earth.

P 37. Quote from the 1980 movie, Airplane.

P 39. Image from the BMW ad, Symbol of Culture on YouTube. [https://www.youtube.com/watch?v=EF0SPhBX1PQ].

P 40. Quote by Christopher Hitchens. The razor was created by and later named after author and journalist Christopher Hitchens.

P 43. Summary verbs definitions from the Cambridge online dictionary definitions of assert, ascertain, asseverate.

P 44. Quote from the opening line of George Orwell's dystopian work *1984*.

P 45. Series of quotes by Voltaire, Oscar Wilde, T.S.Elliot, Picasso, and Steve Jobs. I am sure there are others.

P 49. Lyrics from *'Amazing Song' by One eskimO*.

P 50. Image of Mara carrying away a hiking shoe (one of the last sightings before being eaten), a persistent target and reminder that hiking was more fun than writing.

Chapter 2: Reimagining Learning

P 57. Quote by Bryce Courtenay, Author of The Power of One.

P 59. Infographic recreating the message on the Jackson Hole Tram sign. [https://www.jackson-hole.com/safety] and [https://www.jacksonhole.com/blog/tram-line-etiquette]

P 61. Quote by Aristotle, Posterior Analytics.

Chapter 3: Authentic Learning

P 67. Quote from Good Will Hunting, Sean Maguire, played by Robin Williams. Directed by Gus Van Sant. Written by Ben Affleck and Matt Damon.

P 69. Quote from Johann Wolfgang von Goethe, "Italian Journey" [https://www.guten-berg.org/cache/epub/53205/pg53205-images.html

P 75. Infographic on Agile and AI process.

P 80. Quotes from the Jackson Hole Tram Sign, Quote from Steve Jobs iPhone introduction, first line of A Prayer for Owen Meany by John Irving.

Chapter 4: Understanding AI

P 83. Quote from William Shakespeare, The Taming of the Shrew (c. 1593-94), Act I, scene 2, line 160.

P 84. Image of the trailer from trailer for the Beethoven X - The AI Project. View at [https://vimeo.com/642290986]

Chapter 5: AI and the Learner

P 105. Quote from Lewis Carroll. Alice in Wonderland.

P 109. Image of a Binary Star system from the JWST Telescope. [https://webbtelescope.org/contents/media/images/2020/57/4777-Image?Tag=Binary%20Stars].

P 111. Infographic of learning profiles.

Chapter 6: The Challenge We Face With AI

P 119. Quote from Thomas Jefferson to Nathaniel Macon, January 12, 1819.

Chapter 7: Adapting Intelligence

P 137. Quote from The Age of AI: And Our Human Future: Henry A Kissinger, Eric Schmidt, Daniel Huttenlocher.

P 150. Screenshots of YouTube videos of the rollout of the iPhone 7 in 2007.

Chapter 8: Build an Authentic AI Style Guide

P 153. Quote by The Phantom Tollbooth by Norton Juster.

Chapter 9: AI Impact on Learning

P 167. Quote by James Baldwin from The Creative Process, Creative America, Ridge Press, 1962.

P 171. Infographic of SmarterMedium's learning development process.

P 173. Infographic visualizing the agile methodology metaphor with images from the time spent at Kitty Hawk by the Wright Brothers.

P 174. Infographic on creating an AI Acceleration Engine.

P 175. Infographic highlighting the AI rotor at the heart of the content acceleration process.

P 176. Infographic highlighting the fixed controls or Stator that control the spin, speed and direction of the rotor.

P 176. Quote from the Elements of Style by Strunk and White.

Chapter 10: AI, Learning, & Story

P 185. Martin Scorsese: 'Irish storytelling connects with everyone.' [https://www.rte.ie/entertainment/2020/1018/1172364-scorsese-irish-storytelling-connects-with-everyone/].

P 190. Infographic on the Learning Story form process.

Part 3: Assisting Intelligence

P 203. Quote from Marvin Minskey In Managing an Information Security and Privacy Awareness and Training Program (2005) by Rebecca Herold, p. 101.

P 204. Image of a cairn in the Himalayas- Himachal Pradesh, India.

Chapter 11 Build Authentic

P 207. Quote from Aspen Ideas to Go: Artificial Intelligence and the Future of Everything, on Jul 5, 2023 with Google CEO Eric Schmidt and the head of MIT's College of Computing, Daniel Hutenlocher, Walter Isaacson moderates.

P 211. Infographic lists four images.

1. One of the first images released by the JWST. [https://science.nasa.gov/mission/webb/multi-media/images/].

2. Image from the trailer of Plant Earth 2. The entire catalog of videos from the BBC is a tour deforce of awe inspiring imagery, music and nature. [https://www.youtube.com/watch?v=c8aFcHFu8QM].

3. Historic image of the first human powered flight [https://www.loc.gov/collections/wilbur-and-orville-wright-papers/articles-and-essays/photography-and-the-wright-brothers].

4. A musical sketch from Beethoven that can be transformed into inspiring music. Music Division, The New York Public Library. (1810 - 1811). Sketches for the "Archduke" trio, op. 97 Retrieved from [https://digitalcollections.nypl.org/items/dfcfa580-7598-0131-c1cc-58d385a7bbd0].

P 213. Infographic of the Agile Methodology process applied to the Wright Brothers iterative development.

Chapter 12: Assisting Intelligence

P 225. Quote from Through the Looking Glass by Lewis Carroll.

P 230. Image of the Laurentian Library reading room viewed from the top of the stairs. Image by Mike O'Brien and Sydney O'Brien.

Conclusion: Ancora Imparo

P 237. Quote by Johann Wolfgang von Goethe, sourced from Wikiquotes.

P 239. Quote by Hubert Joly, The Heart of Business.

P 240. Image of Mara walking in the snow, January 2023.

About this Book

P 243. Quote from Farnam Street blog by Shane Parrish, 'Writing to Think'.

P 246. Image of SmarterMedium Logo.

P 247. Image of Assisting Intelligence Logo.

P 247. Font images from the 1529 Champs Fleury, natural and humanistic elements governing the design of geometric shapes. Geoffroy Tory, Champ Fleury. Translated into English and annotated by George B. Ives -1927. Images based on this version. [https://archive.org/details/champfleury00tory/].

P 247. Image of Book and Laptop. iStock photo [Stock photo ID:1270839889].

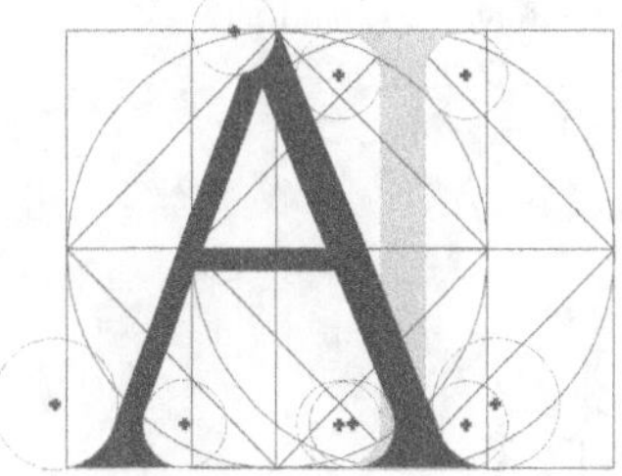

Index

Indexes likely started as concordances of words included in works like the Bible. The first Bible concordance was compiled for the Vulgate Bible by Hugh of St Cher (d.1262), who employed 500 friars to assist him.[1] With the printing press interest in organizing content by topic grew. Unlike an AI, which lacks the ability to attribute it's knowledge, below is the carefully caffeinated index for this book, capturing context, and nuance as well as curation of sources for further scholarship. Thankfully with the advent of MS Word indexing, no monastic order was required.

Hubspot, 48, 89
Human Genome Project, 109

I

IBM, 86
If You Give a Mouse a Cookie, 229
Inboarding, 259
Incunabula, 19, 22, 23, 24, 26, 210, 255
Index Librorum Prohibitorum, 231
Instagram, 256
iPhone, 63, 80, 134, 135, 150, 151
Isaac Asimov, 255
Italian Renaissance, 230

J

Jackson Hole, 58, 59, 63, 70, 71, 72, 74, 76, 80,
    112, 169, 170
Jackson Hole Tram, 212
James Baldwin, 167
James Webb Space Telescope, 20, 109, 210
Jeff Bezos, 245
Johann Wolfgang von Goethe, 71
Johannes Gutenberg, 18
John Herchenroeder, 159
John Hersey, 214
John Irving, 80
John Lennon, 210
John McCarthy, 85, 121
Jon Meacham, 187
Jonathan Haidt, 110, 124, 229, 252
Joseph Campbell, 189
Joseph Pulitzer, 122
Journalistic Six, 183
Julian Birkinshaw, 145
Jurassic Park, 109, 210

K

Kitty Hawk, 172, 173, 213, 269
Knowledge to Potential, 170
Konstantin Grcic, 107
KSAs, 156, 168, 170
Kurt Vonnegut, 189

L

La Commedia, 20, 21, 22, 24, 25
Laura Joffe Numeroff, 229
Laurentian Library, 230
Lee Sedol, 18, 27, 232
Lego, 168
Leonardo da Vinci, 23, 25
Lewis Carroll, 105, 225, 252
Lexis Nexis, 177, 178
Logos, 68, 69
London, 107
Lorenzo de Medici, 20
Lorenzo the Magnificent, 230
Louisville Courier-Journal, 159

M

Macbeth, 102
Machine Learning, 88, 91
Madlib, 54
Mara, 32, 33, 34, 46, 174, 240, 260
Marcel Proust, 187
Martin Scorsese, 185
MasterClass, 254
Meta, 108, 121, 123, 124, 228, 264
    Meta AI, 143, 149, 264
Michael Goldman, 106
Michelangelo, 67, 71, 230, 231, 233, 245
Microsoft, 21, 41, 87, 89, 92, 127, 143, 149, 198
    Copilot, 21, 35, 41, 87, 92, 222
    Microsoft Power BI, 89
Midjourney, 89
Millennials, 108, 109, 121
Mira Frick, 107
MIT, 33, 88, 211, 251
    MIT Technology Review, 33, 88, 251
Monty Python, 181

U

U.S. Holocaust Museum, 106
Uber, 35
University of Adelaide, 189
University of Vermont, 189

V

Venice, 21, 22
Voltaire, 45

W

Wabi-sabi, 145, 146
Warren Miller, 72
Willa Wonka, 34
William Randolph Hearst, 122

Winston Churchill, 208
Wizard of Oz, 109
World Economic Forum, 120
Wright Brothers, 172, 173, 213, 214

X

X, 92, 123

Y

yellow journalism, 122, 123

Z

Zen and the Art of the Internet, 140, 141, 142, 145, 245

References, Notes & Citations

If writing a book is a marathon, this section details all the resources that fueled the training and helped me cross the finish line during the two years of work on this book. From the books and articles that provided the foundation of my knowledge to the websites that offered invaluable data and insights, every reference is a testament to the incredible journey that brought this book to life. Just like a marathon, it took me much longer than expected, but it was worth it. I am deeply grateful to all the authors, researchers, and thinkers whose ideas and authentic knowledge have shaped this work.

Introduction:

[1] AP news story released to the world announcing the 5 games match on March 9, 2016. "Google's software beats human Go champion in first match" [https://apnews.com/international-news-general-news-7570cf6ac013484fb7f7ba8c16a2856a]

[2] Read more about the historic match at Wired Magazine, "In Two Moves, AlphaGo and Lee Sedol Redefined the Future" [https://www.wired.com/2016/03/two-moves-alphago-lee-sedol-redefined-future/] and How Google's AlphaGo Beat a Go World Champion from the Atlantic Magazine [https://www.theatlantic.com/technology/archive/2016/03/the-invisible-opponent/475611/]. For more on the technology side, read MIT Tech Review, Five Lessons from the AlphaGos Historic Victory. [https://www.technologyreview.com/2016/03/18/161507/five-lessons-from-alphagos-historic-victory/]

[3] For more information on the letter to the pope. [https://ilovetypography.com/2019/06/10/the-popes-romance/]. John Boardley wrote a book on the early history of type in *Typographic Firsts*.

[4] Information on the size and scope the Gutenberg Bible [https://apnews.com/article/gutenberg-bibles-morgan-library-scripture-2ff65c3cdbeda696c861fef5db8b18ee]

[5] See the Wikipedia article for more information on how these early books sought to mimic the work of scribes. [[https://en.wikipedia.org/wiki/Incunable]

[6] For more information the early Bard mishap and how the New Scientist called them out read, [https://www.newscientist.com/article/2358426-google-bard-advert-shows-new-ai-search-tool-making-a-factual-error/]

[7] Versions of the La Commedia along with all their issues may be viewed digitally at the Bodleian and other libraries. [https://digital.bodleian.ox.ac.uk/objects/1ba80701-8b5b-4fc9-9252-b6101c99e791/surfaces/3b98e06a-9e6f-4f0a-8a1c-3e135ab5f66e/].

[8] The story of the printing of La Commedia is covered on printing revolution website along with the fascinating details of a printing press startup. [https://www.printingrevolution.eu/dante-1481/].

[9] Learn how Venice became the hub of printing in Europe. [https://www.bbc.com/travel/article/20190708-the-city-that-launched-the-publishing-industry].

[10] Review the innovations and the making of the Octavo format in the Smithsonian Magazine. The Man Who Changed Reading Forever. [https://www.smithsonianmag.com/travel/aldus-manutius-printing-type-face-typography-italics-venice-180956855/]

[11] The history of the desktop publishing Aldus corporation. [https://en.wikipedia.org/wiki/Aldus_Corporation]

[12] For more information on Jenson, reference John Boardley's book on the early history of type in Typographic Firsts.

[13] Geoffroy Tory's Champ Fleury is available at the Library of Congress for digital viewing. [https://www.loc.gov/resource/rbc0001.2009rosen0994/?r=-0.117,-0.075,1.229,0.787,0] For more information on the visual display of typography visit and Tory's influence visit Books On Books Collection – Geofroy Tory-https://books-on-books.com/2021/06/21/books-on-books-collection-geofroy-tory/]

[14] Follow the growth of Da Vinci's shelves and book collection with the digital exhibit of the books know to be in his possession. The books were assembled based on references within his notebooks made during his lifetime. [https://www.mpg.de/13409753/leonardo-da-vinci-reflected-in-his-library].

[15] Statistics on book production provided by Statistica. [[https://www.statista.com/statistics/1394867/europe-manuscript-production-century-region-historical/]

Chapter 1: Brainstorming with a Golden Retriever

[1] Interesting article on the basis of AI hallucinations from the MIT Technology Review, Why does AI hallucinate? [https://www.technologyreview.com/2024/06/18/1093440/what-causes-ai-hallucinate-chatbots/#:~:text=It's%20all%20hallucination,that%20makes%20trusting%20them%20hard].

[2] How Businesses Are Using Artificial Intelligence In 2024, Forbes Advisor. [https://www.forbes.com/advisor/business/software/ai-in-business/]

[3] Data: The Fuel Powering AI & Digital Transformation, Forbes, https://www.forbes.com/sites/cognitiveworld/2019/02/06/data-the-fuel-powering-ai-digital-transformation/?sh=1e0f870b578b

[4] How Generative AI is Changing Creative work? Harvard Business Review. [https://hbr.org/2022/11/how-generative-ai-is-changing-creative-work?ab=at_art_art_1x4_s04]

[5] Statement from the NYTimes article How Schools Can Survive and Maybe Even Thrive with AI this fall. [https://www.nytimes.com/2023/08/24/technology/how-schools-can-survive-and-maybe-even-thrive-with-ai-this-fall.html/]

[6] Read Expanding AI's Impact With Organizational Learning. MIT Sloan Review. https://sloanreview.mit.edu/projects/expanding-ais-impact-with-organizational-learning/.

[7] Read How Businesses Are Using Artificial Intelligence In 2024. https://www.forbes.com/advisor/business/software/ai-in-business/.

[8] Read Will Chatbots Teach Your Children? https://www.nytimes.com/2024/01/11/technology/ai-chatbots-khan-education-tutoring.html

[9] For more information on how a generative AI chat differs from traditional search read: https://prerender.io/blog/traditional-search-vs-ai-powered-search-explained/

[10] The information regarding the flu and the responses were synthesized using Google and Bing search as well as Microsoft Copilot. The responses were also crafted from content from the Mayo Clinic website and the CDC. Influenza (flu) - Symptoms and causes - Mayo Clinic. https://www.mayoclinic.org/diseases-conditions/flu/symptoms-causes/syc-20351719. Flu Symptoms & Complications | CDC. https://www.cdc.gov/flu/symptoms/symptoms.htm. The voice text was made to mimic the responses a voice assistant would give and again text was created from responses from a generative AI. Additional sources were referenced to create realistic content. Flu Symptoms: Headache, Sore Throat, Chills, and More - Healthline. https://www.healthline.com/health/flu-symptoms. Do I Have The Flu? Flu Symptoms, Treatments, and Prevention. - WebMD. https://www.webmd.com/cold-and-flu/ss/slideshow-flu-symptoms-treatment. First Signs of the Flu: What to Do If You Get Sick - Healthline. https://www.healthline.com/health/influenza/what-to-do-first-sign. Flu symptoms: Should I see my doctor? - Mayo Clinic. https://www.mayoclinic.org/diseases-conditions/flu/expert-answers/flu-symptoms/faq-20057983.

[11] BMW ad campaign. https://www.adsoftheworld.com/campaigns/the-symbol-of-culture

[12] BMW is in the vanguard of the use of AI in advertising. https://www.press.bmwgroup.com/global/article/detail/T0388053EN/the-new-bmw-i7-progressively-staged:-star-photographer-nick-knight-creates-expressive-futuristic-photo-series?language=en

[13] Google search conducted February 2, 2024.

[14] That Hitchen would make a great AI dog trainer, is an example of his razor.

[15] Christopher Hitchen's razor. https://en.wikipedia.org/wiki/Hitchens%27s_razor

[16] "Sophist ." The Oxford Pocket Dictionary of Current English. Encyclopedia.com. 21 Feb. 2024 [https://www.encyclopedia.com].

[17] Explore the linkages of sophistry and AI. [https://time.com/6299631/what-socrates-can-teach-us-about-ai/]

[18] Referenced several times in this book, this article gives and important understanding of AI Hallucinations. [https://www.technologyreview.com/2024/06/18/1093440/what-causes-ai-hallucinate-chatbots/]

[19] Mishaps related to AI. [https://www.jumpstartmag.com/ai-gone-wrong-5-biggest-ai-failures-of-all-time/]

[20] Turns out that we're not the only ones to thinking of "shenanigans" as a great way to describe the activities of an AI. [https://www.engadget.com/ftc-warns-tech-companies-against-ai-shenanigans-that-harm-consumers-175851417.html]

[21] Calling Bullshit: The Art of Skepticism in a Data-Driven World by Carl T. Bergstrom, Jevin D. West.

[22] Calling Bullshit: The Art of Skepticism in a Data-Driven World by Carl T. Bergstrom, Jevin D. West.

[23] Quote sourced from "FTC warns tech companies against AI shenanigans that harm consumers" Engadget. [https://www.engadget.com/ftc-warns-tech-companies-against-ai-shenanigans-that-harm-consumers-175851417.html]

[24] Learn more about what is doomscrolling and it's harmful effects. https://health.clevelandclinic.org/everything-you-need-to-know-about-doomscrolling-and-how-to-avoid-it

[25] Three definitions provided by the Oxford English Dictionary.

[26] Calling Bullshit: The Art of Skepticism in a Data-Driven World by Carl T. Bergstrom, Jevin D. West. Page 37.

[27] Disinformation Researchers Raise Alarms About A.I. Chatbots NYTimes. [https://www.nytimes.com/2023/02/08/technology/ai-chatbots-disinformation.html]

[28] NYTimes analysis of generative image AIs and copyright issues. [https://www.nytimes.com/interactive/2024/01/25/business/ai-image-generators-openai-microsoft-midjourney-copyright.html]

[29] NYTimes analysis of generative image AIs and copyright issues. [https://www.nytimes.com/interactive/2024/01/25/business/ai-image-generators-openai-microsoft-midjourney-copyright.html]

[30] World Economic Forum explains "Who owns the song you wrote with AI? An expert explains" [https://www.weforum.org/agenda/2023/08/intellectual-property-ai-creativity/]

[31] AI models make stuff up. How can hallucinations be controlled? Economist Magazine. [https://www.economist.com/science-and-technology/2024/02/28/ai-models-make-stuff-up-how-can-hallucinations-be-controlled]

[32] World Economic Forum explains "Who owns the song you wrote with AI? An expert explains" [https://www.weforum.org/agenda/2023/08/intellectual-property-ai-creativity/]

[33] Editorial featuring AI images along with Authentic content. [https://www.cleveland.com/news/2023/04/why-i-used-an-ai-tool-to-generate-that-silly-image-of-a-golden-retriever-last-week-letter-from-the-editor.html]

[34] Give the HubSpot AI blog a topic and it will draft a post for you. https://www.hubspot.com/blog-topic-generator.

[35] Brands can also have perceived personas and added value beyond the functional benefits of their product or service offerings. The Business and Management Review, Volume 9 Number 3. https://hbr.org/2021/07/how-to-design-an-ai-marketing-strategy

[36] Brands. So What? 03/17/2018 by David Fowler [https://www.ogilvy.com/ideas/brands-so-what]

[37] AI is the end of brands as we know them. Fast Company. [https://www.fastcompany.com/90915063/ai-end-brands-as-we-know-them]

[38] AI is the end of brands as we know them. Fast Company. [https://www.fastcompany.com/90915063/ai-end-brands-as-we-know-them]

[39] Forbes What is a brand anyway. [https://www.forbes.com/sites/jerrymclaughlin/2011/12/21/what-is-a-brand-anyway/?sh=24895602a1b1]

Chapter 2: Reimaging Learning

[1] The sign at the Jackson Home tram base reads:

> *Safety Message. Our mountain is like nothing you have skied before!*
>
> *It is huge, with variable terrain from groomed slopes to dangerous cliff areas and dangerously variable weather and snow conditions. You must always exercise extreme caution. You could become lost. You could make a mistake and suffer personal injury or death. Protect yourself - understand the trail map and ask questions before you proceed. Obey all trail signs and markers.*
>
> *Please think and be careful. Give this special mountain the respect it demands!*

[2] I was not an expert skier the first time I rode the tram at Jackson Hole. I read the sign; I rode the tram and departed at the peak — into white-out conditions. Other skiers piled out of the tram, popped on their skis, and disappeared into the conditions. To my left, as I exited, the ski patrol was loading the search and rescue dogs onto the tram – their handlers had assessed the conditions at the peak as too extreme for the dogs, and they were headed down. I recalled the safety message on the sign, I assessed the conditions and my abilities. I had an experience like never before—I met search and rescue dogs while riding the tram back down.

[3] Storytelling That Moves People, Bronwyn Fryer, Harvard Business Review.[https://hbr.org/2003/06/story-telling-that-moves-people]

[4] Storynomics: Story-Driven Marketing in the Post-Advertising World by Robert McKee [https://a.co/0hrEG]

[5] Storynomics: Story-Driven Marketing in the Post-Advertising World by Robert McKee [https://a.co/0hrEG]

[6] Storynomics: Story-Driven Marketing in the Post-Advertising World by Robert McKee [https://a.co/0hrEG]

[7] Watch Robert McKee defines story. [https://www.youtube.com/embed/5-N5KWfire0]

[8] Adobe Blog "Where Did the Term "User Experience" Come From?" [https://blog.adobe.com/en/publish/2017/08/28/where-did-the-term-user-experience-come-from]

[9] "Signal to Noise" can be traced to 1923 article, by Arnold, H. D., & Espenschied, L. (1923). Transatlantic Radio Telephony 1. Bell System Technical Journal, 2(4), 116-144

[10] 10 Examples of "False Flag" Attacks - History and Headlines. https://www.historyandheadlines.com/august-31-1939-10-examples-false-flag-attacks/.

[11] Zen and the Art of Cab Driving. Taxi, Episode aired Mar 19, 1981 https://www.imdb.com/title/tt0718556/

[12] "Fake news, disinformation and misinformation in social media: a review" National Library of Medicine. https://pmc.ncbi.nlm.nih.gov/articles/PMC9910783/

[13] Read Jonathan Haidt's The Anxious Generation. There are multiple examples and instances of how social media companies manipulate the display of content to capture and hold attention.

Chapter 3: Authentic Learning

[1] The Art of Persuasion Hasn't Changed in 2,000 Years, Carmine Gallo Harvard Business Review. [https://hbr.org/2019/07/the-art-of-persuasion-hasnt-changed-in-2000-years]

[2] Open Rhetoric. Nicholas Whaley. https://pressbooks.pub/openrhetoric/chapter/aristotles-rhetorical-appeals/

[3] Indiana University Writing Center. The Rhetorical Triangle: Understanding and Using Logos, Ethos, and Pathos. [https://www.lsu.edu/hss/english/files/university_writing_files/item35402.pdf]

[4] The Age of AI: And Our Human Future: Henry A Kissinger, Eric Schmidt, Daniel Huttenlocher.

[5] Approbation definition [https://dictionary.cambridge.org/dictionary/english/approbation]

6 Johann Wolfgang von Goethe, "Italian Journey" [https://www.gutenberg.org/cache/epub/53205/pg53205-images.html]

7 Ski Level Assessment - Jackson Hole Mountain Resort. [https://www.jacksonhole.com/ski-level-assessment]

8 Ride the Tram – An Unforgettable Alpine Experience - Jackson Hole .... [https://www.jacksonholechamber.com/blog/post/ride-the-tram-an-unforgettable-alpine-experience/.]

9 Speaking of Harley Davidson, Don James, chairman and chief executive officer of Fred Deeley Imports Ltd. [https://www.theglobeandmail.com/report-on-business/harley-davidsons-great-ride-to-the-top/article25287390/]

10 Communicating Authentically in a Virtual World, Harvard Business Review. [https://hbr.org/2022/01/communicating-authentically-in-a-virtual-world]

Chapter 4: Understanding AI

1 How Artificial Intelligence Completed Beethoven's Unfinished Tenth Symphony, Smithsonian Magazine. [https://www.smithsonianmag.com/innovation/how-artificial-intelligence-completed-beethovens-unfinished-10th-symphony-180978753/]

2 This genius explains exactly what makes Beethoven's music so exquisite… through maths, ClassicFM. [https://www.classicfm.com/composers/beethoven/news/ted-maths-moonlight-sonata/]

3 Symphonic Equations: A Mathematical Exploration of Music," David Kung [https://www.youtube.com/watch?v=QNuPaFq9q28]

4 AI Completes Beethoven's Unfinished Symphony Nearly 200 Years Later,. Nvidia Blog.[https://blogs.nvidia.com/blog/ai-beethovens-unfinished-symphony/]

5 AI Completes Beethoven's Unfinished Symphony Nearly 200 Years Later,. Nvidia Blog.[https://blogs.nvidia.com/blog/ai-beethovens-unfinished-symphony/]

6 BBC Science. How an AI finished Beethoven's last symphony and what that means for the future of music. [https://www.sciencefocus.com/news/ai-beethovens-symphony]

7 AI Etymology. [https://www.etymonline.com/word/AI]

8 Artificial Intelligence Coined at Dartmouth. [https://home.dartmouth.edu/about/artificial-intelligence-ai-coined-dartmouth]

9 Stanford University Human-Centered Artificial Intelligence Institute (HAI) https://hai.stanford.edu/sites/default/files/2020-09/AI-Definitions-HAI.pdf

10 Britannica Definition. [https://www.britannica.com/technology/artificial-intelligence]

11 IBM Definition [https://www.ibm.com/topics/artificial-intelligence]

12 Cambridge Online Dictionary Definition [https://dictionary.cambridge.org/us/dictionary/english/ai]

13 New Scientist Definition. [https://www.newscientist.com/definition/artificial-intelligence-ai/#:~:text=Artificial%20intelligence%20or%20AI%20simply,mimic%20aspects%20of%20human%20intelligence.]

14 Learn the basics of AI 101 from MIT Opencourse [https://ocw.mit.edu/courses/res-6-013-ai-101-fall-2021/pages/video-and-supporting-materials/]

15 Quote from Prof. Rayid Ghani. Generative ai is a math problem. Left unchecked, it could be a real problem. [https://www.heinz.cmu.edu/media/2023/July/generative-ai-is-a-math-problem-left-unchecked-it-could-be-a-real-problem]

16 All the Math You Need to Know in Artificial Intelligence [https://www.freecodecamp.org/news/all-the-math-you-need-in-artificial-intelligence/]

17 How machine learning works, The Economist Magazine. [https://www.economist.com/the-economist-explains/2015/05/13/how-machine-learning-works]

18 Nvidia Developer intro to LLMs [https://developer.nvidia.com/blog/an-introduction-to-large-language-models-prompt-engineering-and-p-tuning/]

19 What is a Data Lake? Data Lake vs. Warehouse | Microsoft Azure. [https://azure.microsoft.com/en-us/resources/cloud-computing-dictionary/what-is-a-data-lake/].

[20] Nvidia Developer intro to LLMs [https://developer.nvidia.com/blog/an-introduction-to-large-language-models-prompt-engineering-and-p-tuning/]

[21] How Artificial Intelligence Completed Beethoven's Unfinished Tenth Symphony. [https://www.smithsonianmag.com/innovation/how-artificial-intelligence-completed-beethovens-unfinished-10th-symphony-180978753/].

[22] Home | Beethoven X - The AI Project. [https://www.beethovenx-ai.com/].

[23] Beethoven's 10th Symphony Completed By AI: Premiere October 2021. [https://www.udiscovermusic.com/classical-news/beethovens-10th-symphony-ai/].

[24] A digital version of Plinko. [https://phet.colorado.edu/sims/html/plinko-probability/latest/plinko-probability_en.html]

[25] Ode to Joy [https://en.wikipedia.org/wiki/Ode_to_Joy]

[26] History of Beethoven's 10th. [https://en.wikipedia.org/wiki/Symphony_No._10_(Beethoven/Cooper)]

[27] QED [https://en.wikipedia.org/wiki/Q.E.D.]

Chapter 5: AI and the Learner

[1] Can Technology Help Us be More Empathetic? Racism, Empathy and Virtual Reality. Santa Clara University. [https://www.scu.edu/ethics-spotlight/ethics-and-systemic-racism/can-technology-help-us-be-more-empathetic-racism-empathy-and-virtual-reality/]

[2] Behavioral economics, explained. UChicago News. [https://news.uchicago.edu/explainer/what-is-behavioral-economics]

[3] Mira Frick, Yale Economist. Minding bias: A Yale economist examines learning and decision making. [https://news.yale.edu/2022/03/09/minding-bias-yale-economist-examines-learning-and-decision-making]

[4] Six Public Clocks, Canary Wharf. [https://canarywharf.com/artwork/konstantin-grcic-six-public-clocks/]

[5] Imax resolution. [https://en.wikipedia.org/wiki/IMAX]

[6] Las Vegas' Sphere: World's Largest High-Res Led Screen For Live Action And Vfx [https://www.vfxvoice.com/las-vegas-sphere-worlds-largest-high-res-led-screen-for-live-action-and-vfx/]

7 Rijksmuseum digital image of the Night watch. [https://www.rijksmuseum.nl/en/stories/operation-night-watch/story/ultra-high-resolution-image-of-the-night-watch]

[8] What are binary stars? | Space. [https://www.space.com/22509-binary-stars.html].

[9] How to Curate Your Digital Persona - Harvard Business Review. [https://hbr.org/2020/07/how-to-curate-your-digital-persona].

[10] Kissinger, Henry A; Schmidt, Eric; Huttenlocher, Daniel. The Age of AI (p. 159). Little, Brown and Company. Kindle Edition.

[11] Jonathan Haidt's 'The Anxious Generation: How the Great Rewiring of Childhood Is Causing an Epidemic of Mental Illness'.

[12] How to avoid the 'competency trap' BBC [https://www.bbc.com/worklife/article/20200608-what-is-the-competency-trap]

[13] Lessons from the America's Cup for leading high-performance teams IESE Business School. [https://www.iese.edu/insight/articles/lessons-americas-cup-grant-dalton-leading-high-performance-teams/]

Chapter 6: The Challenge We Face With AI

[1] Colorado Search & Rescue Groups Warn Hikers Against Relying Solely On Your Cellphone After Hiker Ignores Calls [https://www.cbsnews.com/colorado/news/colorado-hikers-rescue-cellphone-risks-lost-summit-county-mount-elbert/]

[2] The Most Influential Spreader of Coronavirus Misinformation Online, NYTimes [https://www.nytimes.com/2021/07/24/technology/joseph-mercola-coronavirus-misinformation-online.html]

[3] The Fate of Online Trust in the Next Decade (in 2017) [https://www.pewresearch.org/internet/2017/08/10/the-fate-of-online-trust-in-the-next-decade/]

[4] Disinformation is a threat to our trust ecosystem. Experts explain how to curb it. World Economic Forum. [https://www.weforum.org/agenda/2024/03/disinformation-trust-ecosystem-experts-curb-it/]

[5] Millennials No Less Trusting (or Distrusting) of News Sources. https://www.pewresearch.org/journalism/2015/06/01/millennials-no-less-trusting-or-distrusting-of-news-sources/.

[6] Artificial Intelligence Coined at Dartmouth. [https://home.dartmouth.edu/about/artificial-intelligence-ai-coined-dartmouth]

[7] Search of headlines from the NYTimes for the term 'artificial' turned up several scientific breakthroughs.

[8] New York Times, July 31, 1955, MAN REACHES INTO SPACE—PLANS ARE ANNOUNCED FOR FIRST ARTIFICIAL SATELLITE [https://timesmachine.nytimes.com/timesmachine/1955/07/31/93806986.html?pageNumber=95]

[9] List of Films with AI. [https://en.wikipedia.org/wiki/List_of_artificial_intelligence_films]

[10] Newspaper improvements [https://daily.jstor.org/to-fix-fake-news-look-to-yellow-journalism/]

[11] Yellow to Radio transition[https://cs.stanford.edu/people/eroberts/cs181/projects/2010-11/Journalism/index3f35.html?page_id=8]

[12] Two references for AI Provenance from MIT. AI Provenance [https://www.media.mit.edu/projects/data-provenance-for-ai/overview/] and [https://www.ccc.mit.edu/project/data-provenance-for-ai/]

[13] Yellow to Radio transition[https://cs.stanford.edu/people/eroberts/cs181/projects/2010-11/Journalism/index3f35.html?page_id=8]

[14] Quote from the PEW Research Center[https://www.pewresearch.org/internet/2017/08/10/the-fate-of-online-trust-in-the-next-decade/]

[15] Read Frank McCourt's Our Biggest Fight especially on the chapter that concerns AI and future facing technologies.

[16] Forbes article on X's usage of posts and the challenges of the misinformation. [https://www.forbes.com/sites/petersuciu/2024/07/27/x-uses-posts-to-train-ai-based-grok-but-users-get-little-in-exchange/].

[17] We Asked A.I. to Create the Joker. It Generated a Copyrighted Image. By Stuart A. Thompson Jan. 25, 2024. The New York Times. [https://www.nytimes.com/interactive/2024/01/25/business/ai-image-generators-openai-microsoft-midjourney-copyright.html]

[18] Generative AI Has an Intellectual Property Problem. https://hbr.org/2023/04/generative-ai-has-an-intellectual-property-problem.

[19] Always good to include a quote from Shakespeare. He handles every topic.

[20] A great word choice by our second president; his quote on history and wisdom can be applied to many situations today. [https://www.monticello.org/research-education/thomas-jefferson-encyclopedia/honesty-first-chapter-book-wisdom/]

Part 2: Build Authentic

[1] That iPhone Has a Keyboard, but It's Not Mechanical. By John Markoff, June 13, 2007. NY Times [https://www.nytimes.com/2007/06/13/technology/13phone.ready.html]

[2] Why does AI being good at math matter? MIT Technology Review [https://www.technologyreview.com/2024/01/23/1086944/why-does-ai-being-good-at-math-matter/]

[3] That iPhone Has a Keyboard, but It's Not Mechanical. By John Markoff, June 13, 2007. NY Times [https://www.nytimes.com/2007/06/13/technology/13phone.ready.html]

Chapter 7: Adapting Intelligence

[1] From Aspen Ideas to Go: Artificial Intelligence and the Future of Everything, Jul 5, 2023 [https://podcasts.apple.com/us/podcast/artificial-intelligence-and-the-future-of-everything/id702896920?i=1000619399099] Philanthropist and former Google CEO Eric Schmidt and the head of MIT's College of Computing, Daniel Huttenlocher, Walter Isaacson moderates.

[2] The story behind Zen and the Art of the Internet. [https://en.wikipedia.org/wiki/Brendan_Kehoe]

[3] How can you write a guide when the definition of AI is still in flux. "The tech industry can't agree on what open-source AI means. That's a problem." MIT Technology Review [https://www.technologyreview.com/2024/03/25/1090111/tech-industry-open-source-ai-definition-problem]

[4] WABI-SABI 101 [https://lescollection.com/blogs/journal/wabi-sabi-101#] and [https://en.wikipedia.org/wiki/Wabi-sabi]

[5] Fighting the corporate immune system: a process study of subsidiary initiatives in multinational corporations, Science Direct [https://www.sciencedirect.com/science/article/abs/pii/S0969593198000432?via%3Dihub]

Chapter 8: Build an Authentic AI Style Guide

[1] How can you write a guide when the definition of AI is still in flux. "The tech industry can't agree on what open-source AI means. That's a problem." MIT Technology Review [https://www.technologyreview.com/2024/03/25/1090111/tech-industry-open-source-ai-definition-problem]

[2] A hat tip to Phil Alexander and the wisdom he imparted to me during the early days of BrandMuscle; I use so much of it every day. *"As you can see in the Bell Atlantic demo …"*

[3] For further reading, you may refer to resources such as "Guidelines for Human-AI Interaction" by Microsoft and "Ethics Guidelines for Trustworthy AI" by the European Commission. [https://www.microsoft.com/en-us/research/publication/guidelines-for-human-ai-interaction/] and [https://digital-strategy.ec.europa.eu/en/library/ethics-guidelines-trustworthy-ai]

[4] What is Openwashing AI? NYTimes [[https://www.nytimes.com/2024/05/17/business/what-is-openwashing-ai.html]

[5] What are the OECD Principles on AI? [https://cyber.harvard.edu/story/2019-06/what-are-oecd-principles-ai]

[6] Memorandum for the heads of executive departments and agencies. [https://www.whitehouse.gov/wp-content/uploads/2020/01/Draft-OMB-Memo-on-Regulation-of-AI-1-7-19.pdf.]

[7] Stewarding AI in the Age of Big Tech - hai.stanford.edu. [https://hai.stanford.edu/news/stewarding-ai-age-big-tech.]

[8] Ombudsman was borrowed from Swedish, where it means "representative," and ultimately derives from the Old Norse words umboth ("commission") and mathr ("man"). Sweden became the first country to appoint an independent official known as an ombudsman to investigate complaints against government officials and agencies. [https://www.merriam-webster.com/dictionary/ombudsman]

[9] Ombudsman connection to the news media [https://www.niemanlab.org/2021/03/from-public-to-publics-news-orgs-need-ombudsmen-to-push-for-more-diverse-representation-inside-and-out/]

Chapter 9: AI Impact on Learning

[1] The story of the Wright Brothers flights is summarized on Wikipedia [https://en.wikipedia.org/wiki/Wright_Flyer]. For a more robust telling of their story read David McCullough's The Wright Brothers [https://www.simonandschuster.com/books/The-Wright-Brothers/David-McCullough/9781476728759]

[2] Learn more about a brushless motor and how it's innovative usage is powering many modern conveniences. [https://en.wikipedia.org/wiki/Brushless_DC_electric_motor]

[3] The full quote from The Elements of Style by Strunk and White provides even context to the importance of clear and concise writing. *" Vigorous writing is concise. A sentence should contain no unnecessary words, a paragraph no unnecessary sentences, for the same reason that a drawing should have no unnecessary lines and a machine no unnecessary parts. This requires not that the writer make all his sentences short, or that he avoid all detail and treat his subjects only in outline, but that he make every word tell."*

[4] For more information on the basics of prompts and how to make them more effective read Getting started with prompts for text-based Generative AI tools [https://huit.harvard.edu/news/ai-prompts] and Effective Prompts for AI: The Essentials [https://mitsloanedtech.mit.edu/ai/basics/effective-prompts/]

[5] The famous segue between skits in Monty Python [https://en.wikipedia.org/wiki/And_Now_for_Something_Completely_Different]

[6] One of the most famous references for journalism and how to frame and ask questions., Newspaper Writing and Editing by Willard Grosvenor Bleyer. Read the electronic version available at Project Gutenberg. [https://www.gutenberg.org/ebooks/65884]

Chapter 10: AI, Learning, & Story

1 Martin Scorsese: 'Irish storytelling connects with everyone' https://www.rte.ie October 18th 2020. [https://www.rte.ie/entertainment/2020/1018/1172364-scorsese-irish-storytelling-connects-with-every-one/]

2 Read: Gottschall, Jonathan. The Storytelling Animal: How Stories Make Us Human (pp. 5-6). Houghton Mifflin Harcourt. Kindle Edition.

3 The Story Factor: Inspiration, Influence, and Persuasion Through the Art of Storytelling. by Annette Simmons.

4 Origins of Once Upon a Time from Wikipedia. [https://en.wikipedia.org/wiki/Once_upon_a_time]

5 The Storytelling Animal: How Stories Make Us Human by Jonathan Gottschall, (p. 57). Houghton Mifflin Harcourt. Kindle Edition.

6 Jon Meachum on: The Power of History in Shaping the Present [https://www.youtube.com/watch?v=MhvQWc5D4IQ]

7 Robert McKee Storynomics: Story-Driven Marketing in the Post-Advertising World (p. 76). Grand Central Publishing. Kindle Edition. And for more information on story watch: Robert McKee defines story: [https://www.youtube.com/embed/5-N5KWfire0]

8 Read: FORMS OF THE PLOT Norman Friedman. The Journal of General Education Vol. 8, No. 4 (July 1955), pp. 241-253. For more information on story structure and plots watch: Aaron Sorkin Masterclass.

9 Booker, Christopher. The Seven Basic Plots (p. 18). Bloomsbury Publishing. Kindle Edition.

10 Link: Three, six or 36: how many basic plots are there in all stories ever written? | Books | The Guardian [https://www.theguardian.com/books/booksblog/2016/jul/13/three-six-or-36-how-many-basic-plots-are-there-in-all-stories-ever-written]

11 Hero's journey - Wikipedia. [https://en.wikipedia.org/wiki/Hero's_journey]

12 Robert Heinlein defines three plots [https://en.wikipedia.org/wiki/On_the_Writing_of_Speculative_Fiction]

13 Three, six or 36: how many basic plots are there in all stories ever written? | Books | The Guardian [https://www.theguardian.com/books/booksblog/2016/jul/13/three-six-or-36-how-many-basic-plots-are-there-in-all-stories-ever-written]

14 Read: The Story Factor: Inspiration, Influence, and Persuasion Through the Art of Storytelling. by Annette Simmons

15 Read: Booker, Christopher. The Seven Basic Plots (p. 109). Bloomsbury Publishing. Kindle Edition.

16 Read: FORMS OF THE PLOT Norman Friedman. The Journal of General Education Vol. 8, No. 4 (July 1955).

17 20 Master Plots: And How to Build Them by Ronald Tobias

18 The Thirty-Six Dramatic Situations [https://en.wikipedia.org/wiki/The_Thirty-Six_Dramatic_Situations]

19 Link: The Six Main Stories, As Identified by a Computer - The Atlantic [https://www.theatlantic.com/technology/archive/2016/07/the-six-main-arcs-in-storytelling-identified-by-a-computer/490733/]

20 On the Writing of Speculative Fiction, Wikipedia [https://en.wikipedia.org/wiki/On_the_Writing_of_Speculative_Fiction]

21 Quote from Aristotle Poetics, page 8.

22 Characters, Relationships, Objectives, and Where, or CROW [https://www.pantheater.com/the-improv-acronym-for-success-crow.html]

23 Design Unbound p105 Designing for Emergence. Ann M. Pendleton-Jullian and John Seely Brown.

24 Probably the single greatest story to challenge perceptions and belief, presented in the only meaningful way that could get through. Read John Hersey, the Writer Who Let "Hiroshima" Speak for Itself. By Russell Shorto.[https://www.newyorker.com/culture/culture-desk/john-hersey-the-writer-who-let-hiroshima-speak-for-itself]

25 The Role of Cognitive Dissonance in the Pandemic. Elliot Aronson and Carol Tavris, Social Psychologists, The Atlantic [https://www.theatlantic.com/ideas/archive/2020/07/role-cognitive-dissonance-pandemic/614074/]

26 E.R. Tufte maxim from his course on Information Design. Clearly not original but right.

27 Microsoft Story Labs [https://news.microsoft.com/stories/]

28 The Nike Story? Just Tell It! (fastcompany.com) [https://www.fastcompany.com/38979/nike-story-just-tell-it]

29 Journalism That Stands Apart - The New York Times (nytimes.com) [https://www.nytimes.com/projects/2020-report/index.html]

30 Narrative Persuasion in Legal Settings: What's the Story? Philip J. Mazzocco, Ph.D. Ohio State University at Mansfield, and Melanie C. Green, Ph.D. University of North Carolina at Chapel Hill.

Part 3:

1 Marvin Minskey In Managing an Information Security and Privacy Awareness and Training Program (2005) by Rebecca Herold, p. 101.

2 Learn more about cairns [https://www.nps.gov/articles/rockcairns.htm] and [https://www.advnture.com/features/rock-cairns-meaning].

3 Image of Stone Cairn In Himalayas. Himachal Pradesh, India [https://motionarray.com/stock-photos/stone-cairn-in-himalayas-himachal-pradesh-india-2795970/]

4 Cairns Are Good, Actually [https://www.backpacker.com/stories/essays/opinion/cairns-on-hiking-trails-are-good-actually/]

5 How influencers are mimicking cairns. [https://www.sfgate.com/california-parks/article/yosemite-rangers-give-ok-to-destroy-rock-piles-18201467.php]

Chapter 11: Build Authentic

1 From Aspen Ideas to Go: Artificial Intelligence and the Future of Everything, Jul 5, 2023 [https://podcasts.apple.com/us/podcast/artificial-intelligence-and-the-future-of-everything/id702896920?i=1000619399099] Google CEO Eric Schmidt and the head of MIT's College of Computing, Daniel Huttenlocher, Walter Isaacson moderates.

2 Tim Cook on outdoors [https://www.cnbc.com/2023/04/05/apple-ceo-tim-cook-top-strategy-clearing-his-head-go-outside.html] and [https://www.gq.com/story/tim-cook-global-creativity-awards-cover-2023].

3 In 1948, Winston Churchill said, "Those that fail to learn from history are doomed to repeat it," a rephrasing of George Santayana's 1905 "Those who cannot remember the past are condemned to repeat it." Who both may have borrowed the phrase from Edmond Burke. Churchill and history repeating. [https://liberalarts.vt.edu/magazine/2017/history-repeating.html].

4 Jon Meacham on History [https://www.prsa.org/article/jon-meacham-on-how-the-past-prepares-us-for-the-present]

5 Gottschall, Jonathan. The Storytelling Animal: How Stories Make Us Human (p. 103). Houghton Mifflin Harcourt. Kindle Edition.

6 Cleo Abrams. Visit her YouTube channel. [https://www.youtube.com/@CleoAbram].

7 Read If I Understood You, Would I Have This Look on My Face?: My Adventures in the Art and Science of Relating and Communicating by Alan Alda.

8 If you ever have the opportunity to work on the 5th floor of the Boston Athenaeum, you may encounter a visitor on the window sill. The resident hawks of the Granary Burial Ground often sun themselves on the railing and on occasion lean over to see what your writing about.

9 Read Awe: The New Science of Everyday Wonder and How It Can Transform Your Life, by Dacher Keltner

10 AI on the Sky: Stunning New Images From James Webb Space Telescope to Be Analyzed by AI [https://blogs.nvidia.com/blog/james-webb-first-images/]

11 How Are Webb's Full-Color Images Made?[https://webbtelescope.org/contents/articles/how-are-webbs-full-color-images-made]

12 'Now and Then,' the Beatles' Last Song, Is Here, Thanks ... - WIRED.]https://www.wired.com/story/the-beatles-now-and-then-last-song-artificial-intelligence-peter-jackson/].

13 The infographic lists four images.

    1. One of the first images released by the JWST. [https://science.nasa.gov/mission/webb/multimedia/images/]

2.   Image from the trailer of Plant Earth 2. The entire catalog of videos from the BBC is a tour de-force of awe inspiring imagery, music and nature. [https://www.youtube.com/watch?v=c8aF-cHFu8QM]

3.   Historic image of the first human powered flight [https://www.loc.gov/collections/wilbur-and-orville-wright-papers/articles-and-essays/photography-and-the-wright-brothers]

4.   A musical sketch from Beethoven that can be transformed into inspiring music. Music Division, The New York Public Library. (1810 - 1811). Sketches for the "Archduke" trio, op. 97 Retrieved from [https://digitalcollections.nypl.org/items/dfcfa580-7598-0131-c1cc-58d385a7bbd0]

[14] Compared to reading, how much does video improve learning outcomes? [https://mit-ili.mit.edu/news/compared-reading-how-much-does-video-improve-learning-outcomes]

[15] The Book Is Dead'? Let That Myth Rest in Peace, The Atlantic by Peter Osnos [https://www.theatlan-tic.com/entertainment/archive/2011/05/the-book-is-dead-let-that-myth-rest-in-peace/238241/]

[16] Did technology kill the book or give it new life? BBC News [https://www.bbc.com/news/business-33717596]

[17] Neil Gaiman on the importance of books, libraries and reading. This is an edited version of Neil Gaiman's lecture for the Reading Agency, delivered on Monday October 14 at the Barbican in London. [https://www.theguardian.com/books/2013/oct/15/neil-gaiman-future-libraries-reading-daydreaming]

[18] Henry David Thoreau "A Week on the Concord and Merrimack Rivers." [https://www.guten-berg.org/cache/epub/4232/pg4232.txt]

[19] Definition of cognitive dissonance from the Cambridge Business English Dictionary © Cambridge University Press.

[20] John Hersey And The Art Of Fact. The New Yorker, April 2019 By Nicholas Lemann. [https://www.newyorker.com/magazine/2019/04/29/john-hersey-and-the-art-of-fact]

[21] John Hersey And The Art Of Fact. The New Yorker, April 2019 By Nicholas Lemann. [https://www.newyorker.com/magazine/2019/04/29/john-hersey-and-the-art-of-fact]

[22] From Hiroshima's Devastation, a Wrenching Account of the Human Toll. John Hersey shook Americans by telling the story of history's first atomic bombing from the survivors' point of view [https://www.wsj.com/articles/from-hiroshimas-devastation-a-wrenching-account-of-the-human-toll]

[23] John Hersey, the Writer Who Let "Hiroshima" Speak for Itself. By Russell Shorto. The New Yorker. [https://www.newyorker.com/culture/culture-desk/john-hersey-the-writer-who-let-hiroshima-speak-for-itself]

Chapter 12: Assisting Intelligence

[1] The birth of Artificial Intelligence (AI) research. Lawrence Livermore National Laboratory. [https://st.llnl.gov/news/look-back/birth-artificial-intelligence-ai-research]

[2] The birth of Artificial Intelligence (AI) research. Lawrence Livermore National Laboratory. [https://st.llnl.gov/news/look-back/birth-artificial-intelligence-ai-research]

[3] Computing Machinery and Intelligence [https://en.wikipedia.org/wiki/Computing_Machinery_and_Intelligence]

[4] Ghost in the Machine [https://www.gsb.stanford.edu/insights/ghost-machine-knowing-who-created-robot-makes-it-feel-more-authentic]

[5] Ada Lovelace Biography [https://en.wikipedia.org/wiki/Ada_Lovelace]. Also read the chapter on Ada Lovelace, by Walter Isaacson in The Innovators.

[6] If You Give a Mouse a Cookie, one of the most beloved children's books of all time by Laura Joffe Numeroff. [https://lauranumeroff.com/books/]

[7] If You Give a College Student a Cookie . . . by Alisyia Finley, Wall Street Journal [https://www.wsj.com/articles/if-you-give-a-college-student-a-cookie]

[8] The Anxious Generation: How the Great Rewiring of Childhood is Causing an Epidemic of Mental Illness. By Jonathan Haidt [https://www.anxiousgeneration.com]

[9] Ancora Imparo Michelangelo - Wikiquote. [https://en.wikiquote.org/wiki/Michelangelo.]

[10] For more information on the Laurentian Library [https://textshop.com.au/the-library-michelangelo-de-signed/]

[11] Image by Mike, Sydney and Elke O'Brien visiting the Laurentian Library in Florence Italy. Nov 2024.

[12] [https://www.politico.com/magazine/story/2016/12/fake-news-history-long-violent-214535/] and [https://theangus.rpc.ox.ac.uk/nobody-expects-the-spanish-inquisition/]

[13] For more information on the Relazione [https://en.wikipedia.org/wiki/Relazione]

[14] For more information on the Index Librorum Prohibitorum visit https://en.wikipedia.org/wiki/Index_Librorum_Prohibitorum

[15] From the book Surrender by Bono discussing the writing of Beautiful Day and it's meaning. P382-3.

Chapter 13: Conclusion

[1] Hubert Joly, The Heart of Business. Leadership Principle for the Next Era of Capitalism, p 65.

About this Book

[1] Writing to Think, Shane Parrish, Farnam Street Blog [https://fs.blog/writing-to-think/]

[2] I chose the phrase 'happenstance for mischief' over 'penchant for mischief' because I believe both the chaos caused by Mara and AIs are not deliberate, I know with Mara when she intends to get my attention, and I say with hope for AI. For Mara and especially AIs, their training will inform the occurrence and inclination.

[3] Geoffroy Tory, Champ Fleury. Translated into English and annotated by George B. Ives -1927. Images based on this version. [https://archive.org/details/champfleury00tory/]

AI Lexicon

[1] Farnam Street Blog. "Deductive vs Inductive Reasoning: Make Smarter Arguments, Better Decisions, and Stronger Conclusions" [https://fs.blog/deductive-inductive-reasoning/]

[2] The Curious Case of Commonsense Intelligence, Daedalus MIT Press Direct [https://direct.mit.edu/daed/article/151/2/139/110627/The-Curious-Case-of-Commonsense-Intelligence]

[3] Fascinating research paper from Apple demonstrating some of the reasoning and logic limitations of AI models today. [https://machinelearning.apple.com/research/gsm-symbolic]

[4] MIT Technology Review "We need to prepare for 'addictive intelligence'" [https://www.technologyreview.com/2024/08/05/1095600/we-need-to-prepare-for-addictive-intelligence/]

[5] The Age of AI: And Our Human Future: Henry A Kissinger, Eric Schmidt, Daniel Huttenlocher.

[6] From Teddy Roosevelt's Citizenship in a Republic, 1910. [https://www.theodorerooseveltcenter.org/Learn-About-TR/TR-Encyclopedia/Culture-and-Society/Man-in-the-Arena.aspx]

[7] Fascinating research paper from Apple demonstrating some of the reasoning and logic limitations of AI models today. [https://machinelearning.apple.com/research/gsm-symbolic]

[8] Using a generative AI to expand the alliteration.

[9] Learn more about what is doomscrolling and it's harmful effects. [https://health.clevelandclinic.org/everything-you-need-to-know-about-doomscrolling-and-how-to-avoid-it]

AI Glossary

[1] MIT Technology Review "The Tech Industry Open Source AI Definition Problem" [https://www.technologyreview.com/2024/03/25/1090111/tech-industry-open-source-ai-definition-problem]

[2] Quote from NYTimes article on 'What is Openwashing AI' [https://www.nytimes.com/2024/05/17/business/what-is-openwashing-ai.html]

Index of Index

[1] History of Indexes and Concordance [https://en.wikipedia.org/wiki/Concordance_(publishing)]

www.ingramcontent.com/pod-product-compliance
Lightning Source LLC
Chambersburg PA
CBHW071455140726
47997CB00005B/1729